WAR CRIMINAL

Hirota Koki.

WAR CRIMINAL

The Life and Death of
Hirota Koki

SABURO SHIROYAMA

Translated by JOHN BESTER

KODANSHA INTERNATIONAL LTD.

Tokyo, New York & San Francisco

ACKNOWLEDGMENT

The publishers wish to record their gratitude to Miwa Kimitada, Professor of International Relations at Sophia University, Tokyo, for advice given in preparing the translation.

First published in 1974 by Shinchosha, Tokyo, as Rakujitsu Moyu.

Distributed in the United States by Kodansha International/USA, Ltd., through Harper & Row, Publishers, Inc., 10 East 53rd Street, New York, New York 10022. In South America by Harper & Row, International Department. In Canada by Fitzhenry & Whiteside Limited, 150 Lesmill Road, Don Mills, Ontario. In Mexico and Central America by HARLA S.A. de C.V., Apartado 30–546, Mexico 4, D.F. In the United Kingdom by TABS, 7 Maiden Lane, London WC2. In Europe by Boxerbooks Inc., Limmatstrasse 111, 8031 Zurich. In Australia and New Zealand by Book Wise (Australia) Pty. Ltd., 104–8 Sussex Street, Sydney. In Thailand by Central Department Store Ltd., 306 Silom Road, Bangkok. In Hong Kong and Singapore by Books for Asia Ltd., 30 Tat Chee Avenue, Kowloon; 65 Crescent Road, Singapore 15. In the Far East by Japan Publications Trading Company, P.O. Box 5030, Tokyo International, Tokyo.

Published by Kodansha International Ltd., 2–12–21 Otowa, Bunkyo-ku, Tokyo 112 and Kodansha International/USA, Ltd., 10 East 53rd Street, New York, New York 10022 and 44 Montgomery Street, San Francisco, California 94104. Copyright © 1977 by Kodansha International Ltd. All rights reserved. Printed in Japan.

LCC 76–9361
ISBN 0–87011–275–9
JBC 1093–785266–2361

First edition, 1977

EDITOR'S NOTE

All Japanese names in this book (except the author's) are given in the Japanese order—surname first, followed by the given name. In the section dealing with the Tokyo war crimes trials, some of the English dialogue is retranslated from the Japanese, since it has been impossible to trace the originals. The footnotes have been added by the editor.

PROLOGUE

On the afternoon of December 24, 1948, at the Kuboyama crematory on the outskirts of Yokohama, a small group of men were furtively digging up the spot where the crematory disposed of any ashes not required by the families of the deceased. Japan was under Occupation rule at the time, and it was the eyes of the U.S. army that the men were so eager to avoid. Fortunately, it was Christmas Eve, and they also had the support of the director of the crematory for their plan.

Once they had collected a quart or so of ash, they packed it into an urn and made their escape. Taking their strange burden along the coast to the hot-spring resort of Atami, they hid the ashes in a shrine to Kannon, the Goddess of Mercy, that stood on a hillside outside the town. The shrine, dedicated to the memory of Japanese and Chinese officers and men killed in the fighting in China, had been set up by General Matsui Iwane, commander-in-chief of the Japanese forces in central China, following his return to Japan. During the immediate postwar period, it had almost no visitors and was an ideal spot, both secluded and sacred, in which to conceal their haul.

The ashes included a little of the mortal remains of seven men—six former army officers:

Doihara Kenji (general; director of special service agencies in Manchuria; c.-in-c., 7th District Army; inspector general of military education).

Itagaki Seishiro (general; chief of staff, Japanese expeditionary forces in China; c.-in-c., army in Korea).

Kimura Heitaro (general; chief of staff, Kwantung Army; war undersecretary; c.-in-c., Japanese forces in Burma).

Matsui Iwane (general; c.-in-c., Japanese forces in central China).

Muto Akira (lieutenant general; director of the Military Affairs Bureau of the War Ministry; chief of staff, Japanese forces in the Philippines).

Tojo Hideki (general; war minister; prime minister).
And a single civilian:

1

Hirota Koki (foreign minister; prime minister).

At 2:05 A.M. the previous day, December 23, the seven bodies had left Sugamo prison in two large covered trucks belonging to the U.S. army, preceded and followed by jeeps. At 8:00 A.M. the same day, after arrival at the Kuboyama crematory, they had been committed to the flames under the supervision of American army officers. None of the deceased's relatives was allowed to be present, or even to receive any of the ashes. The U.S. army's Public Information Section announced simply that the bodies had been cremated and the ashes scattered in the same manner as those of other Japanese war criminals already executed. Rumor had it that the American forces had taken them up in a plane and scattered them over the Pacific, presumably fearing that fanatic nationalists might later attempt to make use of them.

They had not, however, taken quite all the ashes, and the rest had been disposed of in the usual place. It was these few remaining ashes that had been dug up in secret and conveyed to the shrine near Atami.

Seven years later, in April, 1955, the Welfare Ministry's Repatriation Assistance Bureau divided the ashes into seven portions which it placed in boxes of unpainted wood and handed over to the relatives of the dead men. Hirota's family, however, refused to accept them. The ostensible reason for this was that a lock of Hirota's hair and some nail clippings had already been placed in the family grave, and that they did not want ashes of uncertain identity.

In April, 1959, a stone tablet was erected in the grounds of the shrine with an inscription in Yoshida Shigeru's hand reading "Monument to Seven Patriots." The unveiling ceremony was attended by Yoshida and former general Araki, representing the dead men's acquaintances, and about a hundred other persons. But no one from Hirota's family was present. The family believed that they were acting as Hirota himself would have wished. He had, by nature, been cut out for a life less crowded and less public than the one he had actually lived; in the grave at least, they felt, they should respect his privacy, however ungracious their attitude might seem.

"Japan has no need of heroes," Hirota had often told his subordinates during his days at the Foreign Ministry. "Our job is to do our best in the service of the emperor." Such a man would never have wished to be ranked in death alongside the "heroes" and the "patriots." He was a plain man who—where dress was concerned, for example—had always felt most at home in an everyday suit. "Mr. Hirota was surprisingly fussy about his suits," one of his former colleagues relates. "He was very particular about measurements and fittings—I suppose it was because he'd been in London as a young man." But Hirota's motive was almost certainly not personal vanity but a simple desire to dress as befitted a diplomat. What made it "surprising," even to someone who knew him well, was that by nature he was supremely unconcerned about matters such as dress. His plain, unmodish personal appearance suggested, rather, the principal of some primary school deep in the country. In military uniform, morning coat, or full court dress he looked out of place, and he heartily disliked wearing them.

"I wonder whether I can really handle the job?" he had lamented, with a diffidence uncharacteristic in a diplomat, following his appointment as Japanese minister to Holland. "All those wretched parties and dinners. . . ." This was in 1927, when he was already forty-nine.

He seems to have married a kindred soul, for Shizuko, who was seven years his junior, hated the idea of formal appearances as wife of the minister. Hirota's own distaste for evening dress was matched by Shizuko's dislike of formal gowns and everything that went with them; the mere thought of dressing up and acting as hostess at a party was enough to give her a headache. For that reason, she stayed in Japan with the children while Hirota went alone to take up his post in Holland.

He had already had a fair amount of experience of life abroad as a diplomat—first, a period as a probationer at the legation in Peking, followed by spells at the embassies in London and Washington as third secretary and first secretary respectively. But to represent his country as its minister would obviously necessitate joining in the social round to a considerable extent. Any aspiring member of the foreign service must be, if not infatuated with the gay social life, at least not totally indifferent to its appeal. To dislike dressing up was, in fact, a serious drawback in a diplomat. Hirota's lament was unusual, not to say out of place, in a member of his profession.

Yet this same man had not only become a diplomat but was to reach the highest posts open to him—foreign minister and prime minister—well ahead of Yoshida Shigeru and his other contemporaries at the Foreign Ministry, and in the end he was to find himself, dressed in U.S. army prisoner-of-war uniform, climbing the thirteen steps to the gallows along with Japan's former military leaders.

The course of his life was closely bound up with the fate of Japan's tens of millions of ordinary citizens who lived through the same period. The average Japanese was carried along unwillingly by the tide of the times, and Hirota himself was one of those "average men" who, while trying to avoid being caught, found himself swept along against his will. In that sense, surely, there was nothing remarkable in his family's desire to save him, in death at least, from the need to do what others wished.

In the center of the city of Fukuoka, not far from the prefectural office, stands an unpretentious little shrine to the Shinto deity Tenjin. It is known as the Mizukagami Shrine, or sometimes the Mizukagami Tenman-gu. There are two traditional gateways, one on the southern approach, facing the prefectural office, the other on the northern side, close to the Hashiguchi district.

The Mizukagami Shrine, which has served as a place of worship for the local inhabitants of the area since ancient times, has a distinguished history, and the Chinese characters inscribed on the plaque affixed over the southern gateway were written—as the plaque itself notes—by Prince Kuroda Nagashige, a member of the family that had provided the lords of the local clan during the feudal era preceding the Meiji Restoration of 1868.

The characters for "Tenman-gu" on the plaque of the northern gate bear no signature at all: understandably, for though the hand in which they are written is relaxed and assured they were done by a primary schoolboy with no claim to fame whatsoever.

It would have been different had he been, say, son of the chief representative of the shrine's parishioners; but in fact his father was a stonemason who happened to have worked on the gateway.

The stonemason in question, who was proud of his son's fine hand, sometimes had him write inscriptions for carving on gravestones and the like, and had conceived the ambition of having the boy do the inscription on the gate. He was a hard-working man, known to the locals as "thirty-five" since it was said he did thirty-five days' work a month. A simple fellow with neither hobbies nor vices apart from his work, he was precisely the kind of man to come up with such a fond scheme. . . .

There were discussions with the shrine authorities. Fortunately, the deity Tenjin happened to be the patron saint of calligraphy for children. The boy's script, moreover, was extraordinarily mature for one so young, and the shrine authorities decided to use it—not yielding to an importunate parent, but with the idea that it was appropriate at a shrine to Tenjin and that it would encourage other children. They refused, though, to add the signature of a complete nobody. After all, even the god himself could hardly have known that the boy in question would one day be prime minister. . . .

Physically, the city of Fukuoka has changed entirely as a result of the wartime bombings, and almost everything associated with Hirota's early days has disappeared. About the only thing that remains is the inscription over the gateway.

Not only did those three Chinese characters represent an honor for the youthful Hirota; they were also to have an influence on the whole course of his life.

As a youth, Hirota's father Tokuhei was apprenticed to a small stonemason's business where he worked so diligently that in time he was adopted by the master. Eventually he married Take, daughter of the owner of another small business in the neighborhood that made Chinese noodles. On February 14, 1878, they had a son.

The young couple gave their first-born the name Jotaro—an unpretentious name written with characters meaning something like "sturdy boy"—possibly with the feeling that they would be satisfied if only he grew up strong and hearty. Their hopes were not betrayed, and Hirota Jotaro grew into a sturdy boy.

When in later years Hirota became prime minister, Tokuhei was to declare in high spirits to the reporters clustering round him:

"No, never had a bit of trouble raising the boy. Human beings are like that, you know—give them enough to eat and they grow of their own accord."

Three more children were born after Jotaro. When Tokuhei first went into business, the family lived in a single small room, and it was hard for them to make ends meet. During his first years at primary school, Jotaro himself would often earn the money to buy books and other things he needed at school by going around the streets hawking rushes for tatami mats, or pine needles for kindling which he had gathered himself. Occasionally, he earned pocket money by carrying lanterns in funeral processions.

Both his parents continued, for "thirty-five days a month," to work from before dawn until late at night, and by the time he entered higher primary school the family business was in a position to employ skilled labor from outside, and Jotaro's duties were reduced to occasionally helping with the accounts or running errands.

Besides his calligraphy, he studied hard at other subjects, and always received excellent reports at school. He was the kind of boy, too, who liked to pore over atlases of the world or wander in the hills by himself, where he would sleep beneath the stars.

Tokuhei's intention, of course, was that once this able, well-behaved eldest son of his left higher primary school, he should go into the business and eventually succeed him. There were friends of the family, though, who saw this as a waste of the boy's talent and tried to persuade his father to let him go on to middle school. This was at a time when, even in Tokyo, only four or five pupils out of each class would make it to middle school. At first, Tokuhei dismissed the idea, but the friends persisted. Finally, one of them said, "Look what fine calligraphy your boy's already done for the shrine! Who knows what an expert calligrapher he might become if only you sent him to middle school?"

This argument finally carried the day, and Tokuhei determined to let his son go belatedly to middle school. Young Hirota, who for all his love of study, had always assumed that his schooling would stop at higher primary school as his father had decided, now found an unexpected future suddenly opening up before him. Although the aim at this stage was still that he should succeed his father in the business, he was put into the second grade at the prefectural middle school. By the time he reached third grade, he was already second in a class of 190. From then on until he left school he never missed a day, and earned a steady 90 plus for English and mathematics—the typical kind of boy described in his reports as "attentive and industrious."

Yet he was no mere bookworm. In his spare time, he went to practice *zazen* at a Zen temple, and regularly attended the local judo training center. However many times he was thrown at judo, he would always come back for more, and he often won the championship by sheer stubborn persistence.

The judo center in question was run by an organization known as the Genyosha, and Hirota and his classmates would often go there to attend lectures on the Chinese classics—especially the *Analects* of Confucius—and Chinese poetry. Founded by men such as ultra-patriot Toyama Mitsuru and Hakota Rokusuke, a Meiji-era advocate of democracy, the Genyosha had started life as a political association aimed at acquiring civil rights; its "charter" consisted of three articles:

1. We will revere the imperial family.
2. We will love our country.
3. We will insist on the rights of the people.

However, being situated in a part of the country separated from the continent by only a narrow strip of water—the Sea of Genkai, from which the Genyosha took its name—the association, which from time to time gave aid to refugees of similar sympathies from Korea, naturally had an unusually strong interest in foreign affairs.

It happened that in 1886, when the Chinese North Pacific fleet entered Nagasaki harbor, a group of Chinese sailors attempted to assault a young girl, and when a police officer tried to stop them chased him into the police station and beat him up. The incident, which happened close by and was an obvious insult to Japan, encouraged a tendency in the Genyosha to shift emphasis from civil rights to national rights, and to give the extension of those national rights priority over everything else. It was in such an atmosphere that the Genyosha gave its lectures on the Chinese classics and Chinese poetry (not, it should be noted, that Hirota was, or ever became, a formal member of the Genyosha).

Hirota was in his fourth year at middle school when the Sino-Japanese War broke out in 1894. He and his classmates were filled with youthful ardor at the thought of war with the vast country just across the water, and Hirota even considered volunteering for the army. An even deeper impression was made on him, however, by the Triple Intervention of 1895, following the conclusion of a peace treaty with China. Faced with protests by Russia, Germany, and France, who insisted that Japanese ownership of the Liaotung Peninsula would disturb the peace of the Far East, Japan was forced to return the peninsula, which she had only just acquired at the recent peace conference, shortly after ratification of the peace treaty.

There was little that such a small and weak country as Japan could do in the face of such collusion between three powerful nations and China, but the episode emphasized, nevertheless, the ineffectuality of Japanese diplomacy. In a sense, Japan had won the war but lost at the negotiating table.

The affair left the young Hirota with a deep sense of frustration. Looking about him, he could point to any number of young men who intended to go into the army. But army men alone were no longer enough to defend Japan; without something more, their blood would be shed in vain. What was needed, in short, was really able diplomats. Diplomacy was not a job for everybody, nor did it offer such spectacular opportunities as the army, but it was a field that needed young men just as much as the army itself.

Hirota had already submitted to the Town Hall an application form for entry into the Military Academy. Now, though, he and another youth called Hirata, a close friend from early childhood who shared his feelings on the subject, went together to the Town Hall to retrieve their application forms, having decided to go on to the First Higher School with the aim of becoming diplomats.

His father Tokuhei, also having changed his mind, was now happy to hand on the family business to his second son. This did not mean that he was interested in worldly success for his first son; he was an old-fashioned man whose life had been spent by the Sea of Genkai, and his feeling was that the boy could become an army man, a diplomat, or anything else so long as he was of use to the country—though he himself could not afford to pay Hirota's school fees.

There was stiff competition to get into the First Higher School at the time, but Hirota and Hirata studied together and passed the examination together.

On graduating from middle school, Hirota had changed his given name to "Koki." The name, which meant something like "broadminded and firm of purpose," was taken from a phrase in his beloved *Analects* of Confucius, which used the word in describing the attributes of "the virtuous man," and was intended as a kind of private declaration and constant reminder to himself of his future attitude as a diplomat. Only a very strong determination could have made a boy with such a sense of respect for his parents willingly give up the name that they had bestowed on him. He was so determined, in fact, that he even got the priest of the temple where he practiced *zazen* to register him temporarily as a monk, since this was the only way in which he could officially change his name. Though gentle by nature, Hirota was unwavering once he had made up his mind to something.

Another of Hirota's characteristics was the attention that he paid from an early age to his relations with older men and contemporaries in the same field, and on the need for mutual enlightenment and encouragement; no blind believer in book learning, he valued direct human exchanges, and the absorption of knowledge by contact with others.

While still at middle school he had talked his fellows into forming a group called the "Chikakukai." The group, which took its name from a phrase in the Chinese classics advocating the quest for knowledge, was devoted, ambitiously, to the "study of life," and many of its members were later to become prominent scholars or businessmen.

It had been agreed that Hirota should be helped in paying his higher school fees by a wealthy benefactor, but Hirota, finding that his friend Hirata was also having difficulty finding the money to go to higher school, took it upon himself to do the rounds on Hirata's behalf, find likely benefactors, and persuade them to help. Thanks to this, the two of them went up to Tokyo together in their rough jute kimono, shod in high wooden clogs and with round "coolie hats" of woven bamboo on their heads.

In his second year at the First Higher School, Hirota left the school dormitory—but not, like so many others, in search of the comparative freedom of ordinary lodgings. Renting a small house in Koishikawa (it had three tiny rooms of six, four and a half, and two tatami mats respectively) he invited Hirata and four other friends to share his life there. The idea was not simply to save money, but also to use living under the same roof as an exercise in spiritual discipline and mutual encouragement.

After arriving in Tokyo, Hirota would often call on Toyama Mitsuru—the well-known and influential rightist—and other older men from his own part of the country. Hearing of the new hostel, Toyama was encouraging. "It takes more than one stick of firewood to make a fire," he said. "If several kindred spirits combine forces, then the country is bound to benefit somehow." At Toyama's introduction, Hirota went to call on Soejima Taneomi, who was minister of foreign affairs, and got him to write the new name of the house on a board to be hung over the entrance. The name chosen, "Kokokyo," was taken from the classics and meant "abode of infinite spaciousness."

Life was hard, of course, since they were all poor students who had to work for a living. When they were finally able to afford horsemeat for dinner one day, Hirota exclaimed gleefully "umaka, umaka"—a pun on *umaka*, a dialect form meaning "This tastes good," and *uma ka*, which means something like "Horse, I see. . . ." Hirota had a taste for puns that belied his solemn appearance.

Hirota himself was in charge of the new hostel, with Hirata as his second-in-command. They were close friends, but their characters were diametrically opposed. Hirata would get up at five every morning and, stark naked, work out with weights, accompanying himself with sharp cries of encouragement, then take an English newspaper to read in the toilet. Emerging, he would go out to the well and douse himself with cold water.

For Hirata, the same brisk routine marked the beginning of every day throughout the year. Robust and rosy-cheeked, he was referred to by his fellows as the "red demon."

Hirota, on the other hand, was the "blue demon." Every day,

11

without fail, he rose at six and went to bed at ten, spending every spare minute in between at his desk, poring silently over the *Analects*. On Sundays, he would again spend the morning reading, but in the afternoon he invariably went to call on his mentors. He never missed these visits, even during examinations. The mentors in question were mostly from the same part of Japan as himself, and the most fruitful of all such contacts for Hirota was to be his encounter with Yamaza Enjiro, to whom he was introduced by Toyama. Yamaza, a native of Fukuoka prefecture, who at the time was head of the Political Affairs Bureau at the Foreign Ministry, wielded great influence there—in fact, he was said to be a close confidant of Foreign Minister Komura Jutaro himself.

His positive achievements in the diplomatic field included acting as the driving force behind Komura in the signing of the Anglo-Japanese Alliance of 1902. He was also a champion of good causes, having, for example, privately raised the funds for Sun Yat-sen's escape to Singapore. At the same time, he wrote a distinguished prose, and composed haiku in his spare time. As a result, he had already made a considerable name for himself within the ministry.

For Hirota, it was as though he had been presented with a living example of the ideal diplomat he had always envisaged, an ideal that so far had existed only in his own mind. He promptly determined that he would follow in Yamaza's footsteps.

By now he was a student at the Tokyo Imperial University, but he was not content, as many young men might have been, to wait in comparative idleness until society should provide him with his rightful place in its ranks. He resolved to start immediately to train himself to see, hear, and think in diplomatic terms.

The Anglo-Japanese Alliance had just been signed, and was having all kinds of repercussions both in Japan and abroad. Hirota conceived the idea of compiling a report on public opinion concerning the treaty in various different countries. He was interested in the subject himself, and he felt sure that many other people would find such a report useful. Before anyone else, though, he would show it to Yamaza.

Slow to make a first move, Hirota was good at carrying things through once he had started. Enlisting the help of the other residents of the Kokokyo, he persuaded them to turn to good account their knowledge of English, German, French, and Russian in carefully gathering and translating opinions on the treaty expressed in foreign journals. This done, he edited the results and published them as a book entitled *The Anglo-Japanese Alliance and World Opinion* (Nichiei Domei to Sekai no Yoron).

The book won praise, and was soon sold out. What delighted Hirota still more, however, was that Yamaza recognized the book's worth. From now on, Yamaza began to drop in at the Kokokyo, bringing the occasional parcel containing whisky, steak, and the like. He had realized that Hirota merited something more than the attention he would naturally have paid to another, younger man from his own home district.

One evening in 1903, just before the summer vacation in Hirota's second year at college, Hirota and Hirata were summoned to Yamaza's official residence on "urgent business."

They found Yamaza looking more tense than they had ever seen him before. "Look—" he began, "what would you say to going to the continent during the summer vacation, one of you to Manchuria and one to Siberia?"

Startled but impressed, the two young men were about to agree when Yamaza went on:

"I'll tell you now, though, that you'll have to go prepared to risk your lives." And with his eyes on their faces, he proceeded to explain.

Russia was keenly interested in establishing a foothold in Manchuria and Korea, and Russo-Japanese relations as a result had reached a kind of nadir. For this reason, the Foreign Ministry—if only in order to be prepared for the worst—was interested in collecting as much material as possible that might be of use in appraising the situation. The task meant on-the-spot investigation of local conditions and the climate of opinion, of how far Russian encroachments had proceeded, and so on. Any Foreign Ministry official or army man who went there, even in disguise, would find his movements hampered by constant surveillance, while exposure would mean trouble all round. A student, however, ostensibly traveling to see the world and avoid the heat during the summer vacation, would attract relatively little attention.

Of course—Yamaza added—if it came out that they were traveling under secret orders, they could expect little mercy at Russian hands.

"Blue demon" and "red demon" had been growing increasingly tense, but in the end they spoke with one voice: they understood, they accepted the risks, and were eager to get going.

Yamaza had often told them that China and Russia were crucial to Japan's foreign relations, and that anyone who hoped to become a diplomat must first make a study of those countries. If so, then the proposed journey, for all the personal danger involved, was an ideal chance for the budding diplomat. Armed with their fares and introductions to the local Japanese legations in the countries concerned, they set off: Hirata to Vladivostok via Tsuruga, Hirota to Manchuria via Korea.

The atmosphere in Manchuria, on the eve of the Russo-Japanese War, was menacing. Japan had a legation there, but its influence was negligible, while the Russian presence was all-pervasive. To go as a wandering student did not mean that Hirota could relax his guard. Few Japanese students, in the first place, would be able to afford such a trip. Nor was the place of a kind likely to appeal to most students.

He met constant doubt and suspicion. At times even Hirota himself could tell that he was under surveillance. Sometimes, he would glance from the window of his room late at night to see a Russian military agent standing there in the shadows. Yamaza had not exaggerated the risks involved.

He pressed on nonetheless, to Antung, Tatungkou, and beyond, keenly aware of the signs of spreading Russian influence as he went. At Port Arthur, he found large-scale fortifications being built by the Russian army, and a party of Japanese laborers who had come from Japan in search of employment. Not satisfied with collecting information from these workers, however, Hirota made a contact through whom he himself got a job on the site as a laborer, pretending to be a student working to earn his fare.

Thus, three months later, when he finally turned up at his destination, the Japanese consulate at Chefoo, he shocked the consul with his grimy appearance and unpleasant smell: he had not had a bath for months, and his travels had given him few chances to wash or change his clothes.

On the ship returning to Japan, Hirota set in order the information he had gathered and drew up a detailed report. Back in Tokyo, he went at once to see Yamaza, and presented him with the report.

Yamaza, who opened the report with a mixture of anticipation and apprehension, nodded in growing approval as he read; it was better than anything he had seen produced recently, whether at the Foreign Ministry or elsewhere. There was more than enough data on the matters that Yamaza had wanted to find out about, and the whole document was good enough to be included among the basic materials for weighing up the pros and cons of war with Russia.

Satisfied with the report, Yamaza was also satisfied with Hirota. When he met Toyama Mitsuru—the man who had first sent Hirota to him—he complimented him on a remarkable find. Toyama, in his turn, urged him to keep a strict eye on the young man's progress.

By nature, Toyama disliked all government officials and had originally opposed Hirota's diplomatic aspirations. If every young man became a bureaucrat, he said, it would be like people crowding on one side of a boat: in the end, the boat was bound to tip over. It was better for the country that there should be uncommitted men around as well. Nevertheless, he was so impressed by Hirota's sense of mission and his way of working that he was finally persuaded to put him in Yamaza's hands.

Realizing the enormous potential of this young man, Yamaza made him, and Hirata too, Foreign Ministry advisers even though both of them were still officially students at Tokyo Imperial University. He got them to do a variety of jobs that would not be possible for anyone in a more official position, for which he made them an official allowance. But he was less concerned to help them out financially than to give his protégés a chance, just as soon as possible, to get the feel of diplomacy in action.

With the outbreak of the Russo-Japanese War in 1904, two champions of the Polish independence movement came to Japan as refugees with the aid of a Colonel Akashi. Akashi, also a native of Fukuoka and a friend of Yamaza's, entrusted the two Poles to Yamaza, who in turn gave Hirota and Hirata instructions to act as interpreter and general guide for the refugees. Accompanying them at all times of the day, Hirota had many chances to learn something of Russian politics from the conversation of men who had been personally involved.

A prisoner-of-war camp was subsequently established at Matsuyama, and among the Russian prisoners sent there were large numbers from Poland, which was under Russian rule at the time. Under instructions from Yamaza, Hirota went with one of the Poles to Matsuyama, where they interviewed prisoners and questioned them closely about conditions in Russia and the Russian army. The Polish prisoners, who had no reason to be fond of Russia, talked freely about supplies of arms and food in the Russian army, the defenses of Mukden, and even troop strengths, thereby providing invaluable information for the Japanese military as well as the Foreign Ministry.

Thanks to Yamaza, Hirota, though still a student, was already a diplomat. Nevertheless, when the time came for the actual examination to enter the diplomatic service, both Hirota and Hirata failed because of insufficient marks in English. Yamaza complained bitterly that the examiners did not know a good man when they saw one; but it was too late. It was a painful failure for Hirota, who felt he had disgraced himself in Yamaza's eyes. His ideas, it seemed, had run away with him before he had prepared the ground properly. . . .

For want of any better alternative he entered postgraduate school, where he made a study of colonial policy. At the same time, another older man from the same Fukuoka district as himself arranged for him to work as interpreter to the military attaché at the U.S. legation in Japan. Here again, the aim was not so much to enable him to earn money as to help him with his study of English—and once more Hirota reflected with gratitude on the advantages of having connections with men from the same local community. And when his English had reached a certain stage of proficiency, yet another native of Fukuoka, an older man in the Foreign Ministry, introduced him to a friend from Fukuoka in the Korean Government-General, who gave him a job there as a clerk. He was to go to take up his post, moreover, with a wife, a marriage having been arranged for him by Hirata and other friends who were worried at the thought of his going alone in his present depressed state.

Hirota had long been secretly fond of Shizuko, and it was she who now became his bride. They had known each other since childhood, having grown up in neighboring districts of Fukuoka. It was natural that they should be aware of each other. Almost all boys from the local middle school went on to the Fifth Higher School, and very few, as Hirota did, to the more prestigious First Higher School and still more prestigious Tokyo Imperial University. Shizuko, on the other hand, was known as one of the most attractive girls in the neighborhood. In Shizuko's presence, the already taciturn Hirota would be struck almost literally dumb, and his friends were fond of teasing him about it. Shizuko's father, Tsukinari Kotaro, who had once been an ardent advocate of civil rights, was now living near the Kokokyo, in a state of poverty aggravated by the size of his family.

Despite his reduced circumstances, Tsukinari liked to act as friend and mentor to any young people who came up to Tokyo from Fukuoka with introductions; he promptly took them under his wing, thereby imposing still more hardship on himself. One day Hirota and Hirata, hearing that yet another impoverished student, a girl, had gone to Tsukinari for help, suggested to him that they should take her off his hands by getting her to do the cooking and housework for them at the Kokokyo.

Tsukinari rejected the idea outright. It was too risky, he said, to introduce an unattached girl into a house full of young men. If they wanted a woman to help, they could have his own daughter, since she had been brought up properly and could look after herself.

Hirota was taken aback by this unexpected proposal. He thought it was wrong to ask Shizuko to come alone, and he himself felt embarrassed at the suggestion. Thus he conceived the idea of getting her two younger brothers to come and stay there too, in order to run errands and do other odd jobs. It would make things easier for Shizuko, the Tsukinari family would have three fewer mouths to feed, and Hirota himself would be less embarrassed. So all three of them came to live at the Kokokyo, and every morning Shizuko, before setting off for school, would prepare a meal for a household of nearly ten.

With her oval face, fine nose, and almond-shaped eyes, she had always been the kind of girl to attract attention, but when people saw her now, in her purple pleated skirt, setting off quite happily for school from the student hostel where she worked, the effect was little short of sensational, and there was even a story about it in the papers.

Tsukinari had a sudden rush of requests for his daughter's hand, but he brushed them all aside, saying that he already had someone in mind.

Hirota, in the meantime, had graduated from the Imperial University and abandoned the shaggy mane affected by students for shorter, carefully parted hair. He had left his boyhood behind, and himself felt it would soon be time to get married. A budding young diplomat and Tokyo Imperial University graduate had much to offer as a prospective son-in-law, and Hirota had plenty of offers for an arranged marriage with the daughter of this or that wealthy or distinguished family. But he refused them all. Friends urged him to think more of his own interests, but he saw his future diplomatic career as a means of serving his country rather than a means to worldly success. He had no fancy for being pointed to as a man who had got on in the world thanks to his wife's family.

When self-appointed matchmakers became too pressing, he would tell them that he already had his eye on someone. This was no mere excuse, since at the back of his mind he was constantly aware of Tsukinari Shizuko. In the same way, it was young Hirota whose image lurked behind the refusals of Shizuko and her father. And when the newspaper report forced what had been unspoken into the open,

Hirata took positive steps to arrange the marriage.

Back home in Fukuoka, there was considerable opposition to the marriage from relatives and friends who insisted that he could have made many much more advantageous matches. His mother, Take, however, always replied quite simply, "Any girl Koki chooses is all right with me." Take was a strong-minded woman, and she trusted her son implicitly.

The pair were married very quietly at the Kokokyo in 1905. Hirota was twenty-seven, and Shizuko twenty. For their honeymoon, they went to Enoshima, on the coast not far from Tokyo, where Hirota bought Shizuko a shellwork ring.

"One day, I'll buy you a real diamond," he promised her with a shy smile.

Thus Hirota set off for Seoul not alone, but with a beautiful companion. He continued to study in his spare time, and after eight months took the Foreign Ministry entrance examination again, being granted special leave to return to Tokyo for the purpose. This time, he got good marks in English as well, and was first on the list of successful candidates.

Hirata also passed—as did eight other candidates including Yoshida Shigeru, who much later, as prime minister, was to guide Japan through the difficult postwar years.

The Government-General in Korea was reluctant to let Hirota go, but Yamaza, who was head of the Political Affairs Bureau at the Foreign Ministry in Tokyo, finally prevailed on them to send Hirota back to Tokyo, where he embarked on life as a full-fledged diplomat. Then, after a period spent learning the ropes, he was sent as a probationer to the legation in Peking.

Thus in October, 1907, Hirota found himself in Peking beneath autumn skies that are said to be among the loveliest in the world. The deep blue of the sky and the sparkling clarity of the air immediately attracted the young diplomat. Horse-riding was popular among Japanese residents, and Hirota's colleagues would often ride out together to the Ming Tombs with their stone figures of men and beasts, or farther still to Chuyungkwan.

19

They lived in the foreign concession, a spacious and pleasant area with a river flowing through it, and foreign legations and barracks laid out in orderly fashion. In winter, there were billiards and mah-jongg, or skating in the suburbs for those so inclined. Some diplomats would go to the Western Hills to view the snowy scenery and to compose poems.

Spring would come in with clouds of fluffy willow seeds scattering in the breeze. It would bring winds from Mongolia, too, with a pervasive yellow dust that often turned daylight into premature dusk. In early summer the delicate pink acacias and the silk trees bloomed. As the sun's rays grew fiercer, the great trees that thronged the capital would spread a welcome shade. With its many woods and groves, Peking was a sea of greenery over which the turrets and gateways of the Forbidden City and the Altar of Heaven towered in splendor. There was boating on the Northern Lake and the West Lake, and on clear nights there were moon-viewing parties near the Marco Polo Bridge. . . .

The seasons were beautiful in Peking. Men there still went about their lives in leisurely fashion with living nature and ancient history all about them. It was a different China from the land that Hirota had imagined lying beyond the stormy Sea of Genkai; he welcomed it with a sense of relief, and told himself that it was up to him and his colleagues to establish firm relations with such a country.

But although the seasons in Peking appealed to Hirota, he took almost no part in the seasonal pastimes with which the capital's diplomats amused themselves. The one gathering at which he invariably showed up was the regular dinner at which the younger men among Japanese correspondents, bankers, traders, and soldiers stationed in Peking gathered to discuss Japan's China policy.

At these meetings, Hirota would sit silent while the others took turns in vehemently expressing their own opinions. He never spoke unless his opinion was specifically sought, being less interested in holding forth himself than in absorbing the views of others.

He worked hard every day at the legation. The chief task he set himself—partly in accordance with a suggestion from Yamaza—was to make a survey of "the origins and provisions of treaties between

China and Russia, China and Burma, and China and Annam; treaties between Tibet and India; and the various treaties pertaining to the leases on and trading at Hong Kong and Macao."

Such surveys were more than a mere formality. They also involved a lot of hard work, since the traditional Chinese policy of conducting foreign affairs through the imperial court meant that most negotiations had been carried on in strict secrecy. Hirota went to a great deal of trouble, even making a special trip to Shanghai to search for foreign documents on the subject. In his mind, he could always hear Yamaza saying, "The focal points of Japan's foreign policy are China and Russia. The first requirement for a diplomat is to make a study of Chinese and Russian affairs."

Hirota was almost totally absorbed in these studies, with little time for sightseeing or the various amusements that occupied his colleagues.

After one year and eight months in Peking, Hirota returned to Japan, then was posted to the Japanese embassy in London in 1909. He was replaced in Peking by Matsuoka Yosuke.

Yamaza had preceded him to London, having been transferred from the Political Affairs Bureau to the embassy, where he was now counselor. On leaving for London, he had told Hirota that he hoped Hirota too would come if the opportunity presented itself; he had spoken about it to his successor at the Political Affairs Bureau, he said. The wish had been fulfilled, and Hirota found himself now working directly under Yamaza.

Anglo-Japanese relations at the time involved a number of important questions, such as the revision of the trade treaty and the renewal of the Treaty of Alliance, and a major figure in the political world, Kato Takaaki, had come to London somewhat after Yamaza as ambassador. Kato, who had the broad sweep of the statesman, left all detailed studies of the questions involved to Yamaza, in whom he declared his implicit faith. Yamaza, in turn, with Kato's permission, left all the relevant paper work to his long-established protégé Hirota, whom he asked to draw up preliminary drafts of the two treaties.

21

Likewise, any difficult questions that arose in negotiations with the English were transmitted from Kato to Yamaza and from Yamaza to Hirota, who made a thorough investigation of the issues at stake and presented Kato with draft proposals for dealing with them. Thanks to a repetition of this process, the two revised treaties were eventually safely signed. The three men had evolved a strong working team.

Thus Hirota, though still only a third secretary, won Kato's confidence. Later, when Kato was leaving for Japan to become foreign minister, he asked Hirota to be his private secretary. But Hirota declined. Although the position might provide a shortcut to distinction, Hirota was personally more interested in studying for as long as possible under his respected superior, Yamaza.

Even while he was involved in such top-level diplomatic negotiations, Hirota made a point of going out about the town as much as possible so as to acquaint himself with things English. He would talk to workingmen sitting on benches reading their newspapers, or mingle with the crowds in Hyde Park, listening with them to the speeches of anarchists and socialists and at the same time carefully observing the reactions of the crowd itself.

A colleague of Hirota's complained to Ambassador Kato that such behavior was harmful to the dignity of a diplomat, but Kato paid no attention. "Leave him alone," he said. "Hirota's all right as he is. What he's doing now will be useful some day."

As a result of his studies, Hirota decided at an early stage that Lloyd George, the leader of the Liberal party, was a man worth watching, and carefully gathered material on his political views, character, and behavior (this material was to be of great use in later years when Lloyd George became leader of the nation).

Diplomats in London at the time led a glittering social life. At the instigation of Ambassador Kato and his wife, both Hirota and Shizuko started learning to dance, but it agreed with neither of them and they soon gave up.

Shizuko, who was not used to the gay social life, had little taste for parties; they were hardly the kind of atmosphere where one could mention shellwork rings. At some functions, it was almost oblig-atory to wear expensive rings and other accessories; the wives of younger diplomats would borrow them as the necessity arose from the wives of their superiors, who were, if anything, proud to comply with such requests. Shizuko never did any such borrowing. This attitude of hers gave her a reputation for being difficult to get on with, which made her still more retiring than ever.

Hirota respected her feelings, and never dragged her to parties against her will. Rather than join the social round, in fact, he personally preferred to wander about watching the city. Even so, he himself was in no sense "difficult to get on with." When the younger men drank together, he would often sing his favorite song in a loud voice:

> "When I die
> Oh who will cry for me?
> Only the cicadas
> In the prickly ash tree."

The words appealed to him, and it was the only song he was ever known to sing.

He still had a taste for puns and jokes. One day he was walking with Counselor Yamaza when they came to Trafalgar Square. As they looked up at Nelson's Column, rising fifty-six meters above the surrounding square and its pigeons and guarded by four bronze lions at its base, Yamaza—who was something of a haiku poet—suddenly smiled and said, "How's this?" and he recited:

> "What a surprise—
> Lord Nelson
> Still stiff as a ramrod. . . ."

"Not bad," said Hirota. Then he immediately pointed to the lions and rounded off the poem with two lines of his own:

> "And lions, too—
> At Trafalgar!"

The two men looked at each other and burst out laughing.

Hirota worked in London for five years in all. Finally, Yamaza was called back to Japan, and Hirota was himself summoned home in 1914 to head the First Section of the Trade Bureau. He was thirty-six by now and had three children, two boys and a girl.

Compared with the Political Affairs Bureau, which was concerned with international politics, work at the Trade Bureau, which also concerned itself with matters involving Japanese residents in China, might seem to be less rewarding for a man like Hirota. He occupied himself with important questions affecting the Chinese economy, the anti-Japanese movement, and fishing in northern waters, yet at the same time scanned as many newspapers as possible every day, paying particular attention to the articles on politics.

His predecessor, a hard-drinking native of the southern district of Kagoshima, had customarily kept a bottle of whisky in his desk, which he would sip from at lunchtime while waxing eloquent to the journalists. Even after Hirota took his place, the journalists kept coming through force of habit. They found him totally unlike his predecessor: quiet and serious, yet, when one got to know him, well informed and ready to discuss things fully and frankly. The younger newspapermen in particular began to call on him regularly.

The foreign minister at the time of Hirota's appointment as section chief was Kato Takaaki. As a man in whom both Kato and Yamaza had shown their trust, Hirota was regarded with some interest at the Foreign Ministry. It was the unofficial view that the team of Komura Jutaro and Kato would eventually be replaced by Shidehara Kijuro and Yamaza, and that they in their turn would hand power on to Saburi Sadao and Hirota.

Saburi had been Hirota's contemporary at Tokyo Imperial University, and had preceded him at the Foreign Ministry by a year. His ancestors had been instructors in the art of spearmanship to the daimyo of the Fukuyama clan, and he numbered among his brothers the president of a spinning company and the doctor of engineering who had designed the Shimizu tunnel. A large man with a comfortable background, he had made a name for himself as an oarsman at college. He was said to speak better French than anyone else at the Foreign Ministry, and his wife was Komura's daughter.

In short, he contrasted strongly with Hirota in almost all respects. He had an intellectual—almost aristocratic—and aloof manner, being addicted to solitary hikes in the mountains. In his work he was painstaking and conscientious, and he had soon become a favorite of Shidehara's.

He had started, like Hirota, with a spell of duty in China, then had served in Russia and France. Returning to the ministry, he had been in charge of treaty revision, then had gone to France again. He was firmly set on the road to success.

On May 23, 1914, Mizuno Kokichi, counselor at the Japanese legation in Peking, died suddenly, reportedly of a stomach ulcer. For Yamaza, by then minister in Peking, it meant the loss of his right-hand man. The legation had been understaffed to begin with, so he sent a telegram to the Foreign Ministry recommending that it send Hirota. The ministry decided to comply, and sounded out Hirota, who agreed delightedly. For a diplomat, the chance to work in China—then considered the focal point of Japanese diplomacy—and as assistant, moreover, to a man whom he held in such respect and affection, was not to be missed.

The situation in China at the time was complex and unsettled. The Ch'ing dynasty had collapsed, leaving Yuan Shih-k'ai established in Peking as president with strong ambitions to become emperor. Sun Yat-sen's Kuomintang, on the other hand, had started a second revolution; Yuan had at first collaborated with it, but had later switched to attempts at repression, so that China was virtually split into two camps.

The Japanese reaction to all this was correspondingly complex. The elder statesmen and former prime ministers had long been well disposed toward Yuan, while the younger men at the Foreign Ministry and the so-called "Shina-ronin" (Japanese adventurers in China) supported Sun Yat-sen. Yamaza himself was one of those who, earlier on, had helped Sun Yat-sen to find sanctuary in Japan. To add to the confusion, the local Japanese military were plotting to take advantage of China's divided state to expand Japanese influence there.

Despite the situation, however, Yamaza took no action worthy of the name. He stood by passively, ignoring the evident disappointment of those about him.

What he most feared, in fact, was an open split in China. His idea was to refrain from anything that might provoke such division, and to press ahead quietly with economic development. Moreover, in the absence of any definite policy among government leaders, it was impossible for the Foreign Ministry to take any local action by itself. Yamaza also hoped privately that by not acting he might, conversely, succeed in helping the government make up its own mind.

"From a national standpoint," Yamaza wrote to an acquaintance in the Genyosha, "it is only natural that I should be attacked by the general public. I do not mind. If such criticism of me means that the will of the Japanese people shows itself clearly and the government is thereby prodded into action, it will have the converse effect of backing me up indirectly in the attitude I feel I must take."

It was a difficult position to maintain, and it made Yamaza depend all the more on Hirota for support. On Hirota's side, it gave him something worth living for, and he was fired with new resolve. A new and strong bond of sympathy linked the two men, far separated though they were. A group of businessmen led by Shibusawa Eiichi was making a tour of China at the time, and new plans for economic development were in the making. The thought that Yamaza had lost his right-hand man at such a time made Hirota impatient to get to Peking with as little delay as possible.

But less than five days later, Hirota received another and far more shocking telegram from the legation in Peking. Minister Yamaza himself had passed away, as suddenly as his assistant. The cause of death was given as heart failure. Yamaza had been only forty-nine, still in the prime of life.

The two deaths in such rapid succession prompted on-the-spot rumors that Yuan Shih-k'ai had had the two men poisoned. The story, which sounded probable enough, disturbed the visiting businessmen considerably. Umagoe Kyohei, president of Dai-Nihon Beer and a man normally noted for his courage, called on the party to return to Japan instantly, with the result that Shibusawa's group left China at short notice.

Yamaza's body was brought back to Yokosuka on board a warship. By order of Foreign Minister Kato, Hirota went as the ministry representative to meet it at the wharf in the naval harbor.

It was the rainy season, and a steady drizzle blurred sea and hills alike. It fell silently on the coffin of the man who was to have headed the next generation of Japanese diplomats. Hirota followed the coffin without an umbrella. His trusted senior and mentor, the man who had played an irreplaceable role in his life, had fallen silent. Now there was no one to whom he could turn for advice. It was up to him now to live on, playing the part he had to play, in silence. . . .

He seemed, quite vividly, to hear Yamaza's voice again, giving him words of advice:

"Now that you're in the Foreign Ministry, you should devote at least your first ten years to finding out what diplomacy's all about, without any unnecessary big talk. This is extremely important."

"Komura never kept a diary. Nor do I. A diplomat leaves it to posterity to judge his own actions. He doesn't make excuses for them."

"The diplomat should never take satisfaction in working in the limelight; his duty is to do the work that no one ever talks about."

And:

"To get ahead as a diplomat in Japan, the first necessity is to make a thorough study of China and Far Eastern questions."

Two months after Yamaza's death, the First World War broke out. Japan joined the Allies, blockading Kiaochow Bay and also occupying German-leased Tsingtao. The following year, she demanded special rights in Manchuria and Shantung, and also put forward the notorious "Twenty-one Demands" embodying the general demands on China that she hoped to see realized. This expression of an expansionist policy, designed to acquire rights for Japan while the powers of Europe and America were busy with the war, represented the demands of the military and was drawn up by Koike Chozo, head of the Political Affairs Bureau at the Foreign Ministry, who was persona grata with the military.

The government's intention was to present it to China in the form of an ultimatum. An opposition party, Hara Takashi's Seiyukai, launched a headlong attack on the government on the grounds that the demands would harm Sino-Japanese friendship and violate international trust. Within the Foreign Ministry, Hirota, though he was obliged to participate in the drawing-up of a draft treaty, stubbornly opposed any attempt to present it in the form of an ultimatum. As he saw things, Japan should restrict herself to whatever she could get by negotiation.

Foreign Minister Kato, however, paid no attention whatsoever to Hirota's viewpoint. Originally, Kato himself had been of the view that it would be enough if Japan could only obtain an extension of the lease on the province of Kwantung, but by now the situation had reached the point of no return.

If the minister himself rejected his views there was little Hirota, as a lowly section chief, could do but resign himself to the situation; but he still considered it his duty to carry through his opposition. The Chinese question, as Yamaza had always told him, was of the utmost importance.

He had also told him that a diplomat should act behind the scenes. Hirota accordingly called on Justice Minister Ozaki Yukio, with whom he had been friendly for some time, and asked him to exert his influence on the foreign minister. He was quite well aware that, for a mere section chief, this was going too far, but he thought it necessary in the national interest.

Ozaki worked on Kato, and opposed him at cabinet meetings, but it was too late for him to exert any influence on the government as a whole. The ultimatum was issued. As expected, the Chinese objected, and negotiations threatened to be protracted. The Western powers protested violently; Japan was eventually obliged to give up most of her general demands, and secured only partial rights in the end.

The episode deeply impressed Hirota with the need for a diplomat to have some political influence and backing. "A diplomat can do nothing in isolation," he lamented. "Both Kato and Ozaki are British-style parliamentarians. If only they had got together. . . ." In line with this, Hirota continued his attempts to pave the way for the two men to work together in accord. Before long, he was forced to abandon such activities in the face of criticism from those who considered them presumptuous in a lowly Foreign Ministry official. Nevertheless, shortly after this, when the Kenseikai party was formed with Kato as president, Ozaki also became a member, so that collaboration between the two men became a reality. Thus Hirota, albeit indirectly, had left his mark on the political world.

Essentially, though, Hirota had no interest in political dabbling, much less "presumptuous" campaigning for a cause. It was merely that he found himself in a position where to do so seemed the only possible course for someone with the country's interests at heart. And it was Hirota's refusal to allow such ideas to remain simply ideas that distinguished him from the average run of diplomats.

Hirota's opposition to the Twenty-one Demands was shared by his contemporary Yoshida Shigeru. Not only were they contemporaries, but also—perhaps because they were alike in being not so much professional diplomats with a taste for languages as patriots eager to serve their country—they had a natural affinity, and Yoshida would take every opportunity to call on Hirota and engage him in conversation.

Yoshida had begun his career as vice-consul at the consulate in Mukden, then had spent one year and two years respectively at the embassies in London and Rome, followed by nearly four years as consul in Antung. Closely acquainted with Chinese affairs as he thus was, Yoshida had opposed the Twenty-one Demands. He called on other Japanese consuls to join him in a campaign against the demands, but word of his move leaked out and the campaign misfired.

Yoshida had also served as secretary at the Government-General in Korea, in which capacity he worked directly under Field Marshal Terauchi Masatake as Foreign Ministry representative. However, when Terauchi became prime minister in 1916 and set about forming a cabinet, Yoshida was among those who were ordered back to Japan.

When Yoshida presented himself at the prime minister's official residence, Terauchi greeted him with an invitation to become his private secretary. Yoshida was in two minds. Interested in politics as he was, he found the post immensely tempting. But another consideration deterred him from jumping immediately at the chance. Terauchi, without doubt, was the "man of the moment"—but on the other hand he was no more than that. Self-interest warned Yoshida that it was too early to hitch his wagon to such a star. He had already, in fact, been warned against it by his seniors, who knew of the attraction politics held for him.

Yoshida was the son (by a concubine) of Takeuchi Tsuna, a champion of the civil rights movement in Tosa, but had been adopted by a Yokohama merchant, and was free from financial worries. His wife, moreover, was the daughter of Makino Nobuaki, the minister of home affairs. Makino, the second son of Meiji-era statesman Okubo Toshimichi, was at home among the political establishment and in court circles, and his influence, thus, was not vulnerable to swings of political fortune. With such a father-in-law to back him up, Yoshida could afford to bide his time.

"I might manage to serve as prime minister," replied Yoshida to Terauchi's invitation, with his characteristic blend of facetiousness and a touch of showmanship, "but not as his secretary."

Terauchi, a solemn man, took this quite seriously. "You assume too much; I didn't say I'd definitely decided to take you on," he said irritably, and abruptly dropped the subject.

The foreign minister had issued an order appointing Yoshida to the embassy in Washington, but the order was countermanded just as Yoshida was getting ready to go. His attempt to incite the Japanese consuls in China into a campaign of opposition on the question of the Twenty-one Demands had been held against him. For a while, it even looked as though he might be dismissed, but the fact that he was the son-in-law of Makino Nobuaki, who was held in considerable awe at the Foreign Ministry, saved him and he was appointed acting head of the Records Section, one of the least spectacular jobs in the whole ministry.

Yoshida was disgruntled at the change. His new appointment had been decided on by Shidehara Kijuro, a foreign undersecretary with whom Yoshida had never got on well.

Shidehara was eleven years Yoshida's senior at the ministry. Son of a wealthy farming family in Osaka prefecture, he was punctilious and hard-working. A typical Foreign Ministry bureaucrat, he had a healthy respect for the existing order of things, whether it concerned the international balance of power or discipline within the ministry itself. What was more, he had married the youngest daughter of the Iwasaki family, which made him brother-in-law to Kato Takaaki, and a member by marriage of the Mitsubishi clan. Where the strength of his connections was concerned, he was a worthy match for Yoshida. Shidehara's knowledge of English was outstanding— thanks again to sheer hard work; all day long he sat at the next desk to a foreigner employed by the ministry, and even accompanied him when he went for a walk. Every morning, he would translate the London *Times* leader into Japanese, then translate it back into English and compare it with the original, making repeated additions and deletions. It was no wonder that he preferred men who were good at languages.

Yoshida had an innate aversion to this way of judging others' abilities, and the thought that he had been shunted aside by such a man increased his discontent, which he made no attempt to hide. For some while, he refused to answer the bell which Shidehara used to summon him, and it was not until the end of the year, when he was obliged to go and get the bonuses for the members of his section, that he brought himself to go to the undersecretary's room and reluctantly bow his head to Shidehara.

Such behavior was too much for the ministry to stomach, and Yoshida was once more sent to China, this time as consul in out-of-the-way Tsinan. There he spent an anguished year, until the news that the First World War peace conference was to be held in Paris and that the Foreign Ministry was to dispatch a large delegation, including the pick of its younger men, finally drove him into action.

The great powers such as England, America, and France were all organizing delegations of between one hundred and two hundred members with top leaders as their plenipotentiaries. Japan similarly was to send Prince Saionji as chief plenipotentiary, with an official delegation numbering close on seventy and a total membership of nearly one hundred and fifty. The younger Foreign Ministry officials accompanying Saionji were to include men such as Matsuoka and Saburi, who had joined the ministry two years, and one year, respectively, before Hirota and Yoshida, and who were held to represent the coming generation of Foreign Ministry leaders. Another young man who had only recently graduated from Kyoto Imperial University, Konoe Fumimaro, had also been given permission by Saionji to accompany the party.

The conference offered the ideal international setting for a young diplomat to show his paces. In terms of Yoshida's future, there was a vast difference between watching the proceedings from a distant corner of China and being on the spot as a member of the delegation.

Yoshida was incapable of the same kind of detachment as Hirota. Having been put out to graze for a while, he ought in theory to be lying low, but he determined nonetheless to take active steps to get a position on the team.

Appointments to the delegation were in the hands of Shidehara, who was making all the arrangements for the peace conference. Yoshida was in no position to ask him favors, nor was there any likelihood of such favors being granted. As luck had it, though, the vice-plenipotentiary was Makino Nobuaki. Going over Shidehara's head, Yoshida brought pressure to bear on his father-in-law, and eventually got himself onto the delegation in the capacity of Makino's secretary. (In practice, Yoshida was to prove almost totally unqualified to cope with the miscellaneous tasks involved in the job. On the way home, there was a thorough mix-up with hotels, trains, and ships, which so incensed Makino that he refused to speak to Yoshida for a month.)

Konoe, who accompanied Saionji to Europe, became increasingly convinced as discussions progressed that the views he had outlined in an article entitled "A Protest against 'Pacifism' Which Serves the Interests of Britain and the U.S.," published a little earlier in the magazine *Nihon oyobi Nihonjin* (Japan and the Japanese), were correct:

"The conflict in Europe is one between the powers-that-be and the powers-to-be, between the nations that are interested in preserving the status quo and those that are interested in destroying it. Those interested in preserving the status quo call for peace, those who wish to destroy it incite to war. Pacifism is by no means necessarily identical with justice and morality, nor is militarism necessarily in conflict with them.

"It is England and America who stand to benefit most by the alliance. The rest, lured into participation by the fine talk of justice and humanity, not only stand to gain nothing at all but will find themselves increasingly debilitated economically. This is intolerable, both from Japan's viewpoint and from the viewpoint of justice and humanity. Thus the first thing that Japan, at least, must insist on if there is any question of joining in an international peace pact at the coming peace talks is the abolition of economic imperialism and of discrimination between the yellow and white races."

The way in which the Paris conference—originally inspired by President Wilson's idealistic calls for a lasting peace—ended in vindictive demands by the powers for German reparations, and the way in which a Japanese proposal for racial equality, aimed partly at checking anti-Japanese legislation in the U.S., was sabotaged by Australian and American opposition, impressed Konoe as evidence of the high-handedness of the great powers and of the rule of force. Yet all the while, Saionji and the other Japanese envoys sat for the most part upright and expressionless, seldom expressing any view, to the extent that there were references to the "ivory mask" and "silent partners."

Konoe was intensely frustrated, and his impatience was shared by Matsuoka, who was press secretary to the Japanese delegation.

The topic most directly involving Japan's interests at the conference was the return of Kiaochow Bay. However, in view of Chinese opposition—and the intervention of England and France into the bargain—there seemed little chance of any favorable settlement. Matsuoka grew tired of this passive approach. At the age of thirteen, when his father's business in Yamaguchi had gone bankrupt, he had gone to America and spent nine years working his way through college. As a result, his English was good but, more important still, his life among the lower levels of society in America had taught him that force can only be opposed by force. By nature, moreover, he had always been a strong-willed man eager to have his own way.

One day, during the peace talks, he invited an American journalist to dinner on his own initiative, and told him with every appearance of sincerity that, as things were going, the Japanese delegation might well pack up and go home any day now; in fact, he said, it had already started making preparations to do so. The unwitting journalist promptly wired the report to the American press. Shortly afterward the news got back to Paris, where it added a touch of urgency to the proceedings, just as Matsuoka had calculated it would. From around this time, Matsuoka began to acquire confidence in the conscious manipulation of the media as a way of life.

He was also having doubts about his own future as a career diplomat. Before coming to the conference, Matsuoka had been in collision with Undersecretary Shidehara. Although the general atmosphere at the Foreign Ministry was against Japan's sending troops to Siberia (as part of the "Siberian Expedition" organized in 1918 by the Allies in support of anti-Bolshevik forces), the new foreign minister, Goto Shimpei, was positively in favor. Prime Minister Terauchi, accepting Goto's views without question, had decided that troops should be dispatched, and the necessary papers were drawn up ready for presentation to the emperor for his approval.

There was a considerable stir among the younger men at the ministry when they got wind of this. Matsuoka, who at the time was also serving as private secretary to the prime minister—the job that Yoshida was to have taken—was determined that some outlet should be found for their dissatisfaction. He therefore wrote a letter expressing the opposition of the "Foreign Ministry as a whole" to the sending of troops, and had it delivered to the prime minister.

Terauchi, who read the letter in the car taking him to see the emperor, was so startled by it that he turned back. Summoning Goto, he questioned him closely about the true feelings of the Foreign Ministry, as a result of which he gave up any idea of seeing the emperor for the moment.

Goto, who had suffered considerable loss of face, summoned Matsuoka and the others and gave them a dressing down. Matsuoka took this relatively quietly, but when Undersecretary Shidehara started to reprove him in the same way, Matsuoka rebelled.

"I thought you yourself were opposed to sending troops," he said. "All *we* did was to put it down in writing."

"I'm not talking about the rights and wrongs of the matter," Shidehara replied. "It's your way of doing things I don't like."

"You mean it's all right not to oppose the move?"

"To be *personally* opposed to it is fine, but . . ."

Matsuoka listened to Shidehara with growing depression. If this was an example of the successful career diplomat, then he was considerably disillusioned. Since coming to Paris, too, he had become more and more convinced that he himself was not going to be able always to conform to the strict pattern.

During their long stay in Paris, the members of the Japanese delegation formed all kinds of new personal ties that were to help determine the patterns of later years. Konoe and Yoshida got to know each other, and Konoe and Matsuoka found that they had many things in common. Saburi, Hirota's rival, became a favorite of Saionji's. Saionji himself, though he had earned Japan the label of "silent partner," had shared the same lodgings as French President Clemenceau, chairman of the conference, while he was a student in Paris, and the Japanese delegation accordingly was treated well. Japan itself was recognized as one of the five great powers, and was given a permanent seat on the Council of the League of Nations.

The delegation members were able to return home with renewed pride and confidence in themselves as the men responsible for the future of Japan.

Back at home in the Foreign Ministry building, like a Cinderella left behind while others went to the ball, Hirota had to content himself with reading the reports of the spectacular goings-on in Paris.

In 1919, five years after his appointment as head of the First Section of the Trade Bureau, Hirota was again visited by misfortune. Hirata, one of his closest friends, fell ill and died. The two had been together at middle school in Fukuoka, at higher school, and at Tokyo Imperial University. They had shared life together at the Kokokyo, taken the Foreign Ministry examination together, failed together, then the next year passed together. They might almost have been each other's shadows. It was Hirota who had found a sponsor to pay Hirata's fees, and it was Hirata who had virtually arranged Hirota's marriage when the latter hesitated to make the first move. Ironically enough, it was Hirota who had always been pale and introspective, and Hirata—with his weights and his icy ablutions by the well —who had exuded an air of ruddy good health.

Together, they had set out to be leaders of Japan's diplomacy. Now that was all over. This second blow, coming so soon after the loss of his irreplaceable mentor Yamaza, deeply impressed Hirota with the unpredictability of life.

From the outset, Hirota had had little worldly ambition. His parents' greatest wish had been that he should grow up strong. Furthermore, Zen practice and the example of the old-style patriots among his seniors had encouraged an undemanding attitude to life and a lack of self-interest which these two deaths only confirmed still more strongly in him.

Yet this outlook did not lessen his determination, as the survivor, to work twice as hard as a diplomat to make up for what his friends might have done; he resolved to forget all personal considerations in carrying out the tasks that he was set.

Hirata had served in India, Australia, and Russia, and had been due to take up the post of first secretary at the Japanese embassy in the U.S. When he died, it was Hirota who went to Washington in his stead.

In May, 1919, at the age of forty-one, Hirota arrived in San Francisco—and promptly asked the consul general, who came to meet him, to let him inspect conditions among Japanese immigrants in the area. The consul was dismayed, since he had never visited the settlements himself. Under the wing of a man called Ushijima—one of the more successful immigrants, known locally as the "Potato King"—Hirota spent several days visiting Japanese settlements in the Sacramento district. He also took the opportunity to make a detour to Los Angeles in order to visit orchards and fishing harbors where Japanese immigrants were working.

An extradition campaign was mounting against Japanese immigrants at the time. Japanese representatives in America, at a loss as to what to do for their compatriots, were inclined to turn a blind eye to their existence. Thus the immigrants themselves welcomed Hirota with some emotion, as the first Foreign Ministry official who had ever bothered to visit them. Word of the episode reached Washington, and Hirota had no sooner arrived at the embassy than the press came to interview him. He related his experiences and his feelings about it in awkward English but with evident sincerity.

The ambassador at the time Hirota took up his post was Ishii Kikujiro, a former foreign minister, but he was replaced almost immediately by Shidehara. This spectacular promotion for Shidehara —until now an undersecretary—was arranged by Prime Minister Hara Takashi, who had long been keeping a benevolent eye on him.

Shidehara, who seven years previously had spent something over a year at the embassy as counselor, now found himself its master, seated at the very desk once occupied by such illustrious predecessors as Mutsu Munemitsu, Hoshi Toru, and Komura Jutaro. The

Americans appreciated the fact that he had served as foreign under-secretary under five different prime ministers; and the emphasis in his diplomacy on peace, friendship, and international accord, together with his insistence on maintaining "good faith," ensured him a friendly welcome.

Shidehara put his fluent English to good use—he could also switch to French whenever it seemed more expedient—going out of his way to meet the Americans and engage in an active social life with other members of the diplomatic corps.

At the time of his appointment, Shidehara was forty-eight. His wife Masako, who was nine years his junior, had accompanied Kato Takaaki and his wife (her sister) to England during his term there as Japanese minister. She had been educated there for five years, and her English was correspondingly fluent. She was familiar with Western manners and social etiquette, and had the added advantage of being a daughter of the main branch of the powerful Mitsubishi family. Thus she enjoyed a high reputation as first lady of the embassy; the parties that Ambassador and Mrs. Shidehara held twice monthly at their official residence were much favored by prominent figures in political and diplomatic circles, and came to rank high in the Washington social world.

Ambassador Shidehara had two first secretaries: Saburi and Hirota. In other words, two rivals for the future leadership of the Foreign Ministry found themselves thrown together. In fact, though, the competition was placid and one-sided, very far from the violent clash of swords that the bystander might have hoped for. Saburi, who had served as adviser on the education of the crown prince, as head of the Foreign Ministry's Personnel Section, and assistant to one of the plenipotentiaries at the Paris Peace Conference, had an impeccable record. By comparison, Hirota's credentials were very lackluster. Saburi, moreover, had for long been a protégé of Shidehara's; in Washington the ambassador favored him almost blatantly for any and every task, appealing to him constantly, and even occasionally engaging him in long conversations in French, which nobody but they understood.

Hirota, cut off from the main preoccupations of the embassy, found himself for days on end largely confined to his office. He was not discontent, however, and used the time for his private study. In addition to the newspapers and magazines, he got hold of the latest publications on his own particular fields of interest and perused them for long hours in silence.

He had selected two subjects for special research. One was the influence of the Catholics in Protestant America, the other the American view of China. Even now, far away on the opposite side of the Pacific, he never forgot China for one moment, and was gradually coming to formulate his own view of the correct policy for Japan to adopt toward that country.

"Japan must keep her hands off mainland China," he told his subordinates. "Nor must she do anything to violate the spheres of influence of the Western powers. To do so would be to align the European nations and America against us and jeopardize Japan's whole future. We have inherited a 2,500-year-old legacy from our ancestors, and it is our duty to preserve it for our descendants throughout the next 2,500 years." In its insistence on non-aggression and international accord, this view followed the same lines as those expressed by Shidehara.

Whenever asked, Hirota would expound his ideas patiently to his younger colleagues, and would often ask their views as well. He was more popular among the young embassy secretaries than Saburi, whom they found rather unapproachable. At the same time, he was careful to keep a suitable distance between them and himself.

Among the American reporters who got to know him at this period, there were those who told each other that "Hirota would be a big man some day."

One day, a telegram arrived from the government announcing that Shidehara had been made a baron and awarded the First Class Order of Merit in recognition of his services to the nation. The effect on the embassy was electrifying and Shidehara was surrounded by an admiring crowd eager to offer congratulations.

It was not the first time that an honor conferred on Shidehara had created a stir. Thirteen years previously he had been awarded the

Third Class Order of Merit while still head of the Telegraphic Communications Section. He had been only thirty-five at the time, and the decoration not only set him far ahead of his contemporaries but was in itself unprecedented (Hirota, for example, had still been Fifth Class at the age of thirty-five). Naturally, there had been much speculation within the ministry as to what lay behind the award. Some put it down to Shidehara's being the son-in-law of Iwasaki, while others attacked him out of pure jealousy. The award prompted so much comment, in fact, that the episode became known as the "Third Class Order affair." The same man had now been made a baron and given the First Class Order even though he had only recently taken up his post as ambassador to America. His achievements may have been, as the official citation pointed out, exceptional, but so was the honor bestowed on him.

Amidst all the comings and goings of embassy officials, Hirota had read the cable once and stayed silent. Much to the consternation of his colleagues, he behaved as though nothing of any significance had happened and went on with his work just as usual. Although the effect on those around him was decidedly dampening, his show of indifference was prompted not by any personal objection to Shidehara but by other, more deep-seated convictions. To him, aristocratic titles and carefully graded honors were matters of the utmost unimportance.

The type of men to whom he felt closest were individuals like his father, who spent his days chipping silently at the stone that was his trade; or his father-in-law, that perennial champion of patriotic causes who was always ready, despite his own poverty, to help the aspiring young; or Toyama Mitsuru, content to remain outside the halls of power precisely because of his concern for the country's future. In comparison with the lives of such men, the diplomatic world of titles, honors, and high society was somehow alien to Hirota, nor did he feel that that world contributed in any way to the realization of the true ideals of the diplomat. A diplomat, as much as anybody else, was a patriot working for his country. It was enough for him to do his job properly; honors and other rewards were, rather, to be shunned as an actual hindrance to the real task in hand.

He was quite well aware that his present attitude would be condemned as childish. Why stand by some abstract principle—people would say—when all that was required was a simple word of congratulation? But Hirota was by nature incapable of paying that kind of lip service, which seemed to him a denial of everything he lived for.

It was not particularly pleasant for Shidehara to have his first secretary—the man who, with Saburi, was his closest assistant—assume such an attitude in front of the whole embassy staff. But he said nothing, either then or later, nor did he consciously discriminate against Hirota because of the episode. The fact was that he had already been discriminating against him in the way he looked to Saburi, whom he had raised to the position of counselor, for advice and assistance in every possible situation. At other times, he would go over Hirota's head and call in younger members of his staff such as Ishii Itaro.

Quite apart from any questions of personal feeling, this was Shidehara's customary way of handling people. He always concerned himself with men who were "able" by his own standards—which very often meant linguistic ability—and was indifferent, not to say cold, to everybody else. At one stage, there were even complaints from younger members of his staff that he paid too little attention to the training of his juniors. In Shidehara's eyes, however, diplomats were created not by their superiors but by their own efforts. He always stressed that he had got where he was himself by his own perseverance.

He made great use of "able" men such as Saburi, who loyally obeyed his own orders but remained aloof to the other staff; as he saw it, the Foreign Ministry needed only a handful of outstanding men in order to keep going. In some ways, in short, he was the typical elitist bureaucrat.

Hirota's tour in Washington ended after less than a year and a half. His health had been poor, and his return home was partly for purposes of convalescence. Even so, his new post in the newly established Information Section was something of a sinecure. And in 1921,

41

around the same time that he took up this post, the Washington Conference opened in America.

Ambassador Shidehara became Japanese plenipotentiary along with Navy Minister Kato Tomosaburo and Tokugawa Iesato, chairman of the House of Peers, while Shidehara's trusted right-hand man Saburi, whom Shidehara had also selected to accompany the Japanese delegation to the Paris Peace Conference, went as his assistant, thus adding new luster to an already distinguished record.

Saburi's rival Hirota, however, had so far had absolutely no first-hand experience of international conferences; once again, it seemed, he had missed an opportunity to cut a dash on the main stage of the diplomatic world. Diplomats at the time had an extraordinary preoccupation with such conferences and were extremely loath to be left out of things. Thus Ambassador Ishii, Shidehara's predecessor in Washington, had been so incensed by Prime Minister Hara's failure to include him in the delegation to Paris that enmity developed between the two men, and Ishii had eventually to be replaced.

Hirota was already forty-four, and it began to seem doubtful whether any important international conferences would ever come his way. He ought in theory to have resented this, but his usual lack of self-interest enabled him to apply himself quite happily to his "sinecure."

Even so, there was a fine irony in the task given him. The recently established Information Section, which at first had had no work worthy of the name, now acquired its first real task—to advertise the Washington Conference and the activities of Shidehara and Saburi, and to manipulate public opinion in their favor. There was considerable criticism in some quarters of the outcome of the conference —particularly its restrictions on the construction of capital ships and its call for respect for Chinese sovereignty, items which were seen as representing subservience to England and America—but Hirota worked hard in defense of the Japanese delegation.

Before long, Hirota became second-in-command of the same section. The change seemed to amount to little more than a shift of positions in an unimportant backwater, but Hirota set about his work with the same seriousness as ever. Although the Information

Section was the official outlet coordinating information for the domestic and foreign press, the reporters concerned often tried to worm news directly out of individual departments and sections within the ministry. The result was frequent clashes between the press and the Information Section, and it was always Hirota who bore the brunt of them. He refused to play to the crowd, but neither did he try to sidestep or gloss over issues, which he dealt with head-on, patiently expounding the ministry's point of view.

On one occasion, the argument grew so fierce that a reporter threatened violence. Quietly, Hirota rose and showed by his stance that he was prepared if necessary to use his knowledge of judo in dealing with the other man. This was inappropriate, perhaps, in a high-ranking Foreign Ministry official in his mid-forties, but it was typical of Hirota; if that was how the other man felt, then he was ready to take him on, even if it meant risking his own career. Such aspects of his character, and the obvious sincerity of his manner, impressed the reporters. The view spread, just as it had done in Washington, that Hirota "would be a big man some day," and he won himself many devoted supporters—which was one unexpected harvest of his "sinecure."

It was the same sinecure, in fact, that was to enable him to get back into the mainstream of events at an unexpectedly early date. In the second Yamamoto Gombei government which came to power in September, 1923, shortly after the Great Kanto Earthquake, Ishuin Hikokichi, head of the Information Section and Hirota's immediate superior, was appointed foreign minister and Hirota was selected to head the Bureau of European and American Affairs under him.

Ishuin had come to Peking as minister while Hirota was working in the legation as probationer, and had been keeping a benevolent eye on Hirota ever since. Thus Hirota found himself at last on the path to higher office. Ironically, it was around the same time that Shidehara was put on the waiting list on account of illness and entered on a period of convalescence. He had suffered a recurrence of chronic kidney stone trouble during the Washington Conference, but had insisted on carrying on despite his doctor's advice. His appearance, though, was so pale and wasted, and he was in such obvious pain, that

President Harding expressed the fear that he might barely outlive the conference.

As soon as the conference was over Shidehara went home to rest. He could afford, of course, to take things easy for a while, since he had just completed a major task and had ample personal resources. Shidehara's return involved a characteristic episode which became known as the "Cadillac affair." He had brought back with him a new Cadillac, which he truthfully declared at the Yokohama Customs to be unused—even though, if it had been even slightly used, he could have brought it in without paying any duty. The customs officials concerned kept the figure as low as possible, but even so he had to pay up a considerable sum. Public feeling was divided between admiration for his characteristic rectitude and envy of a man who could bring in a Cadillac fully aware that he would have to pay a high duty. Shidehara himself, unconcerned, retired to his new residence, where he settled down to the life of a semi-invalid.

The political situation, meanwhile, was changing at a bewildering rate. The second Yamamoto government fell after three months as a result of the "Toranomon Incident," in which an attempt was made on the life of the prince regent (the present emperor). The Kiyoura government which succeeded it similarly lasted for less than half a year. Finally, in June, 1924, a coalition government was formed under Kato Takaaki, Shidehara's brother-in-law; and after a bare ten minutes of discussion, Shidehara agreed to take the post of foreign minister under the new prime minister.

It was still less than a year since Hirota had become head of the Bureau of European and American Affairs. In view of past events, it would not have been strange had he been shunted off into a siding at this point, but the new foreign minister left almost all his under-secretaries and bureau chiefs in their old positions. As a dyed-in-the-wool career diplomat, Shidehara was well acquainted with the delicate working of the bureaucratic machinery. He knew that it was rash to reshuffle high-ranking posts every time there was a change of government. He knew, too, that his own achievements as under-secretary for foreign affairs had been possible only because five successive foreign ministers had left him in the same post for a total of four years. Closing his eyes to any personal feelings or past grudges, Shidehara respected the existing order—though he gave the Trade Bureau to his henchman Saburi, whom he intended to use at the impending Peking Tariffs Conference.

The following year, when the second Kato government came into being, Shidehara again became foreign minister, and again retained Hirota in the same post. It was as though he were determined to maintain a noncommittal attitude toward the other man. Hirota, on his side, preserved his attitude of never actively seeking to advance himself. Yet by an odd turn of events, Shidehara was to contribute directly to Hirota's advancement.

It was Yoshida Shigeru who was the unwitting initiator of this development. Following the Paris Peace Conference, Yoshida, who had been a member of the delegation, had gone to the embassy in London, then had spent more than three years in China as consul general in Tientsin. He had returned to Japan for the first time in many years, and was now on the waiting list. Rumor had it that·this time he would get, at the very least, the legation in Sweden. Yoshida himself had just grown accustomed to this idea when Foreign Minister Shidehara said to him unexpectedly:

"I'm sorry about this, but I'd like you to take the post of consul general in Mukden. There's no other good man for the job." Yoshida must have shown his disappointment at the prospect of another term as consul general in China, for Shidehara then added consolingly:

"I'll see that they give you good treatment in terms of ranking."

"What kind of treatment?"

"Grade one of the higher civil service."

Reluctantly, Yoshida resigned himself to going to Mukden. Not long after this, however, he was again summoned by Shidehara.

"I'm sorry about this—" he began again, just as before. "In order to give you grade-one status, formalities require that I should do the same for Hirota, who joined the ministry at the same time. So I put both your names before the cabinet together. Unfortunately, however, the cabinet investigating committee says that although Hirota has spent enough years working within the ministry to be eligible for promotion again, you have not. They can promote Hirota, but not you."

Yoshida, in short, had been instrumental in arranging the promotion of a man uninterested in self-advancement while he himself had got left behind. He objected, but it was too late.

Nonetheless, Yoshida was not the type to suffer a setback without trying to get something out of it. He gave the matter some hard thought, and came up with a request that when he went to Mukden the prime minister should give him a personal letter of recommendation.

Shidehara spoke to his brother-in-law about it.

Having spent years in China, Yoshida knew from bitter experience that in a country where representatives of the Japanese military and various government agencies were struggling among each other to stake out their respective spheres of influence, the authority of the diplomat often went by the board. The legation's military attaché, for example, acted as though the minister and consul were not there at all. This trend promised to be particularly marked at Mukden, which was under the control of the Kwantung Army.*

On the other hand, it would facilitate Yoshida's work greatly if he got the prime minister to certify in his own hand that he, Yoshida, was an important figure assuming the post of consul general at the prime minister's own instigation. It would also, incidentally, help to assuage his own wounded pride.

Faced with this request—emanating from his own brother-in-law and concerning the son-in-law of Count Makino—the prime minister wrote a letter of introduction in which he warmly praised Yoshida, and showed it to Yoshida for his approval before handing it over.

Yoshida was by nature given to head-on confrontations, and the

*The Japanese military force—which became a separate command in 1919—protecting Japan's leasehold in the Liaotung Peninsula and the South Manchurian Railway. The behavior of its higher command, which was determined to promote the rapid development of Manchuria for Japan's benefit, came to typify the way in which the Japanese military in China took the bit between their teeth, acting without reference to, if not in actual defiance of, the government at home.

fact that he went this time armed with such a letter was to be a source of various collisions in the future.

Working under Shidehara, with his belief in international accord, Hirota was able to tackle in earnest the task of improving relations with the Soviet Union, on which he had made a start earlier.

Soviet-Japanese relations at the time, which were suffering from the painful aftereffects of the sending of Japanese troops to Siberia, were in a state of impasse, with no formal diplomatic contacts. As a result, talks had been initiated in Peking between Karakhan and Serizawa, the Soviet and Japanese ministers to China, but the clashes of interest involved and the lack of political stability on both sides made the talks hard going.

Where sheer determination was concerned, Serizawa was one of the Foreign Ministry's best men, but even he began to feel the strain and suggested to the ministry that negotiations should be suspended for a while. Hirota, however, used a combination of reproof and encouragement to make Serizawa persist, and in the end, after a staggering total of seventy-seven meetings, including the preliminary talks, a basic treaty was concluded between the Soviet Union and Japan which provided among other things for the complete withdrawal of the expeditionary force from northern Sakhalin, and the acquisition by Japan of rights where coal, petroleum, and forestry resources in northern Sakhalin were concerned. Thus diplomatic relations were at last restored between the two countries.

Things such as this helped spread the word that Hirota was a man whose opinions were worth hearing, not only because of his experience in the Information Section but also because of his knowledge of the whole field of government. He had many visitors—more visitors from outside, it was said, than anyone else in the Foreign Ministry. Nor were these all concerned with foreign affairs, but included politicians from both the government and opposition parties; men who paid allegiance to none of the existing political forces; businessmen; and even students.

There were some who frowned at the way he associated with a wide range of men cutting across party and factional boundaries, and there were others who saw him increasingly as a man of the future. It was even said that there were three ministers in the Foreign Ministry: Shidehara, the actual minister; Undersecretary Debuchi; and Hirota.

In April, 1927, Shidehara appointed Hirota minister to Holland. This, his first appointment as head of a legation, was in theory a major promotion. The country in question, however, was not China—as Hirota had always hoped it would be—but a small and by now relatively unimportant country far away on the other side of Europe.

It was, in a way, a change for the worse. Why was it necessary to send to Holland a man who had been privately referred to as one of the "three ministers in the Foreign Ministry" and touted as the next undersecretary for foreign affairs? There were some who questioned Shidehara's wisdom in making the appointment, and others who said outright that it was because there were too many "ministers" in the ministry.

One undeniable fact, at least, was that Shidehara had someone else—Saburi—in mind for the legation in China. Saburi was, as ever, progressing steadily along the road to success. After attending the Washington Conference, he had come home and served first as head of the Trade Bureau, then of the Treaties Bureau. And at the Peking Tariffs Conference, he had accompanied the Japanese plenipotentiary more as his right-hand man than as a simple assistant.

The conference, which aimed at restoring China's sovereignty over her trade tariffs, had been proposed by Japan who—having gone to a lot of trouble herself in winning revision of the unequal treaties concluded with foreign powers when she opened her doors to the outside world—understood the Chinese position well. It was natural therefore that China's leaders should have great expectations of Saburi, who had played a major part in the conference. He would be more welcome in China than any other Japanese diplomat, and awareness of this fact influenced Shidehara, who worked steadily to ensure that Saburi should be the next minister to China. The comparison with Hirota was inevitable.

"The legation in Holland isn't a bad post," Shidehara told Hirota hopefully. "I was minister in Holland and Denmark myself."

But that had been when Shidehara was forty-three, and he had stayed there for only a year.

Hirota was forty-nine. An appointment made by Shidehara, moreover, was likely to last for three years at least. Hirota had, in fact, spent three years under Shidehara as head of the Bureau of European and American Affairs, and those three years now began to look suspiciously like a "farewell gift" from the minister. To go to Holland for three years at this stage might well mean that his life as a diplomat was drawing to a close.

All in all, therefore, the prospect of going to Holland could hardly have been a pleasant one. Yet Hirota refused to brood over it. He composed a haiku to mark the occasion:

> A windmill—
> Taking a nap
> Until the next breeze blows.

Not that Hirota's little joke meant that he himself intended to "take a nap" in Holland, or in any way to shirk his duties. Shortly after the appointment was announced, he went to Nagasaki and got a professor at the Nagasaki Commercial College to show him around Nagasaki and Hirado so that he could get some direct feeling for the historical exchanges between Holland and Japan by seeing the sites most closely associated with them.

He even thought of traveling to Holland via Indonesia—then under Dutch rule—to see for himself how the colony was run. But he was also very keen to travel on the Trans-Siberian Railway and see something of post-revolutionary Russia. There were two desirable routes but, unfortunately, only one man.

Hirota wavered, but eventually the Siberian route won the day, thanks to his long-held view that Russia, with China, was one of the nations most crucial to Japan's foreign policy. Even so, he was still interested in finding out about Indonesia, so he decided to have one of his favorite subordinates in the Bureau of European and American Affairs come to Holland as legation secretary and have him take a good look at Indonesia on the way.

The aim, however, was not simply to study Dutch colonialism at work. "They say that whoever controls the tropics controls the world," he told Yoshida. "Any obvious encroachment by Japan would almost certainly give rise to international disputes, but that's no reason why she should hold back in every way. I'd like you to see if there isn't some scope for economic advances in forms that wouldn't make Holland feel threatened."

The task he had set was formidable, but the directions he gave concerning them were painstakingly detailed. He not only selected the spots to be observed, but gave instructions concerning how surveys and observations were to be made, and useful information on how to behave when meeting government officials or making contact with the man in the street. It was almost as though he were sticking his own eyes and ears onto Yoshida before sending him off on his travels.

Hirota had not yet left for Holland when, in 1927, a series of incidents occurred in China. The revolutionary Nationalist army led by Chiang Kai-shek had indulged in an orgy of violence and looting in Nanking on its Northern Expedition, and English and American gunboats on the Yangtze River had retaliated by firing on the Nationalist forces. The Japanese gunboats alone did not join in, the reason being that their captains had been requested by Japanese residents to hold their fire in case Chiang's forces were provoked into retaliatory killings. The rumor got around, however, that it was Foreign Minister Shidehara who had ordered the gunboats not to fire, and he was criticized for presuming, as a mere foreign minister, to interfere with the independence of the supreme command.

This affair was followed by an incident in Hankow in which a Japanese sailor was assaulted. Other countries, such as England and America, reacted to such alarming signs by issuing ultimatums via the diplomatic corps in Peking, rebuking Chiang Kai-shek and threatening military action if he did not take steps to prevent further outrages. Shidehara, however, was opposed to such measures. His justification was as follows:

"Almost all other countries, like human beings, have only one heart, but China has any number. Where there is only one heart, one has but to crush it in order to throw the whole country into a state of paralysis. Thus Japan, say, or England, or the United States, would be completely paralyzed should some foreign country destroy Tokyo, London, or New York by shelling. Since the banks and most other facilities would be cut off at the center, trading would receive a fatal blow. But China, having many hearts, would still maintain a 'pulse' even if one of them were crushed out of existence; it would be impossible to put all of them out of action with a single blow. Should adventurist policies lead to an attempt to conquer China by military force, operations would drag on indefinitely. This might be all right for other nations, but Japan, having important interests in China, is unwilling to embark on such a risky enterprise."

Faced with Japan's refusal, England and the U.S. also gave up the idea of sending troops. Abroad, Japan was criticized for her failure to adopt a spirit of international cooperation, while at home there was mounting criticism of Shidehara's "pusillanimous" policies which—it was claimed—would encourage Chinese aggrandizement without bringing a single benefit to Japan. The army and certain business-men with interests in China were particularly vehement in calling for abandonment of the Shidehara line.

Such attacks, combined with the effect of the Great Depression, toppled the government, which was replaced by a Seiyukai govern-ment headed by General Tanaka Giichi. Shidehara was relieved of his post as foreign minister.

Tanaka at first intended to appoint Honda Kumataro, an advocate of tougher policies toward China, as foreign minister, but a call from the court for more caution in China policies, together with strong opposition to the appointment from within the Foreign Ministry itself, persuaded him to drop the idea and take over the post him-self.

III

Late in the spring of 1927, Hirota arrived to take up his post in a Holland ablaze with tulips and daffodils. He had come alone. He had left his wife and children in Japan partly for the sake of the children's education, but still more out of personal concern for his wife Shizuko. As wife of the minister, Shizuko, who was retiring and ill suited to the social life, would have been obliged to attend all kinds of parties, and sometimes to act herself as hostess.

Hirota could not help calling to mind the dazzling figures that Ambassador Shidehara and his wife had cut as host and hostess at official functions during his own term in Washington. Educated in England, Mrs. Shidehara spoke fluent English; as a member of the famous Mitsubishi family, she had the savoir-faire and personal bearing essential in society. At parties and other such gatherings, she was in her element. Shizuko, in almost complete contrast, was out of her depth. Not that Hirota was dissatisfied with his wife; on the contrary, he tended to share her view of the social life as a waste of time. She had never been very strong, and suffered from chronic neuralgia. Rather than put her in such a position, he preferred to go alone, whatever the inconvenience. So he settled into the tiny official residence near the legation in the Hague together with a young man who acted as his secretary and a Dutch housekeeper.

Life in the Hague began every day with ten minutes of exercises which he had worked out for himself on the basis of standard judo movements. He himself took them in deadly earnest, but the children had always made fun of them as "Father's judo dance."

Hirota was, in fact, a judo enthusiast. He had started training at the Kodokan, the headquarters of Japanese judo, even before going to

52

the First Higher School, and his instructor had declared that if he cared to become a professional judoist, he would go far. He reached the second *dan* while still a student, and the fifth *dan* later. He was particularly good at the more spectacular throws, and would recount his own exploits with a pride unusual in one so reticent. The daily "judo dance" was his way of making up for lack of the real thing.

As before, the exercises were followed by a leisurely "morning bath." A white porcelain Western-style bath full of hot water made a poor substitute for the deep Japanese tub of fragrant wood in which one could soak up to the neck, but he did not feel the day had begun without this morning rite.

After a breakfast prepared by his housekeeper and perusal of the London *Times*, he would walk to the nearby legation along streets shaded by elms and linden trees. At noon, he walked back along the same streets for a simple lunch of sandwiches and coffee.Since lunchtime in Holland customarily lasted two hours, he would doze for thirty minutes or so on a sofa, then walk to work again. When work was over, he would stroll along the canals, or go for a drive.

It was a pleasant town to walk in, with its canals bordered by trees, its old bridges, its red-brick, gabled, medieval houses, and the pots of flowers at its windows. The surrounding countryside was flat and the roads well ordered. It was ideal for driving, and Hirota would tour the fields of flowers when they were in bloom, sometimes stopping by at farmhouses and taking home tulip bulbs that the farmers gave him.

He also tried his hand at billiards. The minister to Sweden, a contemporary of Hirota's who happened to be in the Hague, remarked jokingly that for Hirota to take up billiards must be one of the events of the century. Another pastime popular in the diplomatic community was golf, but Hirota, though he would recommend it to younger members of the legation, never played himself. He also avoided social functions except when it was absolutely necessary, and would often send the legation secretary to stand in for him.

Very occasionally, he would play *go* or mah-jongg with the younger men on his staff. He disliked losing, and was always reluctant to stop playing until he won. Noticing this tendency in himself, he decided that unless he stopped there was a danger of his becoming an addict. This, he decided, would be undesirable in his position, and from then on he began to avoid being drawn into such games, contenting himself instead with watching others play. Even here he would get his pleasure from watching the game as a game, without allowing himself the excitement of supporting one side or the other. In such ways, he managed to maintain the attitude of cool detachment that, in more serious circumstances, he deliberately adopted.

His fellow diplomats were also fond of playing cards, but here again he gradually withdrew from participation. If he found himself with time on his hands and a pack of cards available, he would play patience. Patience, with its monotonous repetition of the same operation that very seldom led to success, offered few of the thrills of other games. But the very "self-effacement" of this pastime, which could be engaged in alone and in which everything depended on the fall of the cards, gradually began to appeal to Hirota. He would go on and on, dealing out the cards in silence broken only by the occasional muttered comment.

Such times apart, Hirota's hours indoors were spent entirely in reading. "I never saw such a man," his Dutch housekeeper would say in despair, "taking so many baths and spending his whole time reading books."

Reluctant though he had been to come to Holland, Hirota was not one to spend his days in useless regrets. He had determined to use his time there as profitably as possible, both for himself and for his country, and concentrated therefore on the advantages of a period of duty in Holland. The country, though small, had once ruled much of the world: what was the secret of its development? Again, to survive though surrounded by larger nations must have required all kinds of effort and contrivances over the centuries; Holland's maintenance of her neutrality in World War I was a case in point. For Japan's sake, therefore, he would learn whatever he could about the secrets of getting by as a small nation. Yet another advantage was that, whereas in a large country one inevitably saw things through that country's eyes, to be in a small country gave one a chance to view the movements of the powers with more objectivity.

Unlike most other diplomats, Hirota was not content to read only books and magazines in English, but specially employed an elderly ex-member of the Dutch Foreign Ministry to read newspapers and magazines in Dutch for him and translate any editorials or commentaries of special interest; he also had him check through any material that promised to throw more light on particular subjects.

The day's reading would be rounded off with the *Analects*, which he read—lying peacefully in bed—in the same edition that he had been using ever since his days at middle school.

Around this time, his contemporary Yoshida was active in Manchuria—though "active" is perhaps too mild a word. Having taken up his post as consul general in Mukden under the personal auspices of the prime minister, Yoshida was generally accounted a figure to be reckoned with. Partly encouraged by this, and partly due to his naturally impetuous nature, Yoshida tackled every problem head-on, even in cases where the Kwantung Army and the South Manchurian Railway were inclined to tread cautiously.

The Tanaka government now in power was pursuing a tough policy toward China, and in 1928, when Chiang Kai-shek's forces passed through Shantung province on their way to quell dissident forces in the north, it promptly ordered Japanese troops into action on the pretext of defending Japan's local rights and interests. This piece of saber-rattling contrasted strongly with Shidehara's opposition to any use of military force by Japan alone. The only result was to fan anti-Japanese feeling, and to provoke the murder of Japanese residents in Tsinan. This in turn led Japan to send in troops a second and third time.

Prime Minister Tanaka was himself doubling as foreign minister, and Mori Tsutomu, a member of the Seiyukai's "positive" faction who had joined the Foreign Ministry as parliamentary undersecretary, had promptly set to work to break down the ministry's traditional insistence on continuity in foreign policy and to spread support for a get-tough line toward China. In what was, in part, an intimidatory gesture, the Japanese minister to China, as well as all consuls general, consuls, and other such officials, were summoned to Tokyo for a grand conference. This conference, which was known as the "Toho Kaigi" (Far East Conference), put forward a new China policy embodying such principles as the use of military force to protect Japanese citizens in China, and "positive and independent action to safeguard the security of Japan's special rights and interests in Manchuria and Mongolia."

Following this, a second Toho Kaigi was held at Dairen. Yoshida, who as consul general in Mukden was a leading figure, acted in close collaboration with Mori as one of the prime movers of both conferences. He also made moves, via his father-in-law Makino, to obtain the approval of the elder statesmen for their conclusions. Gradually, his taste for politics was being translated into action.

On his return to Mukden, Yoshida—acting on the principle that it was for those on the spot to put the policies of the Toho Kaigi into effect—embarked of his own accord on talks with Chang Tso-lin, who controlled the three eastern provinces of Manchuria at the time. Under an agreement of 1909, the Chinese Eastern Railway from Peking to Mukden crossed the Japanese-controlled South Manchurian Railway on its way to the arsenal in the walled city of Mukden, but Yoshida arbitrarily put forward a demand that the railway should be prevented from crossing the Japanese line on the grounds that it might well violate Japanese rights and interests. If Chang Tso-lin did not agree, he threatened, there would be trouble.

Yoshida's imperious attitude was due in part to the fact that Chang, having received aid from the agents of the Kwantung Army, was thus associated with it in his eyes, and partly to what he considered Chang's slighting of local Foreign Ministry agencies. As Yoshida saw things, Chang should have given priority to dealing with representatives of the Foreign Ministry.

On one occasion a staff officer of the Kwantung Army had come to Yoshida with an invitation to dinner from Chang.

"I'm not a Chang retainer," retorted Yoshida acidly. "Does he imagine I'll trot along gratefully whenever he cares to give the word?"

Yoshida's threat of "trouble," coming on top of such incidents, angered Chang Tso-lin.

"Trouble?" he snorted. "Does Japan think it's going to grab Manchuria by force of arms, then?" And he went off to Peking without further ado.

Even the Kwantung Army was taken aback at Yoshida's high-handed way of doing things. Not only had he beaten them at their own game, which was mortifying enough, but he had offended Chang Tso-lin whom they had taken a great deal of trouble in winning over. To have him run off to Peking was adding insult to injury, and the whole staff was up in arms against Yoshida.

With Chang fled and the Kwantung Army after his blood, Yoshida was left in a thoroughly awkward position as consul general. There was nobody who took his side—partly, no doubt, because of the airs he had put on as the prime minister's "personal appointee." Finding himself thus out on a limb, he for once admitted defeat and beat a retreat into the Mukden Red Cross Hospital. He then applied to be sent home, pleading the need for convalescence, and retired to Japan.

Back home, recovery was swift and complete. He promptly set about finding himself a suitable new post, but it was the legation in Sweden that he was eventually offered. The job was not an especially attractive one, but in view of the fact that Hirota—who had joined the Foreign Ministry at the same time and was ahead of him in terms of promotion—was quite happily ensconced in the legation in Holland, Yoshida could hardly decline it. He was discontentedly awaiting his departure date, when Undersecretary for Foreign Affairs Debuchi was appointed ambassador to the United States, thus leaving the undersecretaryship vacant.

The sight of such a desirable post waiting for an occupant tempted Yoshida greatly. He went to see Mori Tsutomu, parliamentary undersecretary, who, being of a like mind, understood how Yoshida felt and promised to recommend him to the permanent undersecretary.

"Not," Mori added in a flat voice, "that it's likely to have much effect."

"Why?"

"Debuchi has already recommended Hirota from the legation in Holland."

Yoshida was thoroughly put out; once again, it looked as though he was going to be outdone by Hirota.

"As you know," Mori added consolingly, "Debuchi is related by marriage to Prime Minister Tanaka. So the P.M. is sure to pay more attention to Debuchi than me. Besides, the people at the Foreign Ministry have been lobbying for Hirota as undersecretary for some time now, and they feel that in terms of precedence the post ought to go to him."

Yoshida was silent.

"I'm sorry, but I'm afraid there's little hope of your being made undersecretary. I think the best thing at the moment would be to forget all about it and take up the post in Sweden."

Yoshida thought for a while.

"In that case," he said, "I'll try having a word directly with Mr. Tanaka. Would you arrange it for me?"

Mori was startled, but Yoshida was not a man to go back on his word.

"The outcome doesn't matter," he went on. "Either way, I'm going to try selling myself for once. If I find it's no use, I'll at least go to Sweden knowing I did everything possible."

Mori had no alternative but to talk to Prime Minister Tanaka and arrange an appointment for Yoshida. The ostensible reason for the visit was to allow Yoshida to pay his respects to Tanaka, who was also foreign minister, before taking up his post in Sweden.

When Yoshida arrived at the official residence, Tanaka launched the conversation by asking what Chang Tso-lin had been doing recently. But Yoshida brushed this aside, saying in effect, "That's not what I've come for today. I'll talk to you about that later." Then, having effectively got Tanaka's attention, he went on:

"To tell the truth, I feel that I'm the best candidate for foreign undersecretary. So I'd like to tell you how I should do things if *I* were in charge of foreign policy." And he proceeded for two hours to air his carefully thought-out views on Japan's China policy and related questions.

Tanaka listened without interrupting, his face turned toward the garden, his expression severe. There was nothing to give Yoshida any encouragement.

The next day, however, a telephone call from Tanaka summoned Yoshida to his villa at Koshigoe. "I'm thinking of appointing you foreign undersecretary," he said unconcernedly. "Would you have any objections?"

Yoshida was hardly likely to demur. For once, he had found someone who could handle him as well as he himself normally handled others. He took a fancy to Tanaka, and was to work thenceforth as his ever-willing agent.

Hirota, far away in Holland, was in no position to have any hand in these proceedings. Even if he had realized what was going on, he would have had no choice but to let things take their own course. He received the news of Yoshida's appointment as foreign undersecretary without emotion; for him, there was nothing for it but to continue his present circumscribed life.

Early in 1928, Hirota received a disturbing letter from home. His mother Take, who was eighty by now, had gone out alone, fallen while getting off a streetcar, and broken a collarbone. Infection had set in and her condition had gone rapidly downhill. In the past she had always been a strong-minded woman, but lately—according to the letter—she kept repeating that she wanted to see her son Koki again before she died.

Left to himself, Hirota would have returned to Japan at once, but in those days it would not have done for a minister to apply for home leave on the grounds of his mother's health. He explained this in a letter, but was shocked a few months later to receive a reply informing him that Take, on hearing that he could not come home, had declared that there was nothing left to live for. She had stopped eating, had resisted all attempts to feed her forcibly, and in the end had died from what was, in effect, starvation.

For some while after this, Hirota could not bring himself to go to the legation, but remained in his residence, mourning and praying before a photograph of his mother. He could not overcome his astonishment that a woman who had always seemed so resilient could do such a thing. After a while, however, his grief seemed gradually to abate and he began, on the contrary, to draw new strength from the episode. If his mother was not afraid of death, then he need not be afraid of it himself; rather, it was something that he could choose freely whenever the necessity should present itself. In this way, his mother still seemed to be encouraging him, even in death.

Take's death made Hirota even more aware of the distance that separated him from Japan. For the first time, his determination to concentrate all his attention on Holland and forget about home began to waver. Holland came to seem excessively cramped, even for a small country. It was, after all, even smaller than Kyushu, the most southerly of Japan's main islands. Now that he had been there for over two years, he began to feel hemmed in wherever he went.

The legation itself, too, was small and inadequate, with no garden nor even a drive. It was joined to another building which housed a dance hall, so that the sound of a band was sometimes audible. It was hardly a fit setting for a man who had once been numbered among the "three ministers in the Foreign Ministry". . . .

During his stay in Holland, Hirota attended the German reparations conference as one of Japan's representatives, and also attended a general meeting of the League of Nations as one of the acting Japanese plenipotentiaries, but neither of the meetings was especially important for Japan or dealt with any subjects of particular interest.

In the meantime, Hirota's rival Saburi had accompanied the Japanese plenipotentiary to the naval disarmament conference in Geneva, and had served as counselor at the embassy in London. Then, when Shidehara became foreign minister for the fourth time in 1929, he was summoned back to Japan and promoted in one step to be minister in China.

Sino-Japanese relations at the time had reached a kind of impasse. The Japanese army's occupation of Tsinan in response to the killing of Japanese residents there (May, 1928) had touched off a renewed anti-Japanese campaign. On the other hand, the Kwantung Army, which had been aiming to set up Chang Tso-lin as a puppet ruler, detaching Manchuria from China and turning it into a kind of Japanese colony, had detected signs of defection in Chang and murdered him by blowing up his special train near Mukden Station.

The Tanaka government, which had admitted to the emperor

that the murder was plotted by the Kwantung Army and which had promised to observe the emperor's request for strict punishment, changed its mind rapidly under pressure from the army and put the blame on Manchurians instead, on the pretext that to reveal the truth would have a harmful effect on the international scene.

The emperor was furious, and declared that he never wished to see Prime Minister Tanaka again. The military, in short, were already beginning to use their position as "the emperor's forces" in order to operate in blatant contradiction of the emperor's wishes.

It was amidst such circumstances that the Tanaka government resigned and a new government came into being under Hamaguchi Osachi.

Shidehara, who thus became foreign minister for the fourth time, once more set about trying to establish a policy of friendship toward China, and brought in Saburi—long his favorite right-hand man—to help him in the task. Saburi, who had already won the goodwill of important Chinese figures at the Tariffs Conference, took advantage of this to press ahead patiently with negotiations for trade and other agreements. This obviously represented a policy of conciliation quite the opposite of the Tanaka government's saber-rattling; talks proceeded smoothly with the Nationalist government, and a thaw seemed to be setting in once more. The Nationalists welcomed the new atmosphere, and Japanese economic circles, which had been distressed by moves such as the boycott of Japanese goods, saw it as a possible way out of their difficulties.

As minister to China and the leading figure in the new friendly advances, Saburi won increasing favor in Japanese political and business circles. Partly because of his distinguished family connections, he had attracted the attention of Prince Saionji, Japanese plenipotentiary to the Paris Peace Conference, which Saburi attended as a member of the delegation, and by this time he was on sufficiently friendly terms with Saionji to have access to him at any time.

Saburi's wife had died in Peking at the time of the Tariffs Conference, and since then he had been living in the Imperial Hotel whenever he was in Japan. He was a figure of considerable standing, firmly established among the elite, striding confidently along the broad road to success while others, such as Hirota in Holland, lingered on obscure byways.

Late on the night of November 28, 1929, little more than three months after he became minister to China, the same Saburi killed himself with a pistol at the Fujiya Hotel in the hot-spring resort of Miyanoshita, Hakone.

Saburi had returned to Japan for consultations with the government, but found Foreign Minister Shidehara and other government leaders preoccupied with working out Japan's attitude to the London naval disarmament conference of 1930. This, together with obstruction by the military and rightists, made it seem unlikely that the talks he had been having with the Nationalist government would bear any immediate fruit, and his suicide was attributed by some to increasing frustration as time went by and opportunities slipped from his grasp.

Another theory blamed his death on a sense of responsibility and disappointment arising from the realization that the agreements he had so confidently entered upon with the Chinese were unrealistic in terms of Japan's present situation.

There were other theories: that Saburi had found life unbearable without his wife; or, conversely, that his well-known fondness for women had got him involved in blackmail. His tall, aristocratic figure was, in fact, a familiar sight in the geisha quarters of Shimbashi and Akasaka. Nor did he restrict himself to the world of geisha, for there were also rumors of affairs with the wives of his subordinates. (Hirota, who disliked such involvements, disapproved strongly of Saburi's private conduct.)

The very number of conjectures made about the suicide meant, of course, that no really convincing motive was apparent at all. Saburi, curiously enough, had left no parting message. In fact, he had left instructions at the front desk of the hotel—a favorite retreat of his—that he should be awakened the next morning and an appointment made with the barber.

What was particularly strange was that though Saburi normally carried around with him a small Colt to protect himself with in an emergency, the weapon found in the dead man's hand was a large pistol of a completely different type. Still odder was the fact that a left-handed man should be holding the pistol in his right hand, and the fact that after death he had apparently drawn a quilt up over his face.

Foreign Minister Shidehara, who was deeply distressed, dismissed the suicide theory outright. If it was murder, then it must have been perpetrated by the military or rightists in an attempt to obstruct Shidehara's foreign policies. Saburi had, in fact, made remarks suggesting that he felt himself to be in danger, and it was for the same reason that he had carried a pistol around with him.

The head of the Foreign Ministry of the Chinese Nationalist government published an unusual statement to the effect that Minister Saburi's death was a great loss to relations between the two countries. The mysterious incident, whether suicide or murder, was perhaps symbolic in its veiled warning to diplomats of the grave personal danger involved in efforts to improve Sino-Japanese relations.

Except in the spring, with its riot of flowers, the climate in Holland is not of the best. Hirota disliked the strong winds, especially the biting westerly winds of autumn and winter, and the depressing mists. The many canals and the rows of old houses, though picturesque, had an ultimately lowering effect on him. Moreover, he had been there for nearly three years, with no particular duties to speak of, and his sense of frustration was steadily mounting. The enforced "nap" that he had accepted as inevitable had gone on too long: the winds that blew about the Hague left the sails of his own windmill motionless. His existence seemed to have been forgotten, and he himself was in danger of forgetting what his own wife and children looked like.

He asked a legation secretary who happened to be going back to Japan to tell Undersecretary Yoshida that, having been there almost three years, he wished to return home for at least a short while. Yoshida, he said, would understand even if the foreign minister (Shidehara) did not. It was one of the few cases in which Hirota broke his rule of not putting his own interests first (and in the light of subsequent events it might almost have been due to some unconscious premonition).

Not only was he feeling cramped in such a small country, but he had already done his job as minister quite adequately. He had acquainted himself with the realities of a neutralist foreign policy, and had made an objective study of the European powers. By now, there was little for him to learn by staying on in Holland. He was asking no favors, and would be content if necessary to be put on the waiting list, but he saw no reason why he should not be recalled to Japan. Even if Shidehara—with whom he had never been on very good terms—should object, he felt hopeful that something would be possible with Yoshida, his contemporary, as undersecretary.

Finding himself foreign minister again under Prime Minister Hamaguchi, with whom he had been friendly since middle-school days, Shidehara set about reestablishing the "Shidehara foreign policy" of international accord. Nevertheless, he left Yoshida Shigeru in the post of undersecretary, thereby drawing criticism from the opposition parties, who pointed out that Yoshida had been collaborating quite happily with former prime minister Tanaka's tough policy toward China. Shidehara, however, being a good bureaucrat, insisted that appointments to important posts should not be lightly interfered with, and left Yoshida where he was.

The two men, unfortunately, did not get on too well together. The previous prime minister, who had served concurrently as foreign minister, had left everything to Yoshida, giving meek approval to anything that Yoshida assured him was all right. Shidehara, however, insisted on reading everything for himself, sometimes even making personal corrections to diplomatic documents in English.

The effect was to leave Yoshida with little to do except lean back in his chair and puff at his cigars. Yoshida's grand airs and Shidehara's bureaucratic efficiency even prompted people in the ministry to joke that Shidehara was really the undersecretary, while Yoshida was the minister. Yet Yoshida had, in a sense, retreated from the limelight.

Such was the state of affairs that confronted the legation secretary when he arrived home from Holland. His first move was to report to Shidehara on his return, and he took this opportunity to relay Hirota's request. Shidehara agreed with surprising alacrity: it was he who had sent Hirota to Holland in the first place, but three years in the same post was too long. Shidehara, moreover, had just lost his right-hand man Saburi, while men such as Mori Tsutomu were gaining increasing influence within the ministry, and a body of younger men in favor of "positive" or hawkish foreign policies was gradually emerging.

Shidehara, sensing a void spreading within the red-brick Foreign Ministry building to which he had grown so attached, wanted to fill the void as far as possible with men whom he could trust. Though there might be difficulties of emotional communication between himself and Hirota, Hirota would at least stand by him in insisting on international accord and maintaining the traditions of the Foreign Ministry. It was no time to leave such a valuable ally languishing in a corner of far-off Europe.

The order for Hirota to come home was issued without consulting Yoshida at all. In March, 1930, Hirota had a final audience with the Dutch queen, then traveled to the Soviet Union, where he boarded a train and crossed the still snowy wastes of Siberia. On his arrival in Manchuli, however, he found unexpected bad news awaiting him at the station. His second son, Tadao, had died suddenly.

Tadao was a quiet, cheerful boy, but he had failed the entrance examinations for higher school (under the old system) for two years running. One more failure that year would have meant that he was liable for drafting into the army. Along with the third son, Masao, he sat for the entrance examination to Waseda Higher School. Masao, who took life more easily, did not go to check whether his name was on the list of successful candidates, and it was Tadao who, on the day, went for both of them. He found that Masao had passed whereas he himself had failed yet again.

Shortly afterward, Tadao killed himself. The day after his suicide, a letter arrived announcing that he had been included in a supplementary list of admissions.

In the Hirota family, the children had always been left to decide for themselves how far their education should proceed, and the parents had never pressed them on the matter. Even so, Hirota's long absence must have given Tadao a sense of responsibility and urgency that drove him to despair when he seemed to have failed.

Hirota, who had only just recovered from the shock of his mother's death, reeled beneath this new blow. In a kind of daze, he allowed the swaying train and ship to carry him the rest of the distance to Japan. And as he prayed before Tadao's ashes on the family altar, the tears streamed down his cheeks.

"Tadao—why did you have to die?" he muttered repeatedly and in vain. Yet somehow, the loss of both his mother and his son had made death seem more familiar and less terrifying. It was as though he looked forward now to his own death, when he could join them again.

Of the presents he had brought back for the children from Holland, one thus became redundant. For his wife Shizuko, who had kept the family going on her own for three years, he had bought a diamond ring in Holland, which was world-famous for diamond-cutting. Thus he fulfilled the pledge he had made more than twenty years earlier at Enoshima, shortly after their marriage, when he had bought her a shell ring and promised to replace it one day with a diamond.

Yet the diamond must have had a cold and empty glitter for them now, as they mourned together the loss of their son.

IV

On the morning of November 14, 1930, Hirota, who was now fifty-two, was standing on the platform of Tokyo station on the way to take up his appointment as ambassador to the Soviet Union. Once more, he was going alone.

It was the beginning of a long journey, to be made almost entirely by rail, tracing in reverse the same route—Shimonoseki, Pusan, Seoul, Mukden, Manchuli—that he had traversed six months earlier on his return from Holland.

It happened that Prime Minister Hamaguchi was also due to board the same limited express as Hirota, on his way to attend special army exercises being held in Okayama prefecture, and the platform was crowded with well-wishers, police, and the like. Hirota had reached the platform ahead of the prime minister and his party. The only people to see him off were his wife, children, and a few others.

He was bidding his family a terse though reluctant farewell—there was no telling when he might see them next—when Foreign Minister Shidehara came up onto the platform.

"It was you I came to see off," he said, "but I got stopped by the station master. He said the prime minister would be here any moment, so would I please wait in the waiting room." He grinned. " 'Me?' I said, 'I'm nothing to do with the prime minister. I came to see someone else off.' And I rushed on up here. You should have seen the station master's face!"

Hirota bowed his head. It was not unheard of for the foreign minister to see an ambassador off when he left to take up his post—he was, after all, his country's representative—but he was grateful that Shidehara should feel as he did in the circumstances. In part, of course, it was the fact that Shidehara was on intimate terms with Hamaguchi that made such a thing possible. Shidehara, moreover, was a bureaucrat who was fond of doing "the correct thing."

They had exchanged a few words when a sharp crack came from the direction of the central staircase. A policeman close to Hirota gave a cry of "They've done it!" and started running. Looking toward the stairs, they saw a man, ashen-faced, sinking to the ground in the center of a small group of people. It was the prime minister.

On the platform, his bodyguards were grappling with a man dressed in kimono. Half-carried by those about him, Hamaguchi was whisked away down the stairs. It was as though the whole thing had been a bad dream.

"What a terrible business," muttered Shidehara, his face grim, "—though Hamaguchi has always said that there's no better way for a man to die than to be killed on the job. . . ." He paused. "Anyway, it's you I came to see off. . . ." And he stayed on the platform.

Hirota was deeply agitated, but he was familiar with Shidehara's punctiliousness, and made no move. Before long, the bell rang. Shizuko and the others still stood there half-dazed. It was a gloomy start to his journey. With a silent nod, Hirota boarded the observation car at the rear of the express. Shidehara watched as the train slowly pulled out of the station, then raced off down the steps.

Hirota heard the details in a train traveling north up the Korean peninsula. Hamaguchi was gravely wounded. The criminal, a member of a rightist organization, claimed that he had plotted to assassinate the prime minister out of indignation at his "misgovernment" and his violation of the independence of the supreme command.

Six months earlier, at the disarmament conference in London, British and American pressure had obliged Japan to agree to limitations on the number of auxiliary vessels she could maintain. The navy, especially, was dissatisfied with this. It held that any decisions concerning military strength were a part of the prerogative of the emperor as supreme commander of the army and navy, and it tried to use the right of top-ranking officers to petition the emperor in order to present its views to him directly.

The Hamaguchi government, on the other hand, and Shidehara and others at the Foreign Ministry in particular, insisted throughout that international cooperation was most important of all, and that any breakdown of the conference should be avoided.

The government, moreover, was pursuing a policy of retrenchment; failure in the disarmament conference would mean an all-out race to build auxiliary vessels, and Japan, far from being able to curtail expenses, would face a rapidly expanding military budget. For this reason, the government did not pass on the military's petition, but hurriedly signed the treaty on its own responsibility. At the same time, it attempted to refute the arguments of its opponents with an interpretation of the Constitution put forward by legal expert Minobe Tatsukichi, who argued that decisions concerning military strength were the prerogative of the emperor in a purely formal sense and that they were thus mainly the responsibility of the government in its advisory capacity.

The military and one section of the right wing, who saw this as a violation of the independence of the supreme command, angrily criticized Hamaguchi, going so far as to claim that he was seeking to strip the emperor of his position as head of the nation's forces and give it to a party government.

The struggle, in other words, was one between the policy of "positive" moves advocated by the military and the Foreign Ministry's policy of international cooperation. The criticism of Shidehara's conciliatory line had been stepped up correspondingly, and the shooting of Hamaguchi occurred just when tension was at its height. As a result, the Hamaguchi government fell. The advocates of the independence of the supreme command had won the day—at least for the time being.

The incident was ominous in its suggestion of the threat posed by the independence and inviolability of the supreme command. It foretold the unleashing of a monster that might be used to dominate the nation's policies, and gave painful warning of the difficult days ahead.

Shortly after Hirota took up his new post, Shidehara switched his contemporary Yoshida from his post as foreign undersecretary to that of ambassador to Italy. The switch represented a promotion in one sense, in that undersecretaries were appointed by the government in the emperor's name, whereas ambassadors were personally appointed by the emperor, but the choice of country was not very flattering. Though one of the European "powers," Italy carried comparatively little weight, and there was not a single outstanding problem between her and Japan at the time. In practice, Yoshida, after an appropriate period of time in which to cool his heels, was being quietly removed from the position of undersecretary.

Another man who, like Yoshida, had been a favorite of Prime Minister Tanaka was Matsuoka Yosuke, who had entered the Foreign Ministry two years before Yoshida and Hirota. At Tanaka's recommendation, he had been made vice-president of the South Manchurian Railway at a time when Yoshida was consul general in Mukden, and the two had joined in on-the-spot advocacy of a "positive" policy toward Manchuria.

On the fall of the Tanaka government, Matsuoka had resigned from the South Manchurian Railway. He had later stood for election in his home district, Yamaguchi prefecture, and was now a member of the Diet. Following the assault on Hamaguchi, when Shidehara became acting prime minister, Matsuoka launched a blistering attack on him in the Diet. In the shadow of the Depression, he claimed, the powers were moving toward formation of an economic bloc. Japan was the only nation left out; she was being forced to make repeated concessions in the name of international cooperation, and to relinquish her economic rights and interests to no purpose; if things continued in this fashion, the nation would be gradually squeezed out of existence.

Though favoring "armed diplomacy," neither Matsuoka nor Yoshida—nor Tanaka Giichi himself, for that matter—had, of course, actual resort to military force in mind; they aimed merely to safeguard and expand Japan's rights and interests by means of diplomatic negotiations backed up by force. They, as much as anyone else, were embarrassed by and indignant at the series of direct moves—beginning with the bomb outrage against Chang Tso-lin—embarked on by headstrong members of the Kwantung Army.

On September 18, 1931, within less than a year of Hirota's arrival in Moscow, the Manchurian Incident occurred.

At the embassy in Moscow, Counselor Amau was thrown into utter consternation by the news, but Ambassador Hirota remained completely unruffled. So marked was the difference between the two that the reporters who rushed to the embassy were understandably perplexed as to which reaction to take as their guide.

Hirota, of course, had no prior knowledge of the affair. It was merely that his experience, and his studies, had shown him the dangers of this kind presented by an expanding military, and by the Kwantung Army in particular, so that the Incident hardly came as a surprise. By nature, too, he was not one to express his personal feelings in displays of alarm or dismay. Furthermore, he had always been taught by Yamaza that the Soviet Union and China were at the heart of Japanese foreign policy; now that he was at the heart himself, faced with a really vital diplomatic question, the important thing was to keep calm.

Hirota prepared his stand cautiously. A stream of inquiries and warnings was flowing in from the Soviet government concerning the progress of the Incident. The only course for a representative abroad was to prevent the ripples spreading by reacting unsensationally yet with as great an impression of sincerity as possible.

With the subsequent occupation of Tsitsihar by the Kwantung Army, the Japanese government sought to avert criticism by instructing Japanese embassies abroad to inform the respective foreign governments that the army would soon withdraw. Hirota, however, sat on his instructions and did not immediately contact the Soviet government. Having gathered information on the situation in Manchuria and the movements of the Kwantung Army, he judged that no immediate withdrawal was likely, and that it would be better to wait for a while and see what happened.

Hirota was already aware of the gap between the ideas of the army and government in Tokyo, and between the army in Tokyo and the army on the continent. Once the army overseas took things into its own hands, orders from supreme command could not be relied on to be effective. The government's powers to hold it in check were still more doubtful.

As Hirota had foreseen, the Kwantung Army not merely failed to withdraw from Tsitsihar, but settled in for a permanent occupation. As a result, those Japanese ambassadors who, as instructed, had notified the governments in the countries where they were stationed found their credibility severely damaged. Moscow was the one exception. People had occasionally criticized Hirota for "shilly-shallying," but in fact it was the ability to do just this—in other words, not to allow himself to be rushed—that was his forte.

The Soviet Union had a number of rights in Manchuria, involving among other things the Chinese Eastern Railway, which was under joint Soviet and Chinese management. The Soviet Union was deeply concerned, thus, about the progress of the Incident, and there were rumors that it was going to station troops along the railway. Hirota responded by negotiating an agreement that the Soviet Union would observe strict neutrality in return for Japanese respect for Soviet rights, and memorandums were exchanged to that effect.

Once the Incident had occurred, Hirota felt that his own task as a diplomat was to prevent the fighting or other repercussions from spreading any further. But a serious difficulty arose. The Kwantung Army decided that it wanted to dispatch troops immediately, via the Chinese Eastern Railway, to deal with an uprising by forces under Ma Chan-shan in northern Manchuria. Since the railway as such was under joint Sino-Soviet management, it would be necessary to get Soviet permission for such a move, and the embassy in Moscow was asked to undertake the necessary negotiations. The situation was urgent; not to act now might mean that the Kwantung Army would seize the railway by force. Hirota hastily began negotiating with the Soviet government.

A provision concerning the Chinese Eastern Railway in the Treaty of Portsmouth said that Japan and Russia pledged themselves to maintain their respective railways in Manchuria solely for purposes of trade and industry, and never for purposes of military strategy. Thus the Soviet Union rejected Japan's request out of hand; since the treaty was so explicit, to agree would, it stressed, damage its prestige.

Hirota was in a dilemma. The Kwantung Army had already assembled at Changchun station, where it waited impatiently. To postpone a reply—and still more to present a refusal—would provoke it into action and lead to a clash between Japan and the Soviet Union. Finally, Hirota fabricated an argument that he hoped might work and tried it on Karakhan, the Soviet representative. Japan, he said, was fully aware of the provision, but there was a question as to the meaning of the phrase "for purposes of trade and industry." At present, the rebel forces in the area were inflicting grave losses on the inhabitants, including those engaged in trade and industry. Thus any move to quell the rebels was not made "for purposes of military strategy," but "for purposes of trade and industry" in the broad sense. This was sophistry, of course, but brazen sophistry was necessary if a crisis was to be averted. Earnestly, Hirota repeated his doubtful arguments.

Fortunately enough, Karakhan had already negotiated with Hirota on many occasions and knew what kind of man he was. Both of them were agreed, moreover, that as diplomats their first aim must be to stave off the pending crisis. Karakhan therefore agreed to go along with Hirota's argument—which would at least not mean a loss of face for the Soviet Union—and set about persuading the Soviet government. As a result, the transport of troops was approved— with the proviso that the regular passenger fares be duly paid!

One outstanding problem between the Soviet Union and Japan at the time was the fishing question. In accordance with long-standing practice and agreement under the Treaty of Portsmouth, Japanese fishing grounds extended as far as Soviet coastal waters, but the gradual expansion of Soviet fishing had given rise to continual disputes.

Negotiations for a Soviet-Japanese fishing treaty agreement had begun, but Hirota was the type who prefers to dig his heels in and proceed with talks on a slow-but-sure basis. As a result, the talks seemed, on the surface, to be making no progress at all, and the Japanese fishing industry was growing visibly impatient. Hirota paid no attention, but patiently pressed ahead with his talks with Karakhan, both sides making gradual concessions, until finally, one year and two months later, the negotiations bore fruit in the Hirota-Karakhan Agreement.

A related problem was the fact that whereas Japan and most other countries set the limits of their territorial waters at three nautical miles, the Soviet Union insisted on setting its own at twelve nautical miles. Any Japanese vessels that entered the twelve-mile limit were being investigated and seized. Japanese public opinion as a whole, and not just the fishing industry, was irritated. Hirota tackled this problem too, and after repeated meetings obtained an agreement that Japan would recognize the Soviet twelve-mile zone in principle, but that the Soviet Union would in practice ignore any Japanese vessels that entered the waters between the twelve-mile and three-mile limits, and refrain from seizing them.

As in the case of the Chinese Eastern Railway, Hirota's efforts succeeded in getting what Japan wanted without wounding Soviet pride. Thanks to this, amicable relations between the two countries were preserved, and the tense atmosphere engendered by the Manchurian Incident was dissipated, the Soviet side adopting a policy of non-intervention despite its dissatisfaction with Japan's moves to establish a separate state in Manchuria.

Moreover, Karakhan came to set great store by Hirota as ambassador, and showed his appreciation by inviting him on a trip to the Caucasus in which his hosts were lavish in their hospitality, laying on transport and giving dinners in his honor wherever he went.

After approximately two years in the Soviet Union, Hirota was relieved of his post and returned to Japan.

The members of his family who came to meet him were startled to find how thin and drawn he was. He was drinking, moreover, to an extent that would have been unthinkable in the old days. Despite the extreme outward calm that he had preserved at the outbreak of the Manchurian Incident, when he carried on as though nothing had happened, he was in fact worn out, both mentally and physically.

He suggested to the Foreign Ministry that ambassadors should be made to serve only one term, and that a man who had been ambassador should be allowed to retire afterward. He himself asked permission to do so, but the Foreign Ministry, pleading lack of precedent, merely placed him on the waiting list.

With the help of a relative, he bought some land at Kugenuma, on the coast about fifty miles from Tokyo, had a small house built there, and moved in. It stood in a grove of small pine trees near the beach, with no other houses nearby: a quiet, out-of-the-way retreat surrounded by greenery.

Hirota's desire to quit the Foreign Ministry was motivated by something more positive than the need for rest or the attractions of life in retirement. "The trouble nowadays is that everyone is under the thumb of the political parties," he would confide to his family. "What's needed is at least one man not in public office who can keep an impartial eye on the state of the world." It was himself, of course, that he had in mind.

He began his self-imposed task by burying himself in the collection of works on socialism that he had bought in the Soviet Union. Whenever he tired of this, he would relax by looking at art books, also acquired in the Soviet Union. Every day, he carefully perused the Japanese and foreign papers, as well as magazines and other material. He rarely went up to Tokyo, but met and talked freely and openly to all who came to see him. He was a better listener than talker, however; he gave his own views straightforwardly when asked, but not otherwise. He tended to hold forth more eloquently and with less prompting when the ideas he was expressing did not represent his own personal feelings.

He enjoyed, too, having his family round him again after such a long interval. Although he had lost Tadao, he still had two sons and three daughters alive and well. His eldest son Hiroo had left college and was working at the Specie Bank, his youngest son Masao was at higher school, and his second and third daughters, Miyoko and Toyoko, were both at school. It was a cheerful, lively household.

In the morning he still amused his family with "Father's judo dance." He often went out walking with his wife or daughters. In spring, it was pleasant to search for truffles among the roots at the foot of the pines. At mealtimes, he talked a great deal with the children; with his sons in particular he would speak animatedly of his experiences abroad and even his views on society and the state. He was a completely different man from the taciturn Hirota known to the outside world.

Around this time the international situation affecting Japan had taken a turn for the worse, the major cause being the Manchurian Incident and Japan's subsequent moves to establish an independent state there.

Following his return, Hirota, who had been in Moscow at the time, was able to obtain various new pieces of information about the outbreak of the Incident. On the night of the Incident, it happened that the consul general in Mukden—Hayashi Kyujiro, a contemporary of both Hirota and Yoshida—was absent attending the wake of a recently deceased acquaintance, and it was Morishima Morito, vice-consul, who was summoned to the special service agency.* Arriving at the agency, which was ablaze with light despite the late hour, he found senior staff officer Colonel Itagaki Seishiro and other officers in a frenzy of activity.

"The South Manchurian Railway, a vital Japanese interest, has been blown up by the Chinese army," the colonel told Morishima. "The army is already in action. I look to you for cooperation."

The abruptness of this announcement prompted Morishima to inquire in turn:

"In action? At whose orders? The army commander's?"

He asked this since he knew that on that day General Honjo Shigeru, commander of the Kwantung Army, was in Port Arthur.

Itagaki, however, was not taken aback.

"The commander-in-chief isn't here," he replied smoothly. "I

---

*The special service agencies were branches of army and navy intelligence attached to Japanese garrisons overseas and specializing in political intrigue.

have the order myself on his behalf, since the incident constituted a sudden emergency."

Morishima was doubtful about this, but things had happened too suddenly for him to do much about it. Nevertheless, since it seemed likely that the Kwantung Army would start by attacking Mukden as a prelude to carrying the fighting still further, he could not refrain from saying one thing:

"If the army's already on the move tonight, it can't be helped, but if it's going to be necessary to occupy Mukden, even temporarily, am I right in assuming you'll arrange for the army to move in by diplomatic negotiation?"

Itagaki glared angrily at Morishima.

"I told you that the supreme command's prerogative has come into effect, didn't I?" he bellowed. "Do you mean the consulate general is going to try to interfere with it?"

At this point, a captain called Hanaya, as though trying to please Itagaki, whipped out his sword and struck an aggressive pose in front of Morishima:

"We've no time here for anyone who infringes the supreme command's prerogative!" he shouted.

Beginning that night, bombs were thrown at various points in the area bordering the South Manchurian Railway, which was under the supervision of the consular police. This was an army ruse designed to dismay Japanese consuls into asking the Kwantung Army to go into action on their behalf. However, Hayashi and Morishima, as well as others such as Ishii Itaro, consul general in Kirin, were all men of strength and individuality; refusing to rise to the bait, they called in Uchida Yasuya, president of the South Manchurian Railway, in an attempt to talk sense into the Kwantung Army, and sent a series of top-secret cables to the Foreign Ministry asking it to have the army call off its action immediately.

The result was to deepen still further the already existing rift between the Kwantung Army and Foreign Ministry officials on the spot.

From the outbreak of the Manchurian Incident, Itagaki and other staff officers of the Kwantung Army continually insisted on the "independence of the supreme command"—in other words, on the fiction that military affairs were under the direct control of the emperor. The emperor himself, however, was if anything surprised and distressed by the Incident.

He told Okamoto Aisuke, one of his chamberlains, of his concern for international trust in Japan and for the cause of lasting peace. He was convinced, he said, that this was the best way to ensure Japan's future prosperity and the true happiness of her people. It was extremely regrettable that the military on the continent should have ignored his orders and rashly extended the scope of the Incident, using military force in an attempt to overwhelm the Chinese people. Still more he feared that it would invite interference by the powers and bring Japan and the Japanese to destruction. The fate of Japan's ninety million people and the land that had been handed down to them by his imperial ancestors now rested on his own shoulders. The weight of his responsibility kept him awake at night....

The leaders of the military were appropriately chastened by this news, and the war minister and General Kanaya Hanzo, chief of the general staff, went to the palace to convey their apologies. The military in Tokyo, hearing of the ominous moves afoot in the Kwantung Army, had in fact on two or three occasions dispatched special envoys from staff headquarters and elsewhere in an attempt to calm it down. Foreign Minister Shidehara likewise made repeated protests to General Kanaya.

The military authorities in Tokyo directed the Kwantung Army to stop the Incident from spreading. This was in fact an imperial order, representing an exercise of the emperor's authority as supreme commander of the military, yet the Kwantung Army—the vociferous exponent of the inviolability of the supreme command—disobeyed and continued to take things into its own hands. Chinchow, far removed from the areas bordering the South Manchurian Railway, was bombed, and Tsitsihar was occupied.

This occurred just before the government promised other countries to prevent expansion of the Incident, and the Japanese ambassadors and ministers in those countries found themselves, as we have already seen, in an embarrassing predicament.

At one point Foreign Minister Shidehara, learning via consular officials in Manchuria that one unit was advancing on Chinchow even though it had not been ordered into action, contacted the war minister. A check was made, and the chief of the general staff, submitting the matter to imperial decision, recalled the unit in question to Mukden.

Following this, the military authorities in Tokyo issued repeated orders to the units of the Kwantung Army concerned to "withdraw to the areas bordering the South Manchurian Railway," but the army marched on regardless. In the meantime, Doihara Kenji, chief of the special service agency in Mukden, set about bringing the former emperor of the Ch'ing dynasty from Tientsin as part of a move to establish Manchuria as a separate country.

Both the government and elder statesmen such as Prince Saionji repeatedly deplored the way the Kwantung Army had got out of control. "It is a grotesque state of affairs," lamented Prime Minister Wakatsuki Reijiro, who took over from Hamaguchi in 1931, "when the Japanese army fails to obey the orders of the Japanese government." The view was even privately expressed that the Kwantung Army was in fact no longer a Japanese army but an independent force on its own.

Since the outbreak of the Incident, General Honjo, commander of the Kwantung Army, had been more or less confined to his quarters, where he led a life of enforced piety, meditating and reading the sutras. When he heard the talk of the army's "independence," he wept in horror. But it was not only the Kwantung Army that had got out of hand. General Hayashi, commander of the army in Korea, had sent his forces across the Yalu River and into Manchuria in support of the Kwantung Army before imperial sanction had been received, thus disobeying the rule that "an army commander must not send his forces outside the area under his control without direct orders from the emperor."

The military in Tokyo were not, in fact, standing by completely impassively. In December, 1931, the Wakatsuki government resigned on the grounds of "its lack of political power to deal with the Incident and disagreement among its members concerning reorganization of the cabinet." A new, exclusively Seiyukai government was formed by Inukai Tsuyoshi, and at the strong recommendation of Mori Tsutomu, Hiranuma Kiichiro, and other members of the "reformist" (i.e. right-wing) faction, appointed Lieutenant General Araki Sadao, an ardent imperialist popular among the young officers, as war minister at the early age of fifty-four.

As a result of a reshuffle carried out by Araki, the army set up Imperial Prince Kan'in as its chief of the general staff. The army resented receiving complaints from the foreign minister and his like; with Prince Kan'in—who was not only a member of the imperial family but also a venerated figure within the military—it would be able to exert proper pressure in its capacity as supreme command. The navy followed suit by appointing Imperial Prince Fushimi as its chief of the general staff.

This new military leadership softened its attitude toward the Kwantung Army and began to view its "positive policies" with a lenient eye. And in January of the following year, 1932, the Incident, once again as the result of an army plot, spread to Shanghai.

General Shirakawa Yoshinori, commander of the two army divisions sent on this occasion, was given special instructions by the emperor to "deal with the enemy as quickly as possible, then to wind up the episode and return home without waging a prolonged campaign." In accordance with this imperial request, General Shirakawa brought all belligerent activities by the Japanese army to an end on March 3, by which time the Shanghai area had been cleared of opposing forces.

Somewhat later, however, Shirakawa was killed by a bomb thrown by a Korean during a ceremony in Shanghai marking the emperor's birthday (Minister Shigemitsu, who was with him at the time, lost a leg in the same incident). On hearing of Shirakawa's death, the emperor commented that "Japan had lost a fine officer, who would be missed," and on the first anniversary of the incident sent a poem to the deceased's family eulogizing his bravery in proclaiming a ceasefire; the literal meaning of the poem is, "I recall the bravery that stopped the fighting on the day when girls at home set out their dolls"

(March 3 is the date of the traditional Dolls Festival in Japan).

It was an unusual imperial gesture—a sign, perhaps, of just how rare were those military men who observed the emperor's commands faithfully.

Meanwhile, the Kwantung Army went ahead unchecked, and in March, 1932, the establishment of the puppet state of Manchukuo was announced.

On May 15, Prime Minister Inukai was attacked and killed by a group of naval officers; the silent pressure from the military had stepped up again.

In the government of Saito Makoto, who took his place, Uchida Yasuya, president of the South Manchurian Railway, was appointed foreign minister.

Uchida, who had personally witnessed the Manchurian Incident, knew that the Kwantung Army's independent machinations had passed the point of no return. He considered that the best way to prevent hostilities from spreading any further and help find a solution was to recognize Manchukuo, to restore a normal atmosphere as far as possible in the areas affected, and to get the army to occupy itself with the development of Manchuria. Thus on November 15 the Japanese government recognized the state of Manchukuo; the Diet also gave its unanimous agreement.

As a result, Honjo, commander of the Kwantung Army, was elevated to the peerage, while Itagaki, Ishiwara, and other members of his staff were promoted to important posts in the central military command in Tokyo. On the other hand, diplomats Hayashi, Morishima, and Ishii were removed from Manchuria.

The army's confidence grew by leaps and bounds. All kinds of arguments began to find currency. The emperor's wishes may have been disobeyed, but had it not, in the event, served Japan's best interests? Uncritical loyalty to the emperor's commands—though undoubtedly loyalty of a kind—was only loyalty in the formal sense. "True" loyalty meant anything that promoted the interests of the Empire, even though it might cause the emperor himself some temporary distress. . . .

The Kwantung Army's adventures in Manchuria were not without support from public opinion. Ever since Japan had sent troops to the continent in the Sino-Japanese and Russo-Japanese wars, Manchuria had been a kind of "holy land" for the Japanese. It was also looked on as a kind of "lifeline." It was a land that had claimed "one hundred thousand valiant souls, two thousand million from the national purse," and as such was felt to be something more than part of a neighboring country. Total Japanese investment in Manchuria had, in fact, exceeded ¥1,600 million in 1930, a figure corresponding to seventy percent of all foreign investment in that country. And one million Japanese nationals, including eight hundred thousand Koreans, had already emigrated to different parts of Manchuria. The Japanese had started improving the South Manchurian Railway between Changchun and Port Arthur, and Dairen harbor had been enlarged, while many new coal and ore mines had been opened. In addition, hospitals, schools and other facilities had been constructed in the areas attached to the South Manchurian Railway, and had been thrown open to the Manchurians themselves.

These areas, being guarded by the Kwantung Army and Japanese police, were relatively safe to live in, and there was a steady influx from other regions of people who had suffered from the depradations of warlords and bandits. Manchuria north of the Great Wall was a "masterless land" without any clearly defined ruler, a land where various warlords struggled perpetually among themselves and bandits ran riot in the intervening areas.

At home in Japan, the Depression was at its height. In the towns, only one job was available for every ten persons seeking work. The agricultural villages were even worse off. In northern Honshu in particular, poor harvests due to unseasonal frosts had aggravated chronic poverty still further. Families in poor areas had long been known to sell off their daughters in times of distress, but now, it was said, a soldier setting off to fight on the continent would sometimes be told by his relatives "not to return alive." This was no exhortation to the unfortunate man to lay down his life for his country; it meant that, should he be killed in battle, money would be forthcoming from the government. The desire for money even led, apparently, to unseemly disputes among the bereaved over ownership of the ashes.

To people in such straits, the "masterless" spaces of Manchuria were a land of infinite promise—promise of vast stretches of fertile soil that could be worked, it was claimed, for ten years without use of fertilizers; promise, too, of limitless supplies of minerals beneath the soil.

For a Japan which, unlike the Western nations, had no real colonies to speak of, Manchuria seemed to be the one remaining possibility. Moreover, Ishiwara Kanji and other staff officers of the Kwantung Army had been fired with the ambition of making it not merely a colony but a paradise of prosperity for Asian peoples in general, among them the Japanese. There was much talk of "harmony among the five peoples," and of "building a new state, founded in righteousness."

To use the Japanese army to secure public peace and order, then to found a unified nation in which the various peoples could live together in harmony and prosperity—such was the romantic dream, so at variance with the bloodthirsty realities of plotting for war, that inspired Ishiwara and his fellows, and that was to be accepted by so many of the ordinary public.

Ishiwara and the rest were also, of course, motivated by something more than such youthful flights of fancy. According to Ishiwara's theory, possession of Manchuria and Mongolia was an indispensable military requirement. He foresaw the outbreak, in the not so distant future, of "a true world war, man's last and greatest war," involving principally Japan and the United States. This war would naturally be prolonged, and the mobilization of all Japan's national resources would not in itself be sufficient to ensure victory. She must bring the vast territories and resources of Manchuria and Mongolia into play, building up a huge productive capacity based on a system of cooperation between the various peoples concerned. Only this, he believed, could ensure final victory in the "last and greatest war." Japan must secure Manchuria and Mongolia for herself, even if it meant fighting for them. In that sense at least, the Manchurian Incident was "a war to feed war."

The Soviet Union at the time was preoccupied with internal reorganization and development, while China had still not achieved complete political unity. It was the ideal time for launching a venture in Manchuria.

Seen from the Chinese viewpoint, the existence of Japanese rights and interests in Manchuria was, of course, a violation of her sovereignty and an encroachment on her territories. The anti-Japanese movement gathered strength, and there were increasing calls for the return of Port Arthur, Dairen, and the South Manchurian Railway; the recovery from Japan of the power of consular jurisdiction and policing rights; and the removal of schools set up by the Japanese.

Under the influence of such popular feeling, various provinces of Manchuria issued "edicts prohibiting the illegal sale of national territory," which banned the sale of land to Japanese or Koreans, and moves were even made to recover land already leased. At the same time, taxes were stepped up on Japanese enterprise in the fields of commerce, manufacturing, and mining, and boycotts of Japanese goods were encouraged, with the result that local Japanese residents were becoming increasingly disturbed.

Large-scale harbor works had already been started on Hulutao as a rival to Dairen, and work was going ahead on construction of a new railway network designed to "encircle" the South Manchurian Railway. Here, too, it looked as though Japanese "rights and interests" might be reduced to forms without substance. Unless prompt action was taken, Japan would end up losing all her rights in Manchuria, her "lifeline." The kind of negative approach based on international cooperation adopted by Shidehara would only serve the interests of world forces concerned to maintain the status quo: it would make the Chinese government and warlords still more swollen-headed, and abandon Japan's interests all to no purpose. It was this situation that prompted Matsuoka to put pressure on Shidehara in the Diet.

A sense of crisis, of the need for some action, was predominant among Japanese on the spot, and the prevailing view was that the sudden moves made by the Kwantung Army had cut a way out for Japan just as she had been in danger of being hemmed in. Most newspaper editorials followed this line of reasoning, and it was the same argument that persuaded the Diet to unanimously approve recognition of Manchukuo.

Shortly after the outbreak of the Incident, China (the Nationalist government) moved to put the question before the League of Nations. Japan tried to prevent this by claiming that the question was a local one, that the Japanese government had made up its mind to prevent the Incident spreading, and that a solution could be found by direct negotiations between the Japanese and local Chinese authorities.

The Chinese, however, insisted that the development of the Incident plainly showed that the Japanese army was acting according to a prearranged plan, and that the situation was beyond such simple solutions.

Although Shidehara, who was foreign minister at the time, was pessimistic about the outcome, he summoned the Chinese minister in Japan and through him earnestly sought to persuade China to change her mind.

"I hear," he said, "that your government has brought the Liutiaokou [Manchurian] incident before the League of Nations. I believe this move to be misguided. All that will happen at Geneva is that countries ignorant of the true state of affairs in the Far East will argue among themselves as though in some debating society. Since no country is going to admit it was wrong under such circumstances, everybody will be obliged to make tough speeches seeking to justify his own country. No decent solution will ever be reached that way. I feel strongly that the best course is for Japan and China to negotiate directly. In any case, the League of Nations Covenant stipulates that appeal to Geneva should not be made until every other diplomatic means has been exhausted. You're being too hasty. I'm sure that if only the delegates of the two countries whose interests are directly affected get together, without immediately turning it into an international question, and have heart-to-heart talks, some satisfactory solution can be reached. . . ."

The subsequent handling of the question at the League of Nations was, in fact, to justify Shidehara's fears. The Japanese and Chinese envoys engaged in acrimonious exchanges amidst a general lack of understanding for the special relationship between Japan and Manchuria. And the fact that the Kwantung Army was pressing on regardless provided a constant source of embarrassment to the Japanese delegation.

For example: Sato Naotake, ambassador to Belgium—who was one of the delegates, and had joined the Foreign Ministry one year before Hirota—would say, "Properly speaking, the League of Nations Covenant, as laid down in the preamble, applies to nations that are organized and unified. However, the present dispute has arisen with a country that in many ways can scarcely be described as 'unified.' If the country concerned were a united, constitutionally governed nation like those of Europe, there would be no need for us to protect our rights and interests by force; we could, and most certainly would, have resort to the method of solution stipulated in the Covenant. In the present case, unfortunately, that is not possible."

This would immediately meet with a scathing counterattack from the Chinese delegate:

"The Japanese delegate insultingly refers to China as a country without unity. One wonders, however, whether a country such as Japan—where the army and navy embark on what can only be described as lunatic ventures, and where the government is powerless to hold them in check—can itself be described as 'unified.' Can Japan, whose diplomatic representatives make promise after promise to the Council only to have them scrapped at home, really be accepted as an 'organized' nation? If China, as Japan so insultingly describes her, is truly a country of anarchy and disarray, how is it that Japan demands of the Chinese government that it should negotiate? Why does it not look to the League of Nations to find some solution?"

The League of Nations, ignoring opposition from Japan, voted by thirteen votes to one to allow America—a non-member—to sit on the Council as an observer during debate on the question. The American representative, however, was inclined to give Shidehara's approach the benefit of the doubt and to dispatch the Lytton Commission so as to allow time to observe developments. He considered that there were limits to China's ability to maintain peace and order in Manchuria; the League of Nations fell in with this view, and at one stage was disposed to wait and see whether or not Japan would observe her promise of non-expansion.

At this point a new development occurred that placed the Japanese delegation in a dilemma. An order from Foreign Minister Shidehara arrived directing it to demand that the Council should include a clause in any League of Nations resolution stating that the League would not ask for the withdrawal of Japanese forces. To put forward such a tough demand, precisely at a moment when the League of Nations seemed prepared, for a while, to wait and see, would have spoiled everything. On inquiry, however, it turned out that Shiratori, head of the Information Section, had sent the cable—ostensibly a directive from the foreign minister—on his own responsibility as the result of a suggestion from the army.

Shortly after the establishment of the state of Manchukuo, Shiratori was asked by an American newspaperman when Japan was going to recognize the new country. He annoyed his interlocutor by replying sarcastically, "Japan is in no hurry. She doesn't have any canals to build there"—a snide reference to the fact that when America was planning to build the Panama Canal, she had engineered a revolution in Panama, then recognized the new government with remarkable speed. It was significant that the head of the Information Section should be a man capable of such provocative statements, a man moreover who enjoyed the support of the "positive" faction within the political world and the military.

It was no longer only within the military that younger men were coming to dominate their superiors. Within the Foreign Ministry itself, a "reformist" (rightist) faction had emerged to threaten the peaceful line, and was beginning to advocate an extremely chauvinistic foreign policy.

As for public opinion at home, there was no special reaction at first to the moves within the League of Nations. There was little understanding of the nature of the League, which was frequently dismissed as an organization aimed principally at allowing European nations to discuss European problems among themselves. However, as criticism of Japan gradually mounted within the League of Nations and Japan's isolation began to be reported in dramatic terms at home, public opinion hardened defiantly. The public, unaware that the Manchurian Incident was part of a plot by the Kwantung Army, believed that it had been prompted by an illegal attack by Chinese forces. It was indignant at the idea that Japan should be criticized when everyone ought to be heartily denouncing the outrages perpetrated by the Chinese army.

Even Nakano Seigo—who had been consistently anti-military, opposing the sending of troops to Siberia after the revolution and accusing the military of improprieties concerning their secret service funds, and who as a Minseito Diet member ought to have had access to more accurate information—could say:

"When it saw the railway at Liutiaokou destroyed before its very eyes, the garrison took determined action in a sudden demonstration of the true Yamato spirit. We acted on provocation."

He could even say:

"It is Japan, and not China, that is the victim of aggression in Manchuria and Mongolia. The aggressor is China."

Japan, moreover, was the "leader" of the Far East. There was resentment at the idea of interference in Far Eastern matters by countries unacquainted with the true circumstances, and people were gradually being persuaded that the League of Nations was acting high-handedly. National rallies were held demanding, among other things, Japan's secession from the League of Nations. A meeting held in Hibiya Hall with such patriotic speakers as Toyama Mitsuru, Nakano Seigo, and Tokutomi Soho was attended by a frenzied crowd, and the hall was full to overflowing two hours before the meeting started.

Nor did the League of Nations' attitude of "wait and see" last very long. With the occupation of Chinchow and the subsequent outbreak of the Shanghai incident, fierce criticism was leveled at Japan as a nation quite evidently, by now, bent on aggression. The retirement of Shidehara in December, 1931, still further weakened confidence in Japan's peaceful intentions. The Japanese delegation found itself isolated, its speeches greeted with catcalls and sarcastic laughter.

At this point the delegation was joined by Matsuoka Yosuke as chief plenipotentiary. He had been recommended for the post by Mori, Shiratori, and others of the "positive" faction.

Matsuoka did not leave Japan with the intention of supervising Japan's secession from the League. In theory, he was determined if possible to avoid a rupture. But there was a limit to what he could do at a time when Manchuria already presented a number of faits accomplis directly opposed to the wishes of the League; when the League's own attitude was becoming tougher; and when public opinion in Japan was also hardening in reaction against this.

Matsuoka's mission was a tragic one, yet he did not go without his aspirations and his plans.

At the Paris Peace Conference, which he had attended as press secretary, he had been disappointed to find that, although chief plenipotentiary Saionji and the others had arrived in grand style, bringing cooks and even maidservants with them from Japan, at the conference itself they made scarcely any pronouncements worthy of the name.

His determination to do better himself was all the stronger in that, at the present conference, Japan itself was the focus of discussion. He decided to put Japan's point of view straightforwardly and confidently so as to open the world's eyes to the facts. This he saw as a job for the statesman, not the professional diplomat.

Having worked his way through a provincial college in the States, Matsuoka had confidence in his own English. Thus on December 8, 1932, he walked into the general assembly of the League of Nations and without a manuscript harangued it for one hour and twenty minutes. The speech might, from its content, have been entitled "Japan on the Cross." Matsuoka took the stand that the member nations' failure to understand, or deliberate distortion of, Japan's special position in regard to Manchuria and Mongolia was as wide of the mark as the prejudice and persecution directed at Christ.

"What guarantee is there," he demanded, "that what you call 'world opinion' is not mistaken? We Japanese are resigned to undergoing a period of tribulation. Certain people in Europe and America are seeking to crucify Japan, here and now in the twentieth century.

Yes, gentlemen"—he argued loudly—"Japan is in imminent danger of being nailed to the cross. But we have faith, an unswerving faith, that within only a few years world opinion will change. And just as Jesus of Nazareth was finally understood by the world, so shall we in our turn be understood!"

Matsuoka made no attempt to conceal the note of tragic indignation; he hurled words at them, drunk with his own eloquence, in a performance that would have been beyond any of the career diplomats in the delegation. Thanks to his fluent English, every word and phrase he uttered got home immediately to the assembly, which listened in complete silence. This type of Japanese representative had never before been seen at an international conference; for the first time, Japan was voicing her claims from the rooftops.

The only effect, unfortunately, was to Japan's disadvantage. Far from deepening understanding, his use of the Christian metaphor was distasteful to people in Christian countries, and gave rise to still more undisguised aversion to Japan.

On the basis of the report of the Lytton Commission, a proposal was made that Manchuria should become a special zone with autonomous rights under Chinese sovereignty and that Japan should be asked to withdraw her troops. At China's insistence, this proposal was put before the general assembly, and adopted with forty-two nations out of forty-four voting in favor, one (Japan) voting against, and with one abstention (Siam).

Matsuoka rose in anger and left the hall at the head of the twenty-member Japanese delegation.

On the way home, Matsuoka visited Italy, where he met Mussolini, head of the Fascist party, then went to England and on to America. Here he met with President Roosevelt, and again voiced Japan's claims via the radio and press. Then he crossed to the West Coast, where he visited his alma mater, Oregon State University, and set up a stone over the grave of the woman who had been his benefactress during his days as a student.

To the citizens of Japanese descent who came to meet him, he said, "You should be good Americans; you have no need to be good Japanese." It was a lesson that he had learned himself during his stay as an impoverished student in America, but it was also, in a sense, a reference to the unhappy age that he suspected lay ahead for the Japanese and American peoples.

At home in Japan, Matsuoka's activities at the League of Nations were reported, with appropriate exaggerations, by Shiratori's Information Section. Matsuoka—it was claimed—had proudly advanced Japan's claims in the face of the tyrannical powers and had foiled their schemings. Matsuoka's popularity went up by leaps and bounds.

During his leisurely progress homeward, the adulation reached a peak, and when he finally arrived in Yokohama he found himself welcomed with a fervor appropriate to the return of a conquering hero.

Somewhat earlier, around the same time as Hirota's return to Japan, Yoshida Shigeru had been released from his post as ambassador to Italy and had also come home. He had been in Rome for one and a half years. His stay had been a period of tedium relieved by no events of any importance. The rise of the Fascist party in Italy, moreover, had reminded him unpleasantly of the Kwantung Army's arrogant ways in Manchuria.

Though no pacifist, Yoshida had been an anti-militarist of a kind ever since his clash, as consul general in Mukden, with the Kwantung Army, and in this sense his advocacy of "positive" foreign policies had come to acquire a different nuance from Matsuoka's.

On his return to Japan, Foreign Minister Uchida had said to him, "How about taking the ambassadorship to the United States?" The tone had been both halfhearted and vaguely patronizing, and Yoshida had refused. As a result of Japan's secession from the League of Nations in March, 1933, and the anti-Japanese movement within America, relations with the United States seemed about to enter on a difficult period. To be sent as ambassador at such a time was tantamount to going to clear up in the wake of the "national hero."

Yoshida, moreover, had the feeling that by recognizing, for example, the independence of Manchukuo, Uchida was justifying one by one the actions of the Kwantung Army. The fact that Uchida had once been president of the South Manchurian Railway suggested that he might well be willing to compromise in other such ways.

Yoshida's contemporary, Hirota, was leading a leisurely life in retirement at Kugenuma. Yoshida, too, had a mind to stay put for a while and observe trends within Japan. Uchida did not press him any further to take the post.

Uchida was by far their senior. He had served as foreign minister in the second Saionji government less than five years after Hirota and Yoshida had joined the Foreign Ministry. He had been foreign minister again in the Hara, Takahashi, and Kato governments, and had been made a count in recognition of his services. This "grand old man" of the diplomatic world had been persuaded by Prime Minister Saito in July, 1932, to occupy the post of foreign minister for the first time in ten years in order to tide things over in the absence of any other suitable candidate to succeed Shidehara.

Uchida, too, had been working in the interests of peace and international cooperation, even though in a less conspicuous way than Shidehara. In his previous period as foreign minister, he had cooperated with the powers in the establishment of the League of Nations. He had overcome opposition from some quarters at home in order to sign the Washington naval treaty in the same period, and again, in 1928, the Kellogg-Briand Pact.

The phrase "sign in the names of their respective peoples" which occurred in the anti-war Kellogg pact had been picked on by the right wing and the military, and had created a great stir. Uchida was on his way home from signing the treaty in Paris, his mind already preoccupied with how to deal with opposition at home, when, in London, he found Hirota, then minister to Holland, waiting for him. Hirota had heard of the problem and had set his subordinates to work, as a result of which he had discovered that "in the names of" was susceptible to various interpretations. He had come, armed with references, especially to inform Uchida. They were to prove useful in helping Uchida tide over the storm and have the treaty safely ratified.

Despite his undoubted achievements, Uchida was already advanced in years. He had lost his old patience and become short-tempered and crotchety. Increasing deafness, moreover, made him speak in a loud voice that always seemed to be ready for a quarrel.

Back at the Foreign Ministry for the first time in a decade, this elderly man found much to irritate him—not least the emergence of a hawkish "reformist" faction not only in the military and political parties, but even within his own ministry. He was affronted by the way that men such as Mori Tsutomu—in Uchida's eyes still the merest fledglings—were proceeding unbidden with their "positive diplomacy," and even going over to the opposition to attack the government on the Manchurian question. In an exchange between Uchida and Mori in the Diet, the latter demanded to know "whether, in the event of Japan's being subjected to pressure from other countries, the government was prepared to stand up to them," thereby implying that the government's weak approach was a cause for concern. The antipathy that Uchida had long felt for Mori came to the surface, and in an attempt to silence the other man effectively he declared, in his most lordly manner: "Should any other nation interfere with Japan's doing what she believes to be right, then let it. Japan will go ahead, even if it means reducing her territory to scorched earth."

This rash utterance made in the heat of the moment was given prominence in the press and caused considerable controversy. Some applauded it, while others criticized it as a return to ".diplomacy of the sword." The final result, though, was that Uchida's approach to foreign relations became known—with little reference to his true intentions—as "scorched-earth diplomacy," and branded as xenophobic and bellicose.

Within the Foreign Ministry itself, a number of problems arose to plague the aging minister. Undersecretary Arita and Tani Masayuki, head of the Asia Bureau, disapproved of the way Shiratori, along with Mori and others of like mind, were regularly fraternizing with the military in the geisha houses and restaurants of Akasaka, and attempted to have Shiratori packed off as minister to Sweden. The latter, however, resisted this move with the backing of the military. Foreign Minister Uchida wavered, but finally issued the order appointing him. Even so, Shiratori stayed put. As a result, Undersecretary Arita resigned, and his place was taken by Shigemitsu Mamoru.

Shiratori also called for the establishment of an advisory board within the Foreign Ministry to act as a kind of staff headquarters for debating and drawing up foreign policy. This proposal, motivated in part by Shiratori's dislike of the Asia Bureau, was supported by the "reformist" faction within the ministry, and began to look like becoming a reality.

The Privy Council now began to advocate instead the revival of the foreign policy research board that had existed at the time of the Terauchi government. This peculiar body, a gathering of Privy Council members and representatives of the army and navy organized to discuss foreign policy, acted as a kind of second and superior Foreign Ministry; it had given Uchida a great deal of trouble during his earlier term as foreign minister, and he had eventually succeeded in doing away with it. Now, thanks to Shiratori, its specter had arisen to threaten the old man again. His first concern after Undersecretary Shigemitsu took office was, thus, to get him to see Shiratori safely off to his new post in Sweden.

Uchida had originally insisted on perusing all official letters and cables that arrived each day, classifying them and giving consideration to each of them himself. But the volume of such documents had swelled enormously compared with ten years previously, and Uchida's own strength had sadly waned. His attempts to keep going at the old pace, together with the pressure of a host of problems at home and abroad, sapped his energies visibly. His health impaired, he was finally obliged to resign in September, 1933 (he died less than six months later).

The transitional period over, it was time now for a "younger man" to take over. That "younger man" would have to be someone who could both stand up to the military and exert a firm control over the ministry. After consulting many people both within the ministry and outside, Uchida selected Hirota. One factor in his decision, no doubt, was the reliability and attention to detail that Hirota had shown at the time of the Kellogg-Briand Pact controversy.

Within the Foreign Ministry, an overwhelming majority favored the appointment. With his air of good faith and his refusal to lean either to right or left, Hirota had few enemies. Some people saw this as a fault in itself, but it also meant that he was a reassuring figure at such a time. He was slow and cautious, and was not the type to go about bragging of what he intended to do. He had vision, yet he built his edifices patiently, one brick at a time. When the occasion arose, moreover, he could play the politician with the rest of them.

His experience in the Information Section had also given him a feeling for the type of approach needed in such an age, and he found advocates in unexpected quarters outside the ministry—Konoe Fumimaro, for example, and Lieutenant General Matsui Iwane, who was a military councillor. All alike seemed to agree, however, that Hirota would bring a breath of fresh air to the post of foreign minister.

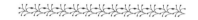

V

In the summer of 1933, a popular song called "Tokyo Ondo" took the capital by storm. In homes, in the streets, over the radio, a record of the song by singing-geisha Katsutaro was to be heard over and over again, from morning to night, and the whole city, it seemed, beat time to it as though possessed. As the sun went down, the same song would float out from stages set up for the annual Bon dance in open spaces and on street corners. Men and women in cotton summer kimono were joined by casual passersby, and all would dance in a ring, on and on, often far into the night.

The words of the song were trivial, almost childish, with a suggestion, somehow, of extreme ephemerality. The readiness of the public, young and old, to abandon itself to it so wholeheartedly was reminiscent of the way a song-and-dance called "Does It Matter?" swept the country in the final days of the Tokugawa shogunate. To some observers, it looked like the mood of irresponsible euphoria that precedes a great social upheaval. To others, though, it looked suspiciously as though the Ministry of Home Affairs and the local veterans' associations had deliberately popularized the song as an outlet for popular frustrations.

But all the while this frivolous ditty was echoing about the streets, another, very different type of song was beginning to make itself heard, quietly at first yet with frightening intensity, in other and less conspicuous places:

> The waves are clamorous o'er the depths of Milo;
> The clouds swirl angrily o'er Wushan:
> We stand amidst the muddied currents of the world,
> Ready for action, fired with righteous wrath.

The words were by one Mikami Takashi, a lieutenant in the navy.

> *Those in power are swollen with pride,*
> *But have no sincere concern for the nation.*
> *The wealthy flaunt their riches,*
> *Yet care nothing for the welfare of society.*

The title of the song was "The Song of Young Japan," but it was popularly known as "The Song of the Showa Restoration."* It was a favorite among young officers, and gradually spread to the lower ranks and among students also.

> *Brave warriors united in justice,*
> *In spirit a match for a million—*
> *Ready like the myriad cherry blossoms to scatter*
> *In the spring sky of the Showa Restoration.*

The song made sense, and conveyed a clear call to action; indeed, it even bade farewell to song itself, as something no longer necessary:

> *But let us leave these lamentations—*
> *Gone is the time for idle grieving!*
> *The day has come when our swords*
> *Shall gleam with the blood of purification!*

Already, in October, 1930, Lieutenant Colonel Hashimoto Kingoro and a number of other field-grade officers on the active list, together with Okawa Shumei and other civilian rightists, had formed the Sakurakai (Cherry Society). With the connivance of certain leaders of the military, they had planned a coup d'état that involved bombing the prime minister's official residence and surrounding the National Diet, but the plot misfired in March the next year (the incident was subsequently known as the "March plot").

In October of that year another coup d'état was planned by

---

*"Showa Restoration" was a term (formed by analogy with the Meiji Restoration of 1868, which saw the fall of the Tokugawa shogunate and the restoration, in theory, of power to the emperor) much used in the 1930s as a rallying cry by the younger army officers and others who wished to rid society of "corrupt" politicians and establish a new order more directly centered on the emperor.

Hashimoto and other radical elements in the Sakurakai, but the association was split by internal dissension arising in part from the extravagant life-style of its leaders, and an informer gave the game away. The ringleaders, however, got away with confinement to their quarters—with freedom, moreover, to summon their favorite geisha whenever they chose.

In February, 1932, the rightists assassinated former finance minister Inoue Junnosuke. In March, another rightist murdered Baron Dan Takuma, president of the Mitsui Bank. On May 15, six naval officers including Mikami Takashi (author of the words of the song), twelve army cadets, and ten rightists raided the prime minister's official residence, the residence of Lord Privy Seal Makino, the Metropolitan Police Headquarters, and the Bank of Japan. Prime Minister Inukai Tsuyoshi, unperturbed, made his famous plea, "You can shoot me any time. Let's hear what you have to say." But they brushed his suggestion aside and gunned him down.

Again in July, 1933, there occurred the Shimpeitai (Soldiers of the Gods) incident, in which the right wing plotted unsuccessfully a large-scale coup to overthrow the government in the name of the "Showa Restoration."

It was just at this period of increasing discord both at home and abroad that Hirota was summoned to become foreign minister. The appointment came as a surprise to Hirota, who had settled comfortably in his villa at Kugenuma and was quietly following his belief in the need to observe the world situation without reference to party or personal interests.

Of the two contemporaries, it was Yoshida Shigeru who was more interested in the post of foreign minister. Following his rejection of the ambassadorship to the United States, he had made an unhurried tour of Europe and America as special envoy, an appointment he received thanks to the good offices of Undersecretary Shigemitsu. On his return home, he had not only made a report to Prime Minister Saito but had approached Prince Konoe. He also visited men such as Shidehara, whose views were different from his own, and even requested a meeting with Suzuki Kisaburo, president of the

Seiyukai party. In every case he was playing the role, as it were, of professional sounding board. Around this time, in fact, he was so busy moving about the upper echelons of the political world that his name seemed to crop up inevitably, whatever the topic under discussion.

Matsuoka, the new national hero, was also very much in evidence, whether calling on Prince Saionji or planning the formation of a new party. Yet it was Hirota who was chosen as foreign minister rather than Yoshida or Matsuoka, neither of whom so much as appeared on the list of candidates.

Hirota himself pleaded tiredness from his long stay in the Soviet Union, but Prime Minister Saito was so insistent that he felt obliged, at the very least, to drag himself away from Kugenuma for a while.

He considered the situation. The Saito government was widely viewed as a "half-and-half" government. Prime Minister Saito himself was a respected navy veteran, and his war minister was Lieutenant General Araki Sadao, who was popular among the younger army officers, but the cabinet also included many men associated with the political parties, men such as Takahashi Korekiyo, Nakajima Kumakichi, Nagai Ryutaro, and Hatoyama Ichiro. Would he, Hirota, be able to carry through his own wishes as foreign minister?

Hirota met the prime minister and questioned him concerning two points. First: he personally felt that Japan's foreign policy henceforth should adhere to the principle of "gradually increasing international trust and furthering the cause of justice throughout the world" that had been set forth in the imperial edict declaring Japan's secession from the League of Nations. Would it in fact be so?

Second: he felt that foreign policy should be principally the initiative of the foreign minister and that the prime minister should cooperate with the foreign minister just as far as possible. What was the prime minister's view?

Saito replied that those were indeed his own wishes, and it was decided that Hirota should join the cabinet. Faced with such a challenging task, Hirota stirred himself into action. He had once written: "A windmill—/ Taking a nap/ Until the next breeze blows." Now the breeze was blowing again, a breeze that threatened to become a gale. The nap had been brief and the windmill must turn busily once more.

Hirota left the villa at Kugenuma and moved to his house in Harajuku. The house was surrounded by a hedge and stood on about seven hundred square meters of land, close behind the Dojunkai apartment houses (the first modern apartment blocks to be built in Tokyo, and still to be seen in Harajuku today). There was an official residence for the foreign minister, but out of consideration for his self-effacing wife Shizuko he decided to make Harajuku his base and return to Kugenuma at the weekends.

Hirota summoned the foreign ambassadors and ministers in Tokyo in order to pay his respects on taking up his new appointment. He greeted American Ambassador Grew especially cordially, grasping Grew's hand between his own in a warm handshake. "There are no special problems where America is concerned at the moment," he told the other man. "I hope both countries will endeavor to appreciate each other's special positions so that there is no misunderstanding or suspicion." He also expressed the conviction that the main task before him in taking up this unexpected appointment was to promote friendly relations between Japan and America.

Short though their conversation was, Grew carried away the impression that Hirota had spoken not "diplomatically," but in all sincerity. The previous foreign minister, Uchida, had disliked giving interviews—partly because he was old and hard of hearing—and would dismiss almost all the problems that Grew brought to him with a brusque "I really don't know," or "I'll think about it." Hirota's appointment at least suggested the possibility of discussions that really went to the heart of the matter, and Grew looked forward to his visits to the Foreign Ministry with a new interest.

Not everyone, unfortunately, greeted Hirota's appointment with the same goodwill.

Foreign Undersecretary Shigemitsu, whom Hirota retained in the same position, was wary of Hirota and said in private to Harada Kumao, Prince Saionji's secretary: "I'd like you to ask Prince Saionji to give the new minister a word of warning in case he's too inclined to fall in with suggestions from members of the Privy Council and especially Viscount Kaneko, who comes from the same part of the country as himself. Hirota is inclined, if anything, to the right, and it would be a good idea if the prince said something about that too while he's about it."

Harada told Prince Saionji what Shigemitsu had said, but Saionji showed no reaction at all.

It was true, of course, that ever since his days at Tokyo's First Higher School, Hirota had been friendly with Toyama Mitsuru and other men of nationalistic inclinations from the same part of Japan as himself. This made some people suspect him of rightist sympathies, but in fact for Hirota it had been no more than a passing phase, and he ceased to have any exaggerated sense of comradeship with his fellows from Fukuoka.

Back in Fukuoka itself, a supporter's group entitled the "Koki Association" was formed to "encourage the man responsible for Japan's foreign policy in this time of emergency," and more than four hundred people attended an inaugural ceremony held at the prefectural hall. But Hirota himself did not attend, and although the Koki Association held many subsequent meetings, Hirota almost always sent a substitute.

Shigemitsu need not have worried: Hirota's loyalties were to his job rather than to any local ties. In autumn of the same year, a meeting was held by a Privy Council committee to discuss again a plan for setting up an advisory body in the Foreign Ministry. At this meeting, Viscount Kaneko adopted a rather overbearing attitude toward the government: "I believe," he said, "that in addition to the bureaucrats at the Foreign Ministry the government should appoint three or four elder statesmen as advisers, or should set up a foreign policy board of inquiry. Either way, the Foreign Ministry ought to make sure it is adequately equipped to deal with the present crisis—and I feel that we are the men for the job."

Prime Minister Saito, who had promised Hirota that the Foreign Ministry should have the principal say in determining foreign policy, firmly rejected the suggestion: they must have confidence in the authorities responsible, he said. Next, Hirota spoke. He pointed out that during the lifetimes of elder statesmen such as Princes Ito and

Yamagata, important proposals had sometimes been decided on in consultation with them. At the moment, Prince Saionji was being kept in adequate touch both directly and indirectly with the situation. But what other "elder statesmen" did they think there were, apart from Saionji?

Kaneko was stumped for an answer. He was highly indignant, but to no avail; even within the Privy Council there were forces opposed to him and his supporters, and there was maneuvering behind the scenes by the government, so that his suggestion eventually came to nothing.

Where the plan for an advisory body was concerned, it was finally decided to reduce its scale and to establish in the Foreign Ministry a "research section" which would gather materials and make any studies necessary in drawing up foreign policies. Thus the controversial question which had first been raised by Shiratori and which had given the elderly Uchida so much trouble was sidestepped, and everybody at the Foreign Ministry heaved a sigh of relief.

Shortly after Hirota joined the Saito government, five conferences on important questions of defense and foreign policy were held by a group consisting solely of the prime minister, finance minister, foreign minister, and war and navy ministers.

Prime Minister Saito was an admiral who had served as navy minister in five governments during the early decades of the century. Finance Minister Takahashi likewise had served in his present post —including times when he held the post concurrently with another position—on six occasions since the 1910s. He qualified as an "elder statesman," having served as prime minister also in 1922. Both of them were in their seventies, and had dragged themselves out of retirement on the understanding that this was a national, suprapartisan government.

On the other hand, War Minister Araki and Navy Minister Osumi were younger, go-ahead men with the weight of the military behind them. Awareness of the crisis facing Japan put them, in their official capacities, still more on their mettle.

The Washington naval agreement was due to expire three years later, in 1936. Japan had always been intensely dissatisfied with this treaty, and Navy Minister Osumi, for one, was extremely worried at the idea that Japan might repudiate it, thus eventually touching off a war between the U.S. and Japan.

The army under Araki, on the other hand, took a tougher attitude. It held that outstanding problems involving the Soviet Union should be solved by resort to military pressure, and that if this led to hostilities Japan should seize the opportunity to deal a blow to Soviet military strength in the Far East. For this purpose, Japan should move quickly to step up her defenses.

Araki was considered one of the army's leading experts on Russian affairs. He was also a leader of the so-called "Imperial Way faction"*—it was he who first used the phrase "imperial army"—and had consistently advocated "national reconstruction" and a tougher foreign policy. He was on friendly terms with politicians of the right such as Mori Tsutomu and Hiranuma Kiichiro. Araki was also popular among the young officers as a man of action who despised anything devious, and his name had been raised by the planners of the aborted coups d'état as a possible leader of the military's revolutionary government. He himself had stated publicly his belief that the officers responsible for the May 15 incident should be judged not for the crime itself but for the purity of the motives that underlay it. A natural affinity seemed to exist between himself and the younger breed of officers, and the combination of awe and respect in which he was held was complemented by his commanding appearance, in which a magnificent handlebar moustache played a large part.

Thus Hirota, as the new foreign minister, found himself set down between two withered old statesmen on the one hand and two younger, fiery-tempered military men on the other. Hirota and Araki were almost exactly the same age, but Araki was well known, almost a

*One of two factions within the army (the other being the "control faction") which believed that drastic measures were needed to rescue the nation from "corrupt" politicians. The more revolutionary of the two in its domestic approach, it was concerned abroad chiefly with the Russian threat and the need to consolidate Japan's position in Manchuria. The "control faction," disposed at home to affirm the existing order, was more concerned with China and the South.

public idol, whereas Hirota was a career diplomat who had been "taking a nap until the next breeze blew," and as such was virtually unknown to the public. At the conferences of the five ministers, Araki ignored Hirota as though he were some young upstart, holding forth on his own, with a great deal of emphasis and frothing at the mouth, concerning Japan's future course.

The five-minister conferences had, in fact, been initiated by Araki himself, who claimed that limiting them to the five ministers in question would give the discussion of national policy a purer and more impartial tone than was possible at ordinary cabinet meetings, which were attended by ministers with party backgrounds.

Araki quite naturally, therefore, put an extraordinary amount of energy into the meetings. At the very outset, he presented a "basic outline of imperial policy," and demanded that it be made the focal point of discussion. This program took as its premises an increasing threat of war and growing uneasiness at home concerning the nation's livelihood, and called for expansion and reinforcement of national defenses as well as drastic political reforms to help cope with the crisis. In short, it was an attempt to embody in the actual government of the country Araki's ideals of a nation focused on the emperor.

Hirota countered by demanding to know where exactly the danger of war lay. The military, he said, were too much obsessed with war, when the real question ought to be how war could be avoided. Diplomacy, in other words, should be the first priority.

The army and navy ministers could, of course, make no effective reply.

"War," Hirota asserted, "occurs when diplomacy reaches an impasse. At the moment, however, there is no area of Japanese diplomacy in which such an impasse exists. Admittedly, Japan has left the League of Nations, but that does not mean that she is at loggerheads with any particular nation."

He countered Araki's theoretical abstractions with more practical considerations. There were no important outstanding problems between Japan and America at the moment, he said. In China, where the Nationalists had succeeded more or less in unifying the country, diplomatic negotiations should be easier than when Japan had had to deal with a country divided. Moreover, the leadership of the Nationalists included many men who were pro-Japanese, or at least well acquainted with Japanese affairs, so that if only Japan showed good faith in negotiating, China might well change her own attitude to some extent. There were signs, in fact, that China was prepared to give tacit recognition to the independence of Manchukuo as a fait accompli. Rather than demand rights and interests, Japan should take the lead in promoting policies of friendship—by, for example, doing away with extraterritoriality.

The chief problem was relations with the Soviet Union, and a major point here was the negotiations for the purchase of the Chinese Eastern Railway. This railway had been constructed by Russia and managed jointly by Russia and China, but the establishment of the puppet state of Manchukuo had made things difficult for the Soviet Union. The Soviet Union's national finances, on the other hand, were in dire straits and, partly to help make ends meet, the Russians had decided to sell the Chinese Eastern Railway to Manchukuo. Negotiations had already begun. In theory, Japan was acting as intermediary in these negotiations, but in practice it would be Japan who would do the buying.

The negotiations, however, had reached a deadlock, partly because of the huge sum—approximately two hundred and fifty million yen—which the Soviet Union had first demanded, and partly because of a toughening in the Soviet stand due to an incident in which Manchukuoan authorities had arrested a Soviet employee of the railway in question.

Certain sections of the Kwantung Army were openly criticizing the Foreign Ministry for shilly-shallying over something that could be had for the price of a few rounds of ammunition. As Hirota pointed out to Araki, however, the price would be infinitely greater if such a move were to lead to war. He also persuaded Araki that amicable diplomatic relations with the Soviet Union were a necessity for the safety and smooth development of the state of Manchukuo, which the army itself had taken so much trouble to set up.

As such discussions proceeded it was, if anything, Hirota who began to get the upper hand over Araki and Osumi. At one meeting of the five ministers, Araki and Osumi both tried to force a discussion of the need for more arms, Araki postulating a war with the Soviet Union and Osumi a war with the United States. Hirota, however, launched a scathing counterattack.

"To take Russia's case as an example—" he demanded, "do you think that we could go to war against Russia and still maintain friendly relations with all other countries?" In such an event, he stressed, it was likely that America and England would unite in alliance. It was possible, too, that America and the Soviet Union would join hands and even persuade China to join them. Did Araki and Osumi's theories about national defense take such prospects into account? And if so, did they really believe that Japan could arm herself adequately to tackle such formidable opposition? The war and navy ministers found themselves temporarily at a loss for words.

Hirota was not one to make spectacular attacks in debate. He pursued his argument frankly, logically, and with infinite patience. The result was that Araki was obliged to modify his first impression of this "upstart," and to take his arguments seriously. Thus in the end it was Hirota who controlled the pace of the discussion. He might be new to ministerial office, but he could draw on a large fund of knowledge and observation stored up during his long "nap."

Before long the five-minister meetings, which had been initiated by the war minister, came to be dominated by the foreign minister instead. The two old men, Prime Minister Saito and Finance Minister Takahashi, were startled to see their new colleague fending so well for himself. Takahashi went along with Hirota, cautioning the two military men and occasionally giving them a dressing down. His own position as the man in charge of finances made him dislike still more the military's "positive" policies. He sought to curb the military's insatiable appetite for expansion by insisting that Japan should not make war actively, but should maintain sufficient arms to ensure that she was not taken too lightly by other nations and had adequate backing in diplomatic negotiations. Japan's military strength, in short, should be, above all, defensive.

Since the two elder statesmen followed Hirota in insisting that priority should be given to diplomacy, the military pair found themselves increasingly on the defensive as the talks proceeded. When Araki began to steer clear of questions of foreign policy and to emphasize domestic unease in Japan, Hirota once more counterattacked. The source of the unease, he insisted, was the disturbance that Japan had created through its behavior in Manchuria. The essential thing, if international misgivings were to be assuaged, was to establish friendly relations with other countries and put Japan's foreign policy on a more settled basis. To step up armament as the military proposed would only work to Japan's disadvantage by creating an impression abroad of a nation in war paint.

Around this time, moves in America to raise tariffs against Japan and impose trade restrictions were causing considerable uneasiness in business circles. Finance Minister Takahashi, echoing Hirota's views, criticized Araki at a conference on domestic affairs that followed these particular five-minister meetings. The real reason for such developments, he declared, lay in the way that the armed forces were looking ahead to 1935 and 1936 as "years of crisis" and going about the country making inflammatory statements suggesting that Japan was on the verge of war with Russia or America. This kind of thing was having adverse effects abroad. At a time when most countries, both in America and Europe, were hoping to manage things as peacefully as possible—to avoid any suggestion, even, of war—a warlike atmosphere in Japan would create a disastrous impression; and this would inevitably have repercussions in the field of trade. The military should be more careful in their words and behavior. There was nothing remotely "critical" about the years 1935–36.

Araki took strenuous objection to this. The military, he insisted, had no intention of going to war immediately. However, it was necessary for Japan to arm herself, since there was indeed a crisis of a kind.

"A crisis of a kind" was a considerable retreat for one who had been speaking in such alarmist tones.

The five conferences of five ministers finally came to an end, and the following points on which agreement had been reached were made public:

107

1. Japan's foreign policy must be based on international cooperation; in particular, steps must be taken to enhance friendly relations with China, the United States, and the Soviet Union.

2. Any increase in Japan's armaments must be such as to forestall any threat to her sense of security or insult to her pride, and due consideration must be given to the state of the national finances.

3. There must be a renewal of all fields of government, together with efforts to rally the national spirit to the needs of the moment.

This extremely mild pronouncement was very different from what had first been expected. It bore the mark, not so much of the headstrong Araki as of the more temperate Hirota and Takahashi. Araki's views were represented only in the third clause—and in a very abstract and perfunctory fashion at that.

Dissatisfaction with Araki arose among the young officers who had been pinning their hopes on him. Some of them even climbed over his garden wall late one night and banged on his door to demand what had become of the promises he had made before becoming war minister. Araki himself seemed, for once, daunted and there were rumors that he was suffering from nervous exhaustion. Men such as General Hayashi Senjuro and General Mazaki Jinsaburo urged him to resign, insisting that things were hopeless with such a cabinet. If he stayed on, he must do something positive. It was impossible to leave things as they were at present. As a result, Araki found himself obliged to take advantage of the pretext afforded by a touch of pneumonia, and resign as war minister. He was succeeded by Hayashi.

Araki's own dismay was matched by the surprise with which his resignation was greeted. Abroad, the disappearance of such a formidably bellicose war minister was generally welcomed, and played a part in relaxing tension.

In his diary for January 23, 1934, American Ambassador Grew wrote:

"Hirota is genuinely doing his best to improve Japan's relations with foreign countries all along the line. He has succeeded in creating a better atmosphere with the United States, mainly through keeping the military comparatively quiet and by exerting a calming influence on the press. . . . It is generally felt that Araki's retirement as War

Minister represents a victory for the liberals and the political parties, and it seems probable that there will be less public rattling of the saber than heretofore."

As though encouraged by Hirota's approach to foreign affairs, there was a resurgence of the forces of liberalism, and criticism of the military by the political parties was stepped up in the Diet, in connection with defense expenditure. In practice, however, most of the questions asked were heavily slanted to serve party interests, and Hirota, who was making his first appearance in the Diet as foreign minister, was disgusted and physically exhausted by the exchanges.

In the meantime, Hirota was making every effort to meet foreign ambassadors and ministers, and to encourage his subordinates and diplomats in embassies and legations abroad. The aspect to which he himself devoted most energy was relations with the Soviet Union, and in particular the still pending question of negotiations on Japan's buying of the Chinese Eastern Railway. Negotiations had been suspended for more than a year and a half, since the time when Uchida was foreign minister, partly on account of the excessive gap between the price asked by the Soviet Union (approximately two hundred and fifty million yen) and that offered by Manchukuo (fifty million yen), and partly because of a number of other disputes that had arisen between Japan and the Soviet Union. Hirota worked hard to urge compromise on both Russia and Manchukuo (i.e. the Kwantung Army), and in February, 1934, negotiations were at last reopened.

On this occasion the Russians, as though to indicate their willingness to compromise, came up with a revised price of two hundred million yen. Even so, this would have placed an enormous burden on Japan (the national budget at the time was around two billion yen in the general account, of which one-third was, moreover, provided by the issue of government bonds). On top of this, when Manchukuo prepared to go ahead with negotiations in appreciation of this major concession by the Soviet side, the Soviet Union promptly demanded an additional thirty million yen by way of retirement allowances for Soviet railway employees. Thus the total differed little from the original figure.

Manchukuo—the Japanese military—hardened its stand. There were some, even, who doubted whether the Soviet Union wanted to sell at all. Over the negotiating table, Hirota confronted Soviet representative Yurenev with this suspicion.

"Of course we want to sell," said Yurenev hastily. "Why—should we cut it by another five million or so?"

"You should cut it by another hundred million!" said Hirota. The two men stared at each other.

Hirota was in deadly earnest. The gap between the two offers was excessive, but he was determined to reach a settlement, come what may. Should the talks break down, it was obvious that the future running of the railway would involve interminable disputes, and might even lead to hostilities between Japan and the Soviet Union. If, on the other hand, the talks were successful, it would mean that peace would be guaranteed, generally speaking, in Manchuria and the surrounding area.

Besides continuing efforts to get the Soviet Union to make concessions, Hirota also had to obtain the agreement of the military and the leaders of the political world. Finance Minister Takahashi and other government members supported Hirota. Even within the military, most of those at the General Staff Office wanted negotiations to continue and were willing to agree to a certain increase in the price. But the "Imperial Way faction" and other advocates of a tougher line toward the Soviet Union called strongly for Japan to break off the talks. There were reports at the time that the Soviet Union's five-year plan had failed. If so, to buy the Chinese Eastern Railway for such a large sum would mean that Japan was rescuing the Soviet Union from its economic straits. Thus the rightists were bitterly opposed to buying the railway on the grounds that it would benefit the enemy, and advocated putting the army into action instead.

American Ambassador Grew mentioned Hirota's efforts in a letter to a friend. The letter first describes how Japanese foreign policy has switched from the irresponsibility of Uchida to Hirota's view of diplomacy as the best means of national defense. It also praises Hirota's wisdom and ability in promoting conciliatory policies toward other countries, and describes the way he forced Araki to resign and his other efforts to exclude the military from the conduct of foreign policy.

"During all these months," the letter goes on, "Hirota worked steadily, and I believe sincerely, to create a friendly basis upon which to deal with China, Soviet Russia, Great Britain, and the United States. His hand was manifest in an immediate toning down of antiforeignism in the press; it was revealed in the renewed efforts to solve the current problems between Japan and Soviet Russia one by one; and it was emphasized to me in conversation in which Hirota showed an eagerness to explore any possible avenue which would lead to an improvement in American-Japanese relations. Certain people considered him a genuine liberal and the strongest Foreign Minister since Komura and Kato."

Even so, Grew's praise of Hirota is not unqualified. He adds:

"Nevertheless, many believe Hirota's moderation to be one of manner and strategy rather than substance. Certainly no one could have come into office last year unless he was pledged to support Japan's continental adventure and unless he profoundly believed in Japan's 'mission to preserve the peace of East Asia.' It is precisely here that we find a deep-rooted antithesis." Grew in short had, in his own way, perceived the subtle difference between Hirota's position and that of Shidehara—another exponent of peaceful foreign policies—in the past, and was watching developments with a mixture of hope and wariness.

An incident known as the "affair of the Amau statement" is significant here. It was Amau who had served as counselor at the embassy in Moscow under Hirota, and had confused the press at the time of the outbreak of the Manchurian Incident by the contrast between his own consternation and the complete imperturbability shown by Hirota. Hirota had since appointed him head of the Foreign Ministry's Information Section in place of Shiratori.

The source of the trouble was a statement made by Amau in the course of a routine press conference. "Japan," he declared in effect, "would resolutely spurn any intervention from abroad that might serve to create trouble between Japan and China." This was taken by an oversensitive press to mean the declaration of a Japanese "Monroe Doctrine" and the exclusion of Great Britain and America from China. The rightist press at home welcomed the statement, while the foreign press gave it widespread and unfavorable attention, producing disapproving inquiries from America and elsewhere.

The statement went against Hirota's true feelings, and he managed to tide things over by calling another press conference himself, and by meeting foreign ambassadors and ministers in order to emphasize that Japan would respect Chinese sovereignty and that the statement implied no encroachment on the existing rights and interests of third parties. Nevertheless, the incident in a way symbolized the delicate position in which he found himself as foreign minister.

In the meantime, appreciation of Hirota's unspectacular but determined efforts gradually spread among the leaders of the political world. This was true of Prime Minister Saito and Finance Minister Takahashi, while Prince Saionji himself was astonished at the valiant showing put on by the new foreign minister.

At that time, to be allowed to visit Saionji at his home at Okitsu was a desire cherished by almost every politician and bureaucrat alike, and a great deal of effort was expended on winning the right to go to "pay one's respects." Hirota's one-time rival Saburi, who had, as it were, a "free pass" to Okitsu, was ipso facto regarded as an important figure, and envied accordingly. Hirota himself had never "paid his respects," nor made any move to do so. It was not until after he became foreign minister that he met Saionji, who was staying at his private residence at Surugadai during a visit to Tokyo.

When Hirota had completed his report, Saionji neither asked any particular questions nor expressed any particular opinions. The impression, rather, was that he was content to leave things to Hirota. He did, however, declare in a serious tone of voice:

"You know, I have a kind of practical philosophy of my own. To take a metaphor from horse-riding, I feel that diplomatic negotiations are rather like a rider tackling an obstacle. He gallops toward the obstacle and tries to clear it. If things go well, of course, he clears it at first go. But if the horse shies or falters in its stride, he goes back and starts all over again. It's much the same with diplomacy."

There was a more personal touch to Saionji's words than one might have supposed; he himself had been foreign minister three times, and his advice sprang naturally from his own experience.

The Saito government fell in July, 1934, as a result of a bribery scandal, and another navy veteran, Admiral Okada Keisuke, became prime minister at Saito's recommendation. The new cabinet, like its predecessor, was a suprapartisan national government, and the four most important ministers including Hirota, Hayashi, and Osumi retained their former positions.

Resuming his post, Hirota was immediately involved in the flurry of activity surrounding the reopening of negotiations on the sale of the Chinese Eastern Railway. In view of the enormous difference between the price asked and the price offered, plus the stiff opposition at home to the purchase as such, the situation seemed hopeless, but Hirota, undismayed, patiently set about persuading those concerned. In his capacity as mediator, he finally hit upon the sum of one hundred and twenty million yen (not including retirement allowances) as a suitable figure, and after much trouble got the Manchukuo authorities to accept it.

When negotiations actually began again, however, Soviet Ambassador Yurenev haughtily rejected the compromise proposal and threatened to break off talks unless Japan proposed a higher figure. The Manchukuo authorities—who were already disposed to bring the army into action and get the railway for next to nothing—were understandably indignant at this rejection of what they saw as a major concession on their side, and their representative (a Japanese) withdrew from the talks.

Faced with this second breakdown, Hirota still refused to give up, and, "starting all over again"—to use Saionji's phrase—embarked on renewed negotiations with those concerned. He realized that the Russians, under strict instructions from home, would be unable to make any further concessions. The only alternative, thus, was to ask further concessions of Manchukuo. This was a daunting prospect, since he was dealing with military men who saw any concession as a disgrace. Any less patient foreign minister would have given up, but Hirota pressed on. After repeated contacts, he finally got the Manchukuo authorities to agree to an increase of twenty million yen, but on condition that payment could be extended over a period of three years.

Following this, Hirota had a rapid succession of meetings with Yurenev at which he continued to press the other to accept the proposal. Finally, Yurenev gave way before Hirota's perseverance— though Yurenev personally, like U.S. Ambassador Grew, was in a sense already disposed to view Hirota favorably. Grew in his diary records Yurenev's impressions of Hirota as follows:

"In this connection Mr. Yurenev expressed a high opinion of Mr. Hirota, for whom he said he had a genuine admiration. He said he considered him a very able and shrewd negotiator but a great deal pleasanter to deal with than Count Uchida, who was merely a mouthpiece of the Japanese military."

Once Yurenev had agreed in principle to Hirota's proposal, further study was devoted to details, and in March, 1935, an agreement was signed. It was the result of fifty-six meetings extending over a period of more than a year.

The successful conclusion of negotiations brought many results. Not merely did it remove the seeds of trouble where the railway was concerned, but that same month the Soviet Union gave permission for the establishment of Manchukuoan consulates in Vladivostok and Khabarovsk, thus agreeing in practice to maintain relations with the new state.

This did not, unfortunately, mean that all outstanding problems between the two countries had been settled. The Soviet Union had recognized Japanese control over Manchuria in the form of the puppet state of Manchukuo, and had sold the Chinese Eastern Railway in line with this, yet at the same time it also started building fortifications on the Soviet-Manchurian border and augmenting its forces there. Such moves irritated the Kwantung Army, and there were more than a hundred border incidents in the course of one year.

The Soviet-Manchurian border had always been a potential source of trouble; it stretched for four thousand three hundred kilometers, and there were quite a few places where its very location was not clear. There was a definite possibility that the increasing frequency and intensity of clashes on the border might lead to a really serious situation.

The Soviet Union responded by suggesting the conclusion of a treaty of non-aggression between the two countries, but the complex political situation in Japan made any such solution unthinkable. This did not mean, though, that Hirota rejected the Soviet suggestion outright. In an attempt to achieve a similar effect, even though a treaty as such was impossible, he proposed the establishment of a committee to deal with border disputes, its aim being to prevent clashes and seek to settle everything by means of peaceful negotiation.

This proposal was strongly opposed by the Kwantung Army. Not only was the army chronically suspicious of the Soviet Union, but it claimed that there was no sense in setting up a committee to deal with disputes when the border itself was not precisely laid down.

Undeterred, Hirota suggested that work should be started on drawing a clearly defined border, while at the same time dealing with any disputes as they occurred. And in line with this reasoning, it was decided to establish a committee with two separate sub-committees entrusted with these tasks. The opposition of the Kwantung Army having thus been diverted, talks went on between Japan and the Soviet Union concerning the committee (which was to come into being under the next government, headed by Hirota himself).

In the Diet session convened in January, 1935, Hirota set forth his views with considerable clarity. His first appearance as foreign minister the previous year had been a tiring business for him, partly on account of his inexperience, but this time he used the Diet as a positive opportunity to explain what he hoped to do. He specifically stipulated that Japan's foreign policy was a policy of "accord." In reply to a questioner in the House of Peers who asked whether "Japan's secession from the League of Nations would not increase her isolation," he replied:

"The League is a kind of meeting place, and absence from those meetings does not mean that diplomatic relations have automatically been severed with the countries who attend the meetings. It is important today that Japan should maintain the closest relations with every country in the world—in short, that foreign policy should be conducted in a spirit of universal accord." Again, when Ashida Hitoshi of the Seiyukai asked him in the House of Representatives whether the government's appraisal of the international situation was not overoptimistic, Foreign Minister Hirota stated firmly:

"My view of what lies ahead for Japan is not—nor could it be—optimistic. A glance at the armament situation affecting various countries shows that, while there may be no immediate danger of war or disputes arising between any particular countries, every nation is devoting vast amounts of money to arms expansion. Under such circumstances I am convinced that, however firmly Japan is set on a course of peace, she still needs, basically, to be well armed. However, as to the future dangers, at least as far as my present convictions are concerned, I am certain that there will never be a war so long as I am in office."

"There will never be a war so long as I am in office"—the words, so resonant and confident, went oddly with a man of Hirota's usual caution and reticence. There was considerable surprise within the Foreign Ministry, and a feeling, even, that he had gone too far.

Hirota, however, was speaking for once not as a professional diplomat, but as a statesman—not, it should be added, of the type who, like Matsuoka, played to the gallery, but the more serious kind motivated by a quest for the truth and love of his country. His conclusion was, in a sense, one that he had reached in the course of dealing with the realities of diplomacy. And it was something, too, to which he personally felt a strong need to give expression. He wanted to commit himself firmly and to transmit his conviction to others.

He had, moreover, acquired confidence in his dealings with the Soviet Union, and was convinced that he could also move slowly, step by step, toward a restoration of friendly relations between Japan and China. All these considerations, together with his cherished belief in the importance of patient diplomatic negotiation, had come together in his denial of the possibility of war while he was in office.

Within a week of this speech, Chiang Kai-shek, head of the Nationalist government, met with Japanese reporters in China and stated that he felt the foreign minister's speech to have been sincere, and that he fully appreciated his attitude. The essential thing for friendship was to get rid of Japanese feelings of superiority toward China and of anti-Japanese emotions within China; he himself, he promised, would work to keep the anti-Japanese movement in check.

Wang Ching-wei, another leading Nationalist figure, echoed this with a statement of his own in which he described the Hirota speech as "largely agreeing with our own long-held views," and welcomed it heartily on China's behalf. Following this, the Nationalist government issued strict orders to newspapers and news agencies throughout China to restrain any anti-Japanese statements and activities.

In his speech, Hirota had gone farther than the conventional talk of "accord." Through it, he had suggested a switch in Japanese policy from the old overbearing attitude toward China to a new, conciliatory approach. Thus the Manchurian question should be solved by a succession of patient efforts over a period of time, and other outstanding questions were also to be negotiated with understanding for the Chinese position. And as proof of his intentions, he immediately set experts to studying the question of the abolition of extraterritoriality.

Still more definitive proof of Hirota's conciliatory approach was given when he elevated the status of Japan's representative in China from minister to ambassador. He placed this suggestion before the cabinet with barely a word to the military. The war minister, shocked, expressed his dissatisfaction, but his objections were overridden by Hirota's insistence that the matter chiefly concerned the Foreign Ministry, and the decision was accepted by the cabinet.

This switch in diplomatic status meant recognizing the other country as a major power, relations with whom were of primary importance. At the time, America, England, Germany, and other powers all considered China worthy of nothing more than a minister, and in deciding to station an ambassador in China, Japan had stolen a march over them. Hirota's decision was promptly transmitted to the Nationalist government by Suma Yakichiro, Japanese consul general in Nanking. Suma described the scene in the following terms:

"Together with interpreter Arino, I visited the official residence of Wang Ching-wei at dusk on an early summer evening. T'ang Yu-jen, second-in-command of the Foreign Ministry, was also present. When they heard the news, their faces flushed; Wang Ching-wei said in his usual sing-song voice—quietly but with barely concealed excitement—'This means that our two countries henceforth can work together in the interests of East Asia.' China, he declared, would immediately take similar steps to elevate her representative in Japan to the rank of ambassador.

"When we left, both of them saw us to our car and Wang himself opened the door for us to get in."

Startled, the other countries concerned made haste to follow Japan's example in raising their own representatives in China to ambassadorial level. China found her diplomatic status greatly enhanced overnight, and the Nationalist government came to set great store by Hirota's conduct of foreign policy.

The army, however, not only disapproved strongly of Hirota's attempts at conciliation, but began what seemed deliberate moves to undermine them. Immediately following the promotion of Japan's minister, a terrorist attack against important pro-Japanese figures in the Japanese concession in Tientsin gave the Kwantung Army a pretext to cross the Great Wall and advance into North China. Near Chang-chia-k'ou, a special service agency of the Kwantung Army under Colonel Doihara Kenji provoked trouble with the Chinese. The outcome was a number of agreements, such as the Ho-Umezu (June, 1935) and Chin-Doihara agreements, which though differing in name were alike in having been concluded under military pressure and in embodying Japanese demands for the withdrawal of Chinese forces, the expansion of cease-fire zones, and the abolition of anti-Japanese organizations. They were the beginnings of a plot to set up similar autonomous governments on the periphery of Manchukuo.

The terrorist incident within the Japanese concession which had provided the excuse for sending in troops was said to have been instigated behind the scenes by the chief of staff of the Japanese garrison in China. It was, in fact, a favorite trick of the special service agencies under Doihara to employ local defectors to create such incidents. Thanks to the increase in national defense expenditure, the secret funds available to these Doihara agencies were said to equal the total secret funds for the whole of the Foreign Ministry, and this vast sum of money was used freely to finance the gathering of information and the promotion of various conspiracies. It followed naturally, therefore, that where China was concerned the agencies prided themselves on having more information at their disposal than Foreign Ministry representatives on the spot, a fact which encouraged still further their tendency to ignore the ministry.

When the Kwantung Army began its move southward, the Nationalist government proposed to the Foreign Ministry that a solution be sought through diplomatic channels. Hirota sent Kuwashima, head of the East Asia Section, to the General Staff Office where he negotiated with Lieutenant General Okamura Yasuji, but Okamura rejected the Foreign Ministry's request out of hand: "The question involves matters under the jurisdiction of the military commander, and is not amenable to diplomatic negotiation. The army is content to leave things to the military commander to deal with on the spot."

This was tantamount to telling the Foreign Ministry to mind its own business. Okamura, moreover, added insolently, "The real trouble is Chiang Kai-shek's spurious pro-Japanese attitude. You should get him to give up his double-faced policies toward Japan." In January, 1935, Hirota had stated in the Diet that he had not the slightest doubt concerning Chiang Kai-shek's sincerity where the improvement of Sino-Japanese relations was concerned. Thus Okamura's statements were a direct challenge to, and a gesture of contempt toward, Hirota.

China was understandably irritated by these moves by the Japanese army, and doubts began to be expressed concerning the patient efforts that Hirota had made so far. It was Japan, not China—the doubters said—whose foreign policy was double-faced, and Hirota's conciliatory moves were no more than a cover. As a result, an assassination attempt on the pro-Japanese Wang Ching-wei left him severely wounded, while T'ang Yu-jen, second-in-command of the Chinese Foreign Ministry, who was a graduate of Keio University and also pro-Japanese, was murdered. Doihara's special service agencies went ahead with their undercover activities, to the extent that a puppet "East Hopei anti-Communist autonomous regime" was actually set up in northern China, and the situation became increasingly involved.

Major General Itagaki Seishiro, chief of staff of the Kwantung Army and a contemporary of Doihara's, had started similar moves in Inner Mongolia also. Another member of the same group was Lieutenant General Okamura, who had shown such a high-handed attitude toward the Foreign Ministry. So was Lieutenant General Isetani who, though in theory military attaché to the Japanese embassy in China, would at times behave as though he had more claim to being Japan's representative than the ambassador himself. In his pronouncements, Isetani seized every opportunity to criticize and revile the Chinese government, or to attack the policies of the powers toward China.

These four generals, all contemporaries and all sharing the same outlook, joined forces in sowing the seeds of trouble. Thanks to them, the anti-Japanese elements in China became increasingly violent, which gave them in turn a welcome opportunity to rally the army to deal with the "menacing situation."

Seeing China thus converted into a stage for the machinations of a handful of ambitious military men, Hirota tried various countermeasures, such as persuading the army command in Tokyo to issue severe warnings to the Kwantung Army, but these showed little sign of having any effect.

Hirota finally realized the prime need to remove the suspicion of "double-faced diplomacy." Mapping out the basic course of his conciliatory foreign policy, he had the Bureau of East Asian Affairs draw up a draft in consultation with army and navy authorities, and after final discussions in which the prime minister was included, the draft was agreed on with the formal approval of the foreign, war, and navy ministers. This constituted what are referred to as Hirota's

"Three Principles on China Policy":

1. China must clamp down on all anti-Japanese statements and behavior. She must free herself of dependence on England and the United States and adopt policies of friendship toward Japan. As practical expression of these policies, she must collaborate with Japan in the solution of specific problems.

2. Eventually, China must accord formal recognition to Manchukuo; in the meantime, she must give tacit recognition to its independence and drop her anti-Manchukuoan policies. Furthermore, she must promote economic and cultural exchanges and collaboration with Manchukuo, at least in the areas of northern China contiguous with that nation.

3. Since Bolshevik forces coming from Outer Mongolia and elsewhere constitute a common menace to Japan, Manchukuo, and China, China must cooperate in establishing such facilities as desired by Japan as a means of eliminating that menace in areas bordering Outer Mongolia.

This apparently arbitrary group of demands toward China was in fact relatively moderate and aimed at "conciliation." Hirota hoped, above all, that it would act as a constraint on the behavior of the army. He summoned Ambassador Chiang and asked him to cooperate in putting the three principles into practice. The ambassador handed Hirota a reply to the effect that the Nationalist government understood the underlying spirit of the principles and agreed to them for the most part. In addition, he impressed on Hirota again that the two countries should "respect each other's independence, work to maintain friendship, and seek solutions to problems by diplomatic means."

At the same time the Foreign, War, and Navy Ministries sent responsible officials to China in order to explain the principles to the Japanese authorities there. The army sent Lieutenant General Okamura, already mentioned above, to Dairen, where he summoned the officers from the local agencies of the Japanese army and described the three principles to them. He got nowhere, however, because of the fierce opposition and protests he encountered. So strong, in fact, was the tendency for the young officers to take things into their own hands that the visit further confirmed Okamura in his own high-handed approach to the Foreign Ministry.

The officers concerned were dissatisfied with Hirota's peace policies. Their minds were entirely preoccupied with the idea of Manchukuo and dreams of other puppet states. They could not understand why the Foreign Ministry did not insist on immediate recognition of Manchukuo by Chiang Kai-shek. Chiang, as they saw it, was in a position where one shove would send him tumbling. His false professions of sympathy with Japan were dictated by his own weakness, which made Japanese backing essential. The Foreign Ministry, thus, should join with the army in putting pressure on him. The time had come for foreign policy to be unified along the lines laid down by the army.

Ablaze with ambition and afraid of no one, the young staff officers insisted that the armed forces belonged to the emperor, and took every opportunity to stress the independence of the supreme command. They were not, in fact, always obedient to the orders of the emperor —i.e. army authorities in Tokyo—but they argued that the establishment of the state of Manchukuo had in the event given added glory to the imperial name, even though the Manchurian Incident had been started contrary to the emperor's will.

Their attitude was confirmed by the fact that the man responsible for the blowing-up of the South Manchurian Railway which led to the Incident had, in the same way as the perpetrator of the Chang Tso-lin bombing, been accorded no punishment worthy of the name, and was in fact well on the way to further promotion.

They were eager to achieve something while they were in China; if high-handed behavior led to trouble, so much the better, and planning to that end was necessary. In their daydreams they saw themselves forever raising the flag of Japan over fresh ramparts, then proceeding with cries of "banzai" to conquer the next objective. . . .

Military authorities in Tokyo were at a loss as to what steps to take. Their official attitude was that such moves were against their wishes, and were the responsibility of a handful of hotheaded officers in China, whose behavior it was impossible to predict.

One of the men at the War Ministry who deplored what was happening—Nagata Tetsuzan, head of the Military Affairs Bureau—was murdered in the ministry in broad daylight. The assassin, an army lieutenant colonel, assumed that he would be able to proceed to his posting on the continent as though nothing had happened. There had already been frequent terrorist incidents and attempted coups d'état by nationalistically minded young officers, and the punishment had always been light. There was a tendency among army leaders to treat such officers as "patriots," even if misguided. No wonder that a man who had assassinated the prime minister could get away with four years' imprisonment (and in fact leave jail after two and a half years as a result of an amnesty proclaimed to mark the birth of the crown prince).

The military were incited to still further excesses by a theory—put forward around that time by Professor Minobe Tatsukichi in a speech in the House of Peers—that the emperor was merely an organ of the state; this theory, they claimed, showed disrespect for the sanctity of the national polity.

Minobe had in fact been marked down for disapproval by the military ever since, at the time of the London naval disarmament conference, he had declared, in his capacity as a constitutional expert, that disarmament did not constitute a violation of the emperor's position as supreme commander.

The military were motivated not only by a desire to get rid of Minobe, but also, by asserting the emperor's absolute inviolability as a "living god," to establish the inviolability of the imperial forces. The emperor himself, however, was disposed if anything to support the "organ of the state" theory, and showed displeasure at such moves by the military. "It seems extraordinarily contradictory that the army should criticize the 'organ of the state' theory," he said. "The Imperial Rescript to the Armed Forces contains the phrase 'I am your leader,' while Article 4 of the Constitution refers to 'the emperor as the head of the Empire. . . .' Both of these show that the emperor is an 'organ of the state.'" He also complained to his chief aide-de-camp, Honjo: "The army talks of the 'organ of the state' theory as compromising the dignity of the imperial family, yet this kind of discussion is itself an insult to that dignity." And he told Honjo to convey his feelings to the war minister.

Nevertheless, War Minister Hayashi, who was a member of the "Imperial Way faction," together with other members of the military, disobeyed the imperial will and stepped up their attacks on the "organ" theory, even going so far as to use veterans' associations throughout the country to distribute pamphlets in which a number of senior statesmen were singled out by name for attack.

The emperor was incensed. "The military attack the 'organ' theory," he complained, "yet by behaving, against my wishes, in this way they are themselves reducing me to a mere agency of the government."

The military, indeed, continued to pursue their own headstrong course, using the emperor in precisely the way he had deplored. Joining with veterans' associations and right-wing organizations, they promoted a view of the national polity as dominated by an emperor who, as a "living god," had absolute sovereignty. This view gradually assumed the proportions of a nationwide popular movement which ended by swallowing up even those political parties that aimed to overthrow the government.

The government, taking the view that the question was merely one of terminology, tried to get Professor Minobe to explain away his theory, but Minobe would not agree; in the end, he was obliged to resign his seat as a member of the House of Peers, whereupon the affair blew over. It had served, even so, to establish firmly the view that discussion of the emperor's position was taboo and to encourage the imperial forces to still further excesses in the name of the independence of the supreme command.

What of Hirota's daily routine at this period?

Getting up at five every morning, he read the papers carefully and thoughtfully. He had once joked that the only things in the papers that one could accept without thinking were the obituaries. . . .

Next, he would do the same set of exercises, incorporating judo-like movements, that the children had once labeled "Father's judo dance." About his health he was always extremely careful, and his routine invariably included a hot bath every morning. Where meals were concerned, however, he made neither requests nor complaints.

124

For lunch at the Foreign Ministry he always had a simple bowl of noodles. The only alcohol he drank normally was a single bottle of saké which he would share with his eldest son over dinner. When he smoked, he used a small, old-fashioned pipe with a tiny bowl. He disliked parties, and rarely went out drinking with his subordinates; if he wanted to drink with someone, he brought him home. Many people came to call on them. Before going to bed, he would take another bath. Then he would round off the day by reading from the battered copy of the *Analects* that he had used ever since his middle-school days, before finally retiring sometime between ten and eleven.

He was popular at the Foreign Ministry because of the thoroughness with which he dispatched business. On principle, he disliked leaving any documents pending on his desk. Twice every morning and every afternoon he had his subordinates bring any relevant documents to him and report to him on their essentials. He would listen with occasional nods and grunts, then when the report was finished would direct that any necessary papers be left with him for instant perusal.

He would also ask persistent questions as to what the other man thought and why. The aim was never to catch him out, but to guide the younger man gently along the right lines of thought. For example, he might say to a member of the Bureau of European and American Affairs, "You're replying, I assume, in your capacity as a member of your bureau?"

"Well, yes. . . ." the younger man would answer with a doubtful expression, whereupon Hirota would go on in a gentle voice:

"You shouldn't. You should think as though you were the man ultimately responsible—the foreign minister. You should consider what instructions *you* would give to such-and-such an ambassador if you were in his position. . . . To do so, it's not enough just to read only the cables that come to your bureau. You should glance through those that go to other sections as well."

The junior would do his homework, then present himself again. Again Hirota would listen with a series of small grunts. Then he would say,

"Good—but it's still not enough."

"What, exactly. . . ?" the other man would query, looking puzzled again.

"Besides the House of Representatives and the House of Peers, Japan has another body with a great deal of authority—the Privy Council. What you always have to bear in mind is how you would explain things to the Privy Council, and how the Privy Council would view the question."

Hirota was perfectly serious. His way of doing things was to amass opinions from as many quarters as possible, and to seek to maintain a constant balance between them all. As he saw it, anything likely to prove excessively irritating in other quarters, or to provoke strong opposition, was unlikely in practice to serve one's own purposes either. If something displeased him in a report from a subordinate, he would take out his little pipe, puff at it furiously, then tap it loudly against the edge of his desk. He made his subordinates work, but never resorted to firing a man even if he proved hopelessly idle. The result was a tendency for people to remain in the same posts indefinitely. When a man in Personnel complained, Hirota said:

"You're still too young in your outlook. No man is any good if you only consider his faults. On the other hand, no man is completely useless if only you try to see his good points and turn them to proper account."

The Foreign Ministry as a whole overwhelmingly supported Hirota as foreign minister, but there was some dissatisfaction with him among the younger men. Those in particular who followed the ideas of Matsuoka and Shiratori and advocated "Imperial Way" policies were vociferous in calling for a "reform" of the Foreign Ministry in conformity with trends in society at large. Hirota detested these men. "They consider only the present," he complained, "and let themselves be carried along without thinking. What would happen to Japan if the country's affairs were left to such an irresponsible crowd?"

There were other young men in the ministry, on the other hand, who tried to counter the military by talking of the emperor's supreme authority in directing foreign policy—as opposed to his supreme command of the nation's forces. But Hirota rejected this kind of approach as unnecessarily provocative, and sought other means of his own to raise the standing of the Foreign Ministry.

For example, there were at the time eleven ambassadors and ministers waiting for appointments, including Yoshida Shigeru. Hirota decided to get them together for an exchange of views and to ask them to visit various parts of the country and hold lecture meetings on foreign policy questions. It was an obvious and effective counter to the lecture tours on defense questions and the national polity that the army was organizing all over the nation.

Hirota also planned to have them tour other countries as special envoys explaining Japan's ideas concerning her policy of conciliation, and to dispatch imperial aides to Japanese embassies and legations abroad. In this, too, he aimed at counterbalancing the stationing of imperial military attachés with the army and raising the morale of Japanese diplomats.

It would be a mistake, of course, to assume that all senior members of the diplomatic world were in favor of peace policies. Matsuoka, for instance, was one of those who criticized Hirota's policies for their pusillanimity; some of his statements, indeed, would have put the army to shame. He considered the Kwantung Army's methods to be halfhearted. In his view, it should get tough and march on to Peking, or Tientsin even; to stop halfway would only invite Chinese contempt.

Hirota was disgusted by such talk. So far as he was concerned, the immediate goal of Japan's foreign policy should be, first and foremost, to conclude a treaty with China and declare to the world the integrity of Chinese territory. In his eyes, the machinations of the Kwantung Army and the expeditionary force in China were a standing disgrace, and he complained constantly around this time that the behavior of the army on the continent was incomprehensible and scandalous.

He would also mutter to those close to him, with a far-off look in his eyes: "The Meiji Constitution will be the ruin of Japan." He foresaw, accurately enough, that the Constitution's recognition of the independence of the emperor's right of supreme command would lead to disaster.

Nevertheless, Hirota was in no sense a negative pessimist. He had declared that there would be no war during his term of office, and he continued his unspectacular efforts to ensure that this was so. He personally visited the army and navy general staffs to stress that he had no intention of going to war with Russia. On a number of occasions, he reprimanded the war minister concerning the actions of the forces stationed in China, and he brought the same subject up at cabinet meetings.

"Japanese forces must under no circumstances cross the Great Wall," he would stress constantly. "Even within the cease-fire zones in which Japan is allowed to station troops, there must be no unnecessary troop movements unless directly commanded by the emperor. Only, in other words, when the cabinet has decided on the move and it is in accord with national policy."

Some men such as Finance Minister Takahashi admired Hirota's stand, but it earned him the dislike of the military.

"The foreign minister talks a lot about peace, but he ignores the needs of national defense. Even at cabinet meetings, he's always trying to get the war minister under his thumb." Hirota knew that this kind of criticism was being leveled at him in the army, having heard of it indirectly through a certain divisional commander. He knew, too, what might happen should the army radicals set their sights on him, but he refused to change his attitude. He was prepared, he said, for the worst.

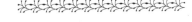 **VI**

At daybreak on February 26, 1936, in a capital blanketed since the previous night by the heaviest snowfall in thirty years, one thousand four hundred officers and men launched a mutiny under the leadership of young officers of the "Imperial Way faction."

Dividing into several units, they attacked the prime minister's official residence, the lord privy seal's private residence, the finance minister's private residence, the official residence of the grand chamberlain, and the private residence of the inspector general of military education. Firing indiscriminately with machine guns they killed Lord Privy Seal Saito, Finance Minister Takahashi, Inspector General Watanabe, and five police officers, and seriously wounded Grand Chamberlain Suzuki. Others such as Prime Minister Okada and former lord privy seal Makino had narrow escapes.

The rebel forces went on to occupy other key points such as the Metropolitan Police Headquarters and the offices of the *Asahi Shimbun,* thus gaining control of the center of the capital.

That morning, Hirota was alone at the foreign minister's official residence. His wife Shizuko disliked the exposure that went with being the foreign minister's wife, and had so far put in only two appearances at official functions. Her daughters, too, were not strong physically. For such reasons, Hirota kept his family at their private home in Harajuku and stayed alone at the official residence whenever he was busy.

Hearing the news of the incident, he contacted other members of the cabinet and hastened to the palace. There, a cabinet meeting was held with Minister of Home Affairs Goto, who had also escaped attack, standing in for the prime minister.

The army insisted that martial law should be proclaimed. Hirota, along with the other ministers, opposed this. Martial law, being a form of military rule, was to be avoided if possible. The mutiny, moreover, was strictly an internal affair of the army's, and as such should be quelled by those in command.

However, when it became clear that persons outside the army were associated with the mutiny, and that the mutiny was on a greater scale than first thought, it was decided to proclaim martial law as the speediest means of getting the situation in hand. On February 29, the mutinying troops gave in.

As premier to succeed Okada, Saionji recommended Konoe Fumimaro to the emperor. He had, in fact, been keeping Konoe up his sleeve as a potential prime minister in case of emergency, even though there was some doubt as to how Konoe would be received by the military. Konoe presented himself at the palace and was asked by the emperor to form a government, but requested time to consider the command. At his next audience, he declined the request on the grounds of ill health. It was extremely unusual for anyone to decline a direct imperial command of this nature, and the fact that Konoe did so is a sign of the difficulties which he foresaw as facing the next premier. Although the incident as such had been brought under control, it had left an ominous atmosphere in its wake. The new prime minister would need to be politically able—and prepared for the worst.

Finding themselves let down by Konoe, the senior statesmen went into a huddle again. The army hoped for the appointment of rightwinger Hiranuma Kiichiro, or of Admiral Suetsugu Nobumasa. To the army's disappointment, however, the name that finally came up was Hirota's. The principal reason for the choice was that the achievements of Hirota's conciliatory policies as foreign minister, his courageous attitude toward the military, and his stable political outlook recommended him highly to men such as Ikki Kitokuro, president of the Privy Council.

Saionji informed Konoe who, partly out of a feeling of responsibility for having declined the post himself, agreed to do his utmost to persuade Hirota. First, he sent Yoshida Shigeru, who was on familiar terms with Hirota, as his messenger. Not only was Yoshida interested in politics himself, but as son-in-law of one of the senior statesmen, Count Makino, he was well acquainted with the circumstances leading up to the choice of Hirota.

It was late at night on March 4, one week after the incident. Hirota, who thought that Yoshida had just come to talk, fell silent when he heard the other's unexpected business. After thinking for a while, his eyes fixed on the floor, he said, "I don't want to accept. I don't believe I'm up to the job, and I've no experience in handling domestic affairs. I intend to remain a diplomat all my life. Besides, I'm not particularly good at politics."

Yoshida did his best to persuade him, but he refused to give in. As a result, Yoshida arranged that the three of them should meet the following morning at Konoe's residence. Hirota went with the intention of joining forces with Yoshida in urging Konoe to take the job, but in fact it was Yoshida who joined Konoe in trying to persuade Hirota. Konoe was particularly pressing.

Though impressed by Konoe's fervor, Hirota insisted that there were other suitable candidates, and started naming military men. But Yoshida waved a hand to stop him and said, quite unexpectedly,

"They want a man in mufti, a man in an ordinary suit."

"A man in an ordinary suit. . . ?" Hirota repeated the words as though he didn't believe them.

"That's right, they don't want any of your military men."

"A man in an ordinary suit. . . ." Hirota muttered to himself over and over again. He half suspected that Yoshida was being disingenuous, but Yoshida could hardly have invented the requirement since Konoe was there with them; it must have come from Saionji or another of the senior statesmen.

The phrase affected Hirota strongly. It fitted well enough—he was indeed an ordinary man, in an ordinary suit. If that was what they wanted in the new prime minister . . .

He could well understand why the elder statesmen did not fancy a man in uniform. Moreover, although Konoe and Hiranuma might be "men in mufti," he suspected that they were more at home in formal attire than in gray flannel. He himself, on the other hand, did not look well in either morning coat or full court dress. An ordinary suit was more his mark, and he himself felt most at home in one. He was a perfectly ordinary man, a man of no particular family background. . . .

Hirota began to feel that he might, after all, have a role to play. The breeze was already blowing, and it was too late to retreat into slumber. There was no guarantee that the windmill might not collapse in the wind, but it had no alternative but to turn as best it could.

The phone rang, and Konoe answered. It was Saionji's secretary, Harada. As he put the phone down, Konoe said,

"Actually, Prince Saionji knows that we're here trying to persuade you. He was so worried that he got his secretary to call and see whether you'd accepted or not."

Further calls came from Saionji at approximately thirty-minute intervals. These calls, too, had their effect on Hirota. Could Prince Saionji really be so concerned about the reaction of someone like himself? If Saionji was worried, moreover, it meant that the emperor also was concerned. If so, then he would have no alternative but to accept with due humility.

So it happened that, somewhat before noon, Hirota told Konoe that he would accept the imperial mandate.

Delighted with the news from Konoe, Saionji promptly called at the palace and recommended Hirota to the emperor. At four the same afternoon, Hirota was summoned to the palace and was commanded by the emperor to form a government.

As Hirota, formally attired in full court dress, stood before him rigid and with downcast eyes, the emperor gave his usual advice to the new prime minister. It enjoined him:

1. To govern the country with respect for the provisions of the Constitution.

2. To exercise restraint in foreign affairs so as to avoid unnecessary friction.

3. To avoid anything that would create any sudden upheaval in the business world.

Hirota had already heard of these three injunctions. In Hirota's case, however, the emperor added one more:

4. To see that the position of the nobility was not endangered.

Hirota glanced up in spite of himself. Though he had heard quite clearly what the emperor had said, he could scarcely credit his ears. He would have liked to check on the exact meaning of the imperial words, which fell like a douche of cold water on the enthusiasm with which he had been preparing himself for the heavy task ahead.

As he left the palace, his shoulders sagged with a sense of shock and desolation.

He called to mind the faces of men such as Saionji, Makino, Kido, and Konoe—all of them "nobility." Closer to home, even, most of the men associated with the Foreign Ministry were either "nobility" or intimately connected with it. Shidehara, the late Saburi, and Yoshida had all married daughters of distinguished families. The generals and admirals from whose ranks so many prime ministers had been drawn were also, in a sense, members of a "nobility" derived from the new privileged class formed by the military.

Looking about him, Hirota had the feeling that he had been hoisted into an exposed position without any defenses. Did it mean, then, that under normal circumstances "a man in an ordinary suit" would have been unqualified to become premier? And had they felt it necessary to make it clear to him, as a rank outsider, just how far he could go?

In the halls of political power, the "nobility"—a mere handful of men compared with the nation as a whole—formed an overwhelming majority. That fact was, in a sense, one of the causes of the recent February 26 incident. Among the various factors that had driven the young officers to action was disgust at the abysmal poverty of the farmers of northern Honshu, from whose ranks so many of the army's soldiers were recruited. Angered at the politicians' neglect of the grass roots, they had called for the overthrow of the corrupt political and financial world, and had dreamed of a national "reconstruction."

Not surprisingly, the incident had shocked and frightened the "nobility" and the rest of the establishment. Although it was they themselves who had brought in Hirota, "the man in an ordinary suit," the fact remained that he was the son of a stonemason, and his wife the daughter of a poor family. Moreover, he was friendly with ultranationalist Toyama Mitsuru, who was an older man from the same part of the country as himself. All things considered, this plebeian prime minister might well prove a double-edged sword; and the "nobility" could not conceal their anxiety lest, by some process or other, he should become involved in some future outburst of calls for reform. . . .

When he arrived home after being installed as prime minister, Hirota was showered with congratulations from all about him. But he merely grunted, with an ungracious expression. It was not until late that night that he told his third son, Masao, what the emperor had said.

"I shall tell the other ministers about the first three items," he said. "But I'll keep the fourth to myself, since I've a feeling it was intended for me alone. I can't help wondering whether the emperor said it because of my humble origins. And I wonder, too, whether he said it of his own free will or whether he was just serving as a mouthpiece. . . ." For a while, he seemed sunk in thought. Then he suddenly muttered, "Anyway, it looks as though I was born fifty years too early."

Heedless of Hirota's inner conflicts, the windmill was turning furiously. The capital remained under martial law, and armed troops were in control of the heart of the city. The prime minister's official residence, still scarred by bullets and marked with the victims' blood, could not be used. It was amidst such a grim, abnormal atmosphere that Hirota installed himself in the foreign minister's official residence to start work on forming his government. He decided to bring in Yoshida Shigeru as his foreign minister, and in the meantime enlisted his help in selecting a new cabinet. The official residence was visited by a stream of ministerial candidates, men whom he and Yoshida had chosen together or who had been recommended by Konoe and other senior statesmen.

The proportional representation of the various parties in the House of Representatives at the time was Minseito forty-four percent, Seiyukai thirty-six, independents and minor groups twenty percent.

The Hirota government was to be a suprapartisan, national body in the same way as its predecessors for several governments past. It would be necessary, of course, to have the major parties represented in the cabinet, and Hirota left negotiations in this connection to Yoshida.

The crucial point in forming any government was the choice of war minister. The posts of war and navy minister were restricted to army and navy officers, including those on the reserve list; civilians were strictly excluded. As a result, the armed forces had frequently got together in the past and refused to provide candidates for the two posts, thus hindering or actually aborting the formation of a new government.

In Hirota's case, the navy was cooperative, and Admiral Nagano was chosen to be navy minister. The real question, though, was the war minister, particularly since an important task facing the new government would be to purge the army so that there should be no repetition of the February 26 incident. Hirota conferred with former vice-chief of the general staff Sugiyama, who came from Ogura, near his own home, and was a long-standing acquaintance. When Hirota suggested that he needed a man bold enough to carry out a drastic purge, Sugiyama recommended that they choose someone so far unassociated with the central command, and named General Terauchi Hisaichi, who had been commander of the army in Korea, among other things. "For one thing," he added slyly, "he's a bit of an innocent." The implication was that Terauchi, knowing little about the affairs of the world, would be more willing than most to listen to Hirota and to carry out a determined reform.

Prince Kan'in, chief of the general staff, former war minister Kawashima, and Nishi Yoshikazu, inspector general of military education, all approved of Terauchi, and since appointments to the post of war minister were traditionally made at the recommendation of all the "Big Three," Terauchi accepted the appointment.

Speed was necessary in view of the seriousness of the situation, and moves to form a new government went on throughout the night. Within twenty-four hours a list of candidates for all the important ministerial posts had been drawn up. At this point, however, the army started obstructive tactics on the grounds that certain of the men whom Hirota had chosen had doubtful qualifications.

Early on the morning of March 6, when General Terauchi arrived at the War Ministry all ready and eager to take up his new post, he found a conference of army leaders already in progress. They had before them a blacklist of "undesirable ministerial candidates":

Yoshida Shigeru (foreign minister)—son-in-law of a liberal senior statesman, Makino Nobuaki.

Kawasaki Takukichi (minister of home affairs)—it was absurd to put a party man in such a post.

Ohara Naoshi (justice minister)—his attitude to the theory of the emperor as an "organ of the state" had been too easygoing.

Shimomura Kainan—vice-president of the Tokyo *Asahi Shimbun*, a liberally inclined daily.

Nakajima Chikuhei—associated with the arms industry and a source of political funds.

In short, Hirota's view of the situation facing the country as demonstrated by his choice of candidates was highly suspect, and the military could not go along with it. Terauchi, therefore, was to decline to join the cabinet. And like a robot, an errand-boy for the army, he was dispatched to see Hirota with a message to this effect. Hirota urged him to change his mind, but this was not within Terauchi's power to do.

Upon returning to the War Ministry, Terauchi issued a statement in which he criticized the lineup of the new cabinet as "characterized by the same old liberalistic approach as ever and devoted to the maintenance of the status quo or to negative policies leading to compromise and retrogression." It was impossible to form a government without a war minister, and Hirota found his efforts frustrated.

Such a situation had not been entirely unforeseen, even by Joseph Grew, American ambassador to Japan, who was one of those who had evaluated Hirota highly as foreign minister. "For me there are no finer people in the world than the best type of Japanese," he had first written in his diary. "I am rather inclined to place Hirota among them; if he could have his way unhampered by the military I believe that he would steer the country into safer and saner channels."

Again, when he heard that Hirota had been commanded to form a government, he wrote: "I am very much pleased because I believe that Hirota is a strong, safe man and that while he will have to play ball with the Army to a certain extent, I think that he will handle foreign affairs as wisely as they can be handled, given the domestic elements which he will have to conciliate. I think too that he wants good relations with the United States, and will do what he is able to do in that direction. . . . If I had had the pick myself, I know of nobody whom I would have more gladly chosen to head the Government, with American interests in view." However, on hearing that Hirota had selected Yoshida as his foreign minister, that same Grew wrote apprehensively that it was "like waving a red rag at a bull."

The situation, in fact, had developed just as Grew had feared. Though resigned to a certain amount of interference from the army, Hirota had set out with the intention of choosing the men he himself thought best, rather than selecting from the start only ministers who would please the military. If the army cared to intervene, he felt, it would at least serve to show it up for the tyrant it was.

In fact, the army had gone much further than Hirota had foreseen. Far from being abashed at their own part in the recent bloody incident, the military set upon this "prime minister in mufti" as though the sight of the snowy capital temporarily pinned beneath the jackboot had only served to encourage them in their excesses.

Hirota's headquarters at the foreign minister's residence, which had been in a cheerful mood at the prospect of a new government before the day was out, was thrown into gloom once more. The gloom was deepened by the presence of Yamashita Tomoyuki, Muto Akira, and other men from the War Ministry, who stalked imperiously about the building with swords at their sides, periodically converging on Hirota.

Beneath the windows, military police were patrolling, and troops with fixed bayonets stood at the gate. In one room of the building, Hirota had gathered Yoshida and others of his staff for consultations. Hirota was tempted to give up the task in despair. Why should he have to put up with the army's arrogant ways indefinitely?

137

But a message had already come from Saionji and other senior statesmen strongly requesting him to go through with forming a government whatever personal trials it might entail. A feeling also existed that for civilians to succeed in forming a government under what was virtually military rule would be a significant feat in itself. Conversely, to give up at this stage would only have a still more harmful effect in every sphere.

Thus it was decided after long deliberation that the civilians should pocket their pride and draw up a new list of candidates embodying such concessions to the military as seemed at all possible. Work on forming a cabinet began again, but Yoshida left headquarters that day never to return. The attack on him was part of a pattern that had begun with the antagonism between him and the army during his days as consul general in Mukden, and, together with the attacks on Professor Minobe over his controversial view of the emperor, were a reminder of how long the army as a whole bore grudges.

On several occasions Yoshida's wife called at Hirota's home in Harajuku and complained that her husband was depressed, but there was nothing that Hirota could do for the moment to help his old acquaintance. A new cabinet list of candidates was drawn up incorporating changes such as the withdrawal of Ohara and Shimomura, and the switching of Kawasaki to the Ministry of Commerce and Industry. Finally, late on the night of March 8, Hirota turned to his staff members and prospective ministers and said with an air of finality, "Well then, I think this will do."

"Just a moment—" put in General Terauchi. He left the room and went to see Yamashita, Muto, and other members of the Military Affairs Bureau who were in another room. About thirty minutes later, he returned.

"The list of ministers," he declared, "includes two each from the Minseito and Seiyukai. This amounts to nothing more nor less than a party government. You must know that the army has requested all along that there should be not more than one man from any single party. The army will not be satisfied unless you reduce the number to one. I cannot accept the post of war minister." And he withdrew to the War Ministry, together with the members of the Military Affairs Bureau, as though to suggest that his words had been a final ultimatum.

Hirota was appalled: he had never expected the army to be as intransigent as this. In the name of the emperor, the army had rudely interfered—not once, but twice—with the process of government-making. It should be no business of the military's whether he chose to include one man or two from each party. Despite the request that he carry through the task of forming a government, he felt that he had suffered in silence long enough; there was no further room for compromise.

He summoned Fujinuma Shohei, who had been named as chief cabinet secretary and who, as a liberal, was among those whose expulsion the head of the Military Affairs Bureau had demanded. Fujinuma telephoned Terauchi at the War Ministry. "We shall announce in tomorrow morning's papers that we have finally failed to form a government on account of obstruction by the military," he said. "Is that all right with you?"

Terauchi sounded flustered. "Wait a moment, will you?" he said. There were sounds of an exchange in low voices, then, "I'll call you back in a little while."

Before long, Terauchi phoned again: "We will .agree to the formation of a government tomorrow if you'll go along with a document that we're sending you now by special messenger."

It was 1:30 A.M. on March 9 when Major Muto Akira, the "special messenger," presented himself with a copy of a declaration for publication. With his piercing gaze and fierce expression, this keen young officer looked as if he were making a sortie into enemy territory.

The declaration he had brought with him ran as follows: "The recent mutiny was not the sole responsibility of the military. Government is corrupt; the political parties must reconsider their behavior, and domestic policy must be reformed." Hirota looked at the document with wry amusement: it was rather like dealing with a bunch of spoiled kids. The contents were sufficiently abstract to require no immediate action. Even so, Hirota sent Muto away and made a few corrections to the declaration for form's sake, then had it delivered to Terauchi. Agreement was thus reached.

It was 2:30 in the morning. Three hours later, Hirota had morning dress sent from his home and set off to pay his respects at the Meiji Shrine. Martial law was still in force, and the excitement engendered by the mutiny still lingered in the capital. Brushing aside the objections of those close to him Hirota went, accompanied by a single secretary, with no bodyguard at all. As he walked up the drive to the shrine, it was still only half light, and a morning mist shrouded the trees on either side. He bowed before the main shrine, reported to the gods on the formation of his government, and sought their protection. The courtyard was quite deserted, and the white pebbles with which the ground was strewn were wet with the cold mist.

On the evening of March 9, when he was to be sworn in at the palace, Hirota again changed into formal attire. He disliked full court dress, which he often complained made him look like a street musician. On this occasion, he told his family in embarrassment that he felt like a hotel doorman.

Following the ceremony, the new cabinet held a brief first meeting. It was past 11:30 P.M. when Hirota returned to the foreign minister's official residence, where a large number of friends and acquaintances, including men from the Foreign Ministry and from his home district, were waiting to toast him. The happiest man among them, though, unaware as he was of the complex emotions assailing Hirota, was his eighty-eight-year-old father Tokuhei, who had come up to Tokyo from his home in the country. Tokuhei the stonemason, the man who people had said worked thirty-five days a month, stroked his white goatee and answered freely everything the reporters cared to ask him.

"He was an obedient boy," he recalled in his thick country accent. "I never had to hit him once. He liked studying, so I just let him study. If I'd made him a stonemason, I suppose he'd have had quite a business of his own by now. When he was leaving middle school, the principal asked me whether I wanted him to go into the army or into government service. So I said, 'Let the boy be what he likes. He can be a horse or an ox for all I care, so long as he serves his

Hirota as a "student" in China (1903).

Hirota, on his appointment as ambassador to Moscow.

The newly appointed prime minister, with his father and wife.

Hirota, as Konoe's foreign minister, at a farewell party for the German ambassador's wife (on his right). The bearded man is Toyama Mitsuru, one of the founders of the Genyosha.

Hamaguchi's assailant, beaming, between two police officers.

A gravely wounded Hamaguchi being carried out of Tokyo Station (Nov. 14, 1930).

Matsuoka Yosuke, in the center of an excited throng, leaves Japan for the League of Nations (1932).

Shidehara Kijuro.

Prince Saionji.

Matsuoka Yosuke.

Yoshida Shigeru (in retirement).

General Araki—war minister in the Saito government.

Joseph C. Grew, U.S. ambassador to Japan, with his wife (the granddaughter of Commodore Perry, the first official American visitor to Japan).

Prime Minister Saito with his new foreign minister, Hirota.

The abortive coup d'état of February 26, 1936; rebel troops surround the Diet building.

Departure for Manchuria.

Commander Matsui Iwane entering the fallen city of Nanking.

Hirota in 1937 with Navy Minister Yonai (in white) and War Minister Sugiyama.

Herbert von Dirksen, the German ambassador.

Kido Koichi.

Konoe Fumimaro.

The trial scene. Hirota is third from left in the prisoners' dock. Kiyose, second-in-command of the defense, is at the microphone.

Sir William Webb.

Comyns-Carr (left) and Keenan.

On board the bus from Sugamo prison to Ichigaya. At the extreme left is Muto; directly behind him are Umezu (left) and Araki. Behind Umezu is Tojo and, beyond him, Matsuoka (with beard). On the right of the picture is Sato Kenryo (in peaked cap), with Kido two seats behind (in glasses). Hirota is at the back of the bus on the left.

Mealtime at Ichigaya. From left to right: Hirota, Togo, Tojo, and Sato.

Hirota's children, just after visiting him in prison. From left to right: Miyoko, Chiyoko, Masao, Toyoko, and Hiroo (his eldest son).

country.' The principal didn't say another word." And the old man laughed. . . .

Seeing his father's delight, Hirota reflected that a stonemason's son could hardly have come any further than he had. He wished that his mother Take, or his second son Tadao, could have seen him too. But that was all—personally, he felt not so much pleasure at having become prime minister as tension at the thought of the difficulties with which he would have to deal. Still unable to use his own official residence because of the lingering marks of violence, he himself realized, better than anyone else, the unnaturalness of the situation he faced.

He was not a convivial man by nature, and the situation sapped still further any desire he might have had to celebrate. Although he was generally considered to feel strong ties with men from Fukuoka, he did not even attend the special gathering held back home to celebrate his appointment. It will be remembered that, in the same way, he had had almost no contact with the supporters' association organized at the time of his appointment as foreign minister.

All kinds of congratulatory gifts including saké were sent to him, but he forwarded some of them to orphans' homes, together with money from his own pocket, and had the casks of saké delivered to a day-laborers' hangout in Ikebukuro, on the outskirts of Tokyo. Some of the press promptly poked fun at this as an attempt by the new prime minister to win popularity; but Hirota was puzzled and pained by their attitude. "In any period, there are always people in distress at the lower levels of society," he complained. "What's wrong in doing something for them? Politics is a matter of deeds, not ideals."

"The man in an ordinary suit" was—and, what was more important, still felt himself to be—the son of a stonemason; "prime minister" was no more than a label newly attached to him. Orphans and laborers were his own kind, and the "nobility" episode had made him feel even closer to them than before.

To the great disappointment of all those fellow Fukuokans in Tokyo who saw themselves—whether at their own or others' recommendation—as potential private secretaries to the prime minister, he chose to take his own third son Masao and a former newspaper reporter from Nagoya to fill the job. He did not ask the Foreign Ministry to provide him with any secretaries.

There was a reason for this. There was no telling when another February 26 incident might occur, and Hirota, though quite resigned to dying himself if necessary, was reluctant to take with him a young stranger with a future.

Since Yoshida Shigeru had proved persona non grata with the military, Hirota himself served concurrently as foreign minister for one month, then appointed Arita Hachiro, ambassador to China. On the day he left the Foreign Ministry, Hirota assembled its senior officials to deliver a few parting words. In this address he said, among other things, "I have taken on the job of prime minister as my final act of service to the emperor. . . ."

"What does he expect?" some of those present murmured. "He couldn't go any higher, could he?" But they had not got the point. In using the word "final," Hirota had meant to indicate his acceptance of the danger of being felled by an assassin. As he told his son Masao, "I'll be content so long as this government manages to purge the army and make clear the distinction between right and wrong." The task, which might sound easy enough, was in fact likely to provoke an intense reaction from the other side. Yet Hirota felt that if only he could manage it he would have no regrets, whatever happened. "If I am to do anything more," he added—meaning if he were allowed to go on living—"I would like to carry out domestic reforms to get to the root of all kinds of popular complaints."

The purge as such was an internal matter for the army, and the restrictions imposed by the independence of the supreme command made it difficult for Hirota to take direct action. Nevertheless, he intended to prepare the way for it as far as he could. The first step had been the appointment of Terauchi, a political innocent with no links with central command, as war minister. At his urging, Terauchi now undertook a series of major steps to punish or transfer to other posts those responsible. The undersecretary for war, the head of the Military Affairs Bureau, and the head of the Military Staff College at the time of the incident were retired or shifted to other posts, and all military councillors and all generals apart from three younger men, including Terauchi, were obliged to resign in token of the responsibility of the army as a whole. At the same time, reappointments involving three thousand officers in all were listed. Those directly responsible for the incident were subjected to a swift court-martial, and the fifteen officers who were the ringleaders were executed; it was the first time that such severe punishment had been meted out in such a case.

Thus a determined purge of the army had been carried out, in theory at least. It would have been rash to assume, however, that this indicated a genuine soul-searching on the army's part. There had long been factional struggles within the military, and a major internal motive for the purge had been the desire of the "control faction" to use the incident as a means of getting rid of the "Imperial Way faction" once and for all.

As part of the purge, the army had proposed a return to the system of choosing war ministers from the ranks of serving officers. The posts of war and navy ministers had originally been confined to serving officers only, but in 1913, under the Yamamoto Gombei government, the system was changed to cover officers on the reserve list too, in order to avoid giving serving officers such an absolute say in military affairs.

The reason put forward by the army for suggesting a return to the old system was that it would be dangerous if generals who had been put on the reserve list on account of their responsibility for the incident were to reemerge as cabinet ministers, thus rekindling factional rivalries and making it impossible to carry through the purge thoroughly.

Since Hirota's principal aim at the moment was to purge the army, he could scarcely reject the proposal outright. He put it before a cabinet meeting, where it met with no particular opposition. Prince Saionji also expressed the view that if one was going to have to listen to a war minister at any rate, one might as well have it straight from the shoulder.

So Hirota agreed. Nevertheless, he got Terauchi to undertake to do away with the understanding, observed hitherto, that any candidate for the post of war minister required the unanimous recommendation of the outgoing war minister, the chief of the general staff, and the inspector general of military education, and replace it with an agreement that the prime minister could select the candidate freely from among serving officers. He also got him to agree that, if necessary, a suitable candidate on the reserve list could be restored to the active list.

In a sense, this left the man charged with forming a government a freer hand than before. Hirota felt that, if anything, he had traded the name for the reality, and had no special sense of having given in to the military. (He had no way of knowing that this episode would be used as material at the Far East Military Tribunal in accusing him of conniving with the military's grab for power.)

In mid-March, president Ikki of the Privy Council had resigned and Hirota recommended Hiranuma Kiichiro as his successor. Hiranuma was a major political figure whose name had been mentioned on several occasions as a candidate for the premiership, but he had contacts with right-wing organizations and was well received among the military. As such he was persona non grata with the elder statesmen, yet Hirota had his own reasons for recommending the man. As Hirota saw it, to leave him out in the cold would only encourage him to plot and subvert; to put him in a position of responsibility would, conversely, oblige him to exert a certain self-restraint and keep him out of mischief. As a condition of Hiranuma's appointment, Hirota got him to promise to sever all connections with rightist factions.

The opportunities for meeting the emperor personally afforded by his new position brought many surprises for Hirota. Whenever he met the emperor, custom required that he sit with his eyes fixed on the small table placed between the emperor and himself, and take care not to look him directly in the face. In Konoe's case, of course, things were different: Hirota had heard that he would talk to the emperor in a relaxed way, with his legs crossed—but then Konoe was by birth a privileged man. . . .

One day when the weather was still chilly, the emperor had a cold, but he took up his position as usual, seated formally on the other side of the small table. The only sign of heating in the room of some twenty square meters was a single electric stove with water steaming in a metal washbasin placed on top of it. Hirota, who knew how royalty lived in Europe, could not help wondering whether this was good enough. Could it be that the emperor had no personal desires, envy, or any similar feelings at all?

But another day, in summer, when the time for compiling the budget was drawing near, this same emperor summoned Hirota and, announcing that he was speaking "in his capacity as supreme commander of the armed forces," named a certain sum as necessary for the army and navy appropriations and asked Hirota as prime minister to see that it was obtained.

Hirota, taken aback, was at a loss for a reply. Even the emperor's final injunction to "decide the matter by debate in the Diet" did not remove the sense of surprise. He felt a perplexity similar to what he had felt on the day of his swearing-in, when the emperor had given his warning about the "nobility." Could the request be the emperor's own idea? Or was it the military using the emperor as a mouthpiece? Although they talked of his inviolability as supreme commander, the impression by now was that they were using the emperor to give orders just as they liked, over the heads of the administration.

Now that the army purges were more or less over, the military were once again switching to a high posture. Together with the repudiation of the Washington and London disarmament agreements, the navy had demanded enormous funds to be devoted chiefly to the building of warships, the aim being to establish Japanese control over the waters of the west Pacific. The army too, as though not to be outdone, had demanded a vast amount to be used mainly in completing "nation-building" in Manchukuo and in stepping up national defense over a wide area—all on the assumption that the potential enemy was the Soviet Union.

At the same time, Hirota himself requested the various ministries to consider ways of effecting the domestic reforms that were the motto of the new government, and to make concrete proposals. These measures were a task that naturally faced the government in the wake of the army purges. The rebellion by the young officers had had its origins in the corruption of party government and the poverty of the masses, so it was imperative to carry out a determined reform of government as it affected the lives of the ordinary people. The task, moreover, seemed particularly appropriate for a prime minister who was himself of humble origins. In the long run his aim was to improve the lives of people who wore workaday suits like himself, or factory overalls, or farmer's clothes, and give them hope for the future.

In response to Hirota's call, the ministries concerned submitted more than thirty draft bills. All of them required budget allocations which would have to be debated along with the military appropriations in the course of drawing up the budget. But the number was too great for them all to be dealt with at once.

Hirota accordingly summoned a five-minister conference—prime minister, finance minister, foreign minister, war minister, and navy minister—to reduce the number of items to manageable proportions for purposes of budget-making. The result was a list of fourteen proposals grouped together under what was known as the Hirota government's "Seven Major Items of National Policy":

1. The stepping-up of national defense.
2. A radical reform of education.
3. A reorganization of the tax system embracing both national and local taxes.
4. The stabilization of the people's livelihood, entailing: (a) measures to forestall natural disasters; (b) the expansion of health facilities; (c) the overhaul and encouragement of the agricultural and fishing economies and the encouragement of small- and medium-scale commerce and industry.
5. The establishment of controls over industry, entailing: (a) the reinforcing of control over the electric power industry; (b) moves to make Japan self-sufficient in liquid fuels and iron ore; (c) the securing of stable sources of fibers; (d) the promotion and establishment of controls over trade; (e) the promotion of aviation and shipping enterprises; (f) the promotion of Japanese development overseas.
6. The laying-down of firm national policies on important mat-

ters affecting Manchukuo; steps to encourage emigration; and the encouragement of investment.

7. The reorganization and improvement of the administrative machinery.

In the meantime, the army and navy decided it would be better to share the field between them rather than engage in eternal rivalry, and to this end drew up their own national policy program. This was reworked with the participation of officials of the Foreign Ministry on account of its bearing on foreign policy, and emerged as the "Bases of National Policy." For example, section 1(c) of this document embodied a favorite army theme:

"The basic concern of Japan's policies on the continent shall be to ensure the healthy development of Manchukuo and to secure the defenses of Japan and Manchuria; to remove the threat from Russia in the north, and at the same time to prepare for any threat from Britain and America; and to promote economic development via close collaboration between the three countries of Japan, Manchukuo, and China."

The navy, which had ambitions of expansion to the south, was taken care of in the following passage:

"(d) To promote the economic development of the Japanese people in southern waters and the outlying areas in particular, and to extend Japanese power by gradual, peaceful means, taking care not to offend other nations, thus contributing, along with the completion of nation-building in Manchukuo, to the amplification and reinforcement of the national strength."

In line with these principles, the immediate aims where national armament was concerned were defined in two sentences:

"(i) The aim for the army shall be sufficient strength to counteract whatever forces the Soviet Union may be able to deploy in the Far East, and in particular to bring its strength in Manchukuo to the point where it could deal a decisive blow to those Soviet forces in the Far East at the very outset of hostilities.

"(ii) The aim for the navy shall be to bring its strength up to the point where it can guarantee control of western Pacific waters against the U.S. navy."

Besides these, officials of the three ministries also put forward their own tentative foreign policy, but it was a rehash of already expressed views, with nothing new to speak of.

The two drafts were put before the five-minister council as "top-secret" proposals, and were confirmed. The other ministers as well as Hirota considered them as statements of the claims of the various ministries concerned, to be used as reference material in debate. With the government committed to the new task of domestic reform, and with various claims for huge military appropriations, the usual methods of tackling the budget would be inadequate; thus the guidelines represented by the two drafts were needed in order to give form to the discussions.

The idea behind this was similar to that underlying the "Three Principles on China Policy" of Hirota's period as foreign minister; rather than allow oneself to be pulled first one way then the other by those directly responsible, one let them have their say first, then drew up a framework of principles, or criteria, and imposed it on them from above.

For all this, Hirota was in complete earnest about those aspects in the "Seven Major Items of National Policy" that seemed to have a particularly close bearing on the lives of the people.

A case in point was educational reform: the aim here was that compulsory education should be extended from six to eight years, and it was decided to carry this out in the following year, 1937. Again, a system of subsidies was put into effect as a means of setting local finances on their feet.

In the economic sphere, the electric power industry was transferred to national management so as to guarantee the cheap and abundant electric power that was needed both by industry and for the well-being of the nation as a whole. Other measures, such as a plan for helping the agricultural communities to get out of debt, improvements in the system of mutual aid insurance in the event of natural disasters, and the passing of a law concerning the welfare of mothers and children, were aimed more specifically at those in the lower strata of society.

The various ministries were directed to draw up the necessary bills with all speed, and to provide justifications for their claims for budget appropriations; finally, everything was ready for the discussion of the budget in the Diet.

Partly as a result of these new undertakings, the national budget swelled to a total of approximately 2,800 million yen, an increase of twenty-two percent over the preceding year, and the word "positive" came to be used frequently of the government's policies both abroad and at home. Where the phrase "positive foreign policies" was concerned, the army doubtless had its own private ideas, but Hirota defined it as meaning that relations with Europe and America would remain the same, whereas Japan's existing policies toward the Soviet Union and China would be intensified. His idea was to keep the military satisfied with the word "positive," while in practice trying, for example, to improve relations with China in accordance with the above-mentioned "Three Principles on China Policy."

On the subject of his own methods, Hirota once confided to a subordinate with whom he was on close terms: "The military are like an untamed horse left to run wild. If you try head-on to stop it, you'll get kicked to death. The only hope is to jump on from the side and try to get it under control while still allowing it to have its head to a certain extent. Of course," he went on with a rueful smile, "it's a hard job to jump on without stirrups, and since you're riding bareback, there's no telling when you'll get thrown off. But somebody has to do it. That's why I've jumped on."

Even after Hirota became prime minister, his wife Shizuko stayed quietly at home as before, rarely making any appearances at the more spectacular official functions. A piano teacher, a woman, often came to give lessons, and the sound of the girls practicing would drift out into the garden. On hot days in summer, Shizuko would stand behind the instructor throughout the lesson, fanning her with a round paper fan. There was nothing at all about her to suggest the wife of a prime minister.

Even now, Hirota observed the same daily routine as ever, beginning with his "judo dance" and his morning bath. There were more visitors than before, and those coming for the first time would be startled to see a prime minister and former career diplomat smoking cut tobacco in an old-fashioned, long-stemmed pipe. With leisurely movements he would take the tobacco out of the small drawer in the smoking set, fill the tiny bowl of the pipe, and light it with a match. Occasionally, he would twist a piece of handmade paper into a spill with practiced fingers, and clean out the pipe. It was a fixed routine.

He would still drink one small bottle of saké every evening with his meal. At home with his family, he talked a lot, giving the lie to his usual taciturn appearance. Sometimes, he would invite his sons to share a bottle of saké with him as they talked. When dinner was over, he would go to the room that led off the entrance hall to see if the police officers on duty were playing *go*. If not, he would suggest they play, and would watch the game's progress intently. Occasionally, on Sundays, he would spend almost half the day in the room by the entrance. In similar fashion, he would watch his children play cards, beaming all the while but making no move to join in. He would often play patience, however, muttering to himself morosely whenever the cards failed to work out.

At weekends, if there was no business in hand, the family would make a beeline for the villa in Kugenuma. But they were bothered there by the noise of a railway that passed nearby, and looked for land to build another house in the neighborhood. There was a promising site at Kataseyama, but when the owner told him that he could have it for ten yen per *tsubo* (3.3 square meters), Hirota gave up the idea; he had heard that it should cost fifteen or sixteen yen at the current rate. "A politician has to be particularly careful when he buys land," he told his sons. "He should never buy it if it's too cheap."

Next, they found a quiet place on the hill behind the Ryukoji temple—but it had no running water. The town authorities promptly offered to lay on water if the prime minister was thinking of buying the land. Hearing this, Hirota once more gave up the idea. Finally, they stopped looking for land altogether, and enlarged their old villa instead. With visitors, bodyguards, and the like, the population of the house sometimes swelled to as many as twenty, and in the end they were obliged to enlarge it on two separate occasions.

Hirota liked to watch the progress of the building work. He would often go out in the morning and gaze at the carpenters in action. Occasionally, even, he joined them for a drink in their shed in the evening after they had finished work. "You really shouldn't," Shizuko would say to him nervously. "They can't relax with you around."

Sunday afternoons at the villa were invariably devoted to talks with the press. Life in Tokyo was too hectic to allow conversation in a relaxed atmosphere, but here there were no interruptions. Hirota had no particular favorites among the reporters, and the various newspapers sent whoever they happened to have on duty at the time. When the weather was fine, they would sometimes take chairs out into the garden and talk beneath the shade of the trees, but usually Hirota sat facing them in one of the guest rooms. He would wear Japanese dress and sit formally on his cushion, legs beneath him and both hands on his lap. Sometimes they would talk for two or three hours at a stretch.

For the reporters concerned, it was a refreshing change to be able to discuss affairs of state with the prime minister in such a pleasant country setting and without the formality and reserve usual on such occasions. They looked forward to the meeting, and some of them compared it to the way people in ancient China would make pilgrimages to discuss matters with some revered sage in retirement.

Reporters being what they are, of course, there were also some who referred to these visits irreverently as "going down to the shack." Despite the enlargements, the building was in fact still remarkably unpretentious for a prime minister's private villa.

"A politician ought to throw his money around a bit," some journalists would tell Hirota, almost as though giving him advice. But he paid no attention. He had no political funds, nor did he try to obtain any. His ethical sense would not allow him to do so, nor would it have accorded with his innate objection to all forms of self-seeking. The only time he helped raise funds was when a campaign was started to build a dormitory in Fukuoka for students from other parts of Asia. On that one occasion, he gave the campaigners his name-card to use when they went to visit prominent businessmen. The response was generous; Mitsui, for example, happily donated twice the expected sum on the grounds that "Mr. Hirota had never asked for money before."

Hirota often went walking on the beach, sometimes with his daughters, sometimes alone with Shizuko.

"How about a walk, Mama?" he would say.

"Yes, dear," she would reply, addressing him as *ansama*, the Fukuoka dialect word.

When their daughters were still young, they would sometimes ask, "Mummy, did you and Daddy marry for love?" and the parents would look embarrassed but nod with a smile. They were still fond of each other, although Hirota was now fifty-eight and Shizuko fifty-one. Seen walking together, they seemed a perfectly ordinary middle-aged couple.

A path led through the grove of stunted pine trees that covered the sandy soil, then out onto the beach, with its view of the island of Enoshima floating like an upturned bowl on the sea a short way up the coast. It was at Enoshima that Hirota had bought Shizuko the shellwork ring in their early married days. The diamond ring which he had brought her later, on his return from the legation in Holland, still sparkled on her finger now.

If the diamond caught his eye as they stood there in the breeze from the sea, he may well have recalled his days in Holland, and the sound of the windmills. And he may have reflected on his own position—himself a "windmill" fated to turn unceasingly in an ever-increasing gale.

And Shizuko, as she watched him staring thoughtfully out at the horizon, may well have felt a touch of uneasiness and wished they could stay there in Kugenuma, without ever returning to the official residence in Tokyo.

But Shizuko, of course, never breathed a word of such feelings. They stood there silent, a couple on the threshold of old age, with the wind from the sea blowing about them.

Around this time, in far-off Germany, a plan was afoot that in later years was to cast a dark shadow not only over Hirota's life but over the whole fate of Japan. Although it involved negotiation between two nations, the talks were in fact carried on behind the veil of privacy afforded by the "independence of the supreme command," and neither Hirota nor the Foreign Ministry authorities were informed until things were quite far advanced.

The talks were first broached in mid-1935 by a German arms dealer and prominent Nazi, who approached Major General Oshima Hiroshi, military attaché at the Japanese embassy in Berlin. In fact, both the military and naval "attachés" had separate offices of their own where they were free from embassy surveillance.

The gist of the German proposals was that since Germany and Japan both found themselves, internationally, in similar situations, and both felt themselves threatened by the Soviet Union, they should join in some form of pact that would act as a restraint on the Soviet menace from both sides. Oshima, whose father had been war minister and had been stationed in Germany during his youth, was pro-German in his sympathies, but was not enthusiastic at first, feeling that such a pact would benefit Germany more than Japan. However, under pressure from the Germans, he passed the suggestion on to the General Staff Office, and in the course of repeated contacts the proposed pact gradually took shape.

In practice, it was not to be the military alliance that Germany hoped for, but a kind of defensive alliance in which both sides guaranteed that if either should be attacked by the Soviet Union the other would engage in no activity likely to benefit the Russians. It was, moreover, to take the form of a private anti-Comintern agreement—avoiding mention of the Soviet Union by name, and pledging cooperation in, for example, the gathering of information as a means of preventing Communist infiltration.

It was not until more than six months after Oshima had first begun negotiations, at a time when the outlines of an agreement were emerging, that the Foreign Ministry got wind of the talks and demanded an explanation from the army. The ministry itself was in a dilemma. Togo, head of the Bureau of European and American Affairs and the man directly responsible, was opposed to the agreement, but Foreign Minister Arita was in favor provided it was not too binding on Japan. A cable of instructions sent to Ambassador Mushanokoji in Berlin at the beginning of May, 1936, said: "The situation in various quarters requires that close relations should be maintained between Japan and Germany. It would be an appropriate time, if Germany should so wish, to conclude an agreement in vague terms, as we told you before your departure, without for the time being making any specific commitments between the two countries."

The prevention of Communist infiltration was considered a self-evident requirement of national policy at the time. It was undeniable, too, that the "threat from the north" had increased; since the outbreak of the Manchurian Incident, the Soviet Union—partly to guard against future moves by the Kwantung Army—had almost trebled its forces in the Far East, and was engaged in construction of military installations on the border. Furthermore, Japan had been isolated from the rest of the world ever since leaving the League of Nations, and public sentiment favored an end to isolation.

War Minister Terauchi and Foreign Minister Arita came together to call on Hirota and present him with what was already on the way to becoming a fait accompli.

"Even if we sign an agreement," Hirota told the two ministers, "it must not be of a kind to give offense to the Soviet Union or any other country. There must be absolutely no presupposition of war, nor any use of the term 'war.' Furthermore, if the main aim is to counter communism, then attempts should be made to have England and other countries also join the alliance."

The army was opposed to any moves to obtain an agreement with England, but the Foreign Ministry insisted that negotiations with that country be begun. Thus—since the conclusion of treaties was, after all, the Foreign Ministry's job, no matter how much the military might do to prepare the ground—the military finally gave in.

Japanese embassies and legations in countries extending from Holland and Belgium as far as Greece were instructed to sound out the respective governments to see if they were interested in joining such an agreement. France, being on traditionally bad terms with Germany, was not included. At the same time, the ambassadors and ministers concerned were instructed to give detailed estimates of each

154

country's reaction. The greatest hopes of all were, of course, pinned on England's participation.

From England, however, there was no response. More accurately, the Japanese ambassador in England made no attempt to sound out English reactions but himself sent back a lengthy cable expressing head-on opposition to the idea of an anti-Comintern pact. The ambassador who thus ignored the Foreign Ministry's instructions was Yoshida Shigeru; in fact, it was Hirota himself who, in an irregular move, had given Yoshida the ambassadorship to England after he had been prevented by the military from becoming foreign minister. Not only was the post one of the most prestigious available to a diplomat at the time, but England was the ideal country for a man with Yoshida's aristocratic inclinations. He had gratefully accepted Hirota's gesture, and was now puffing contentedly at his cigars in distant London, savoring his position and his freedom from the interference of his bête noire, the military.

In Yoshida's eyes, Hitler's Germany and Mussolini's Italy were presumptuous upstarts whom he despised and mistrusted. He believed that they aimed at the destruction of the existing order, and that their calls for the construction of a new world were directed in large measure at England and the United States. A country such as Germany, however, could not hope to compete with the overwhelmingly greater natural resources and economic and military power of Britain and America. From the viewpoint of her own self-interest, Japan would have nothing to gain in joining with Germany. Why should Japan need to conclude such a treaty—conclude it, moreover, in a way to suit the ideas of the military—at a time when flexibility was the most necessary thing for her foreign policy? Although such an agreement might not be felt as a very serious commitment at the moment, sooner or later its implications would deepen both politically and militarily. How could he be expected to propose anything so foolish to England?

Major Tatsumi, military attaché at the embassy in London, was ordered by the General Staff Office to try to convert Yoshida, but in the end found himself won over instead to Yoshida's viewpoint. As a result, Major General Oshima made a special journey from Germany to England and spent a long time trying to persuade Yoshida, but the only result was complete disagreement. Major Tatsumi later reported the scene at dinner that evening as follows:

"Mr. Yoshida chatted cheerfully, giving no sign of having just been engaged in difficult discussions for a full three hours, but Oshima looked extremely sour and announced that he was going back to Berlin the next day. I tried to persuade him, now that he was in London, at least to come and have a meal at the military attaché's office, but he would have none of it. So I phoned for a flight reservation, and the next morning he returned to Berlin in high dudgeon.

"After he had left, I asked Mr. Yoshida how things had gone. 'Just as I said they would,' he replied, and I remember well his adding, 'Germany's bitten him quite badly, hasn't it?' "

Even if Yoshida had obeyed instructions, there was little likelihood that England would have been interested. The British foreign secretary, in fact, was subsequently to express opposition in Parliament to the formation of any anti-Comintern bloc. The Japanese Foreign Ministry had hoped, even if England could not be persuaded to join in such a pact, to secure some kind of agreement ensuring friendly relations with Britain and promising, for example, respect for British rights and interests in China. But since Ambassador Yoshida refused even to mention the Foreign Ministry directive to the British side, the ministry was obliged for the moment to abandon its goal where Britain was concerned.

Thus Hirota, who had pinned his hopes on the maintenance of friendly relations with England, found them frustrated from the start by an old acquaintance whom he himself had appointed. And the anti-Comintern pact, just as Yoshida had feared, was to lean increasingly in the direction of a military alliance involving Japan, Germany, and Italy alone.

During his period at the Foreign Ministry, Hirota, in a talk to younger officials of the ministry, had startled them by confessing, "The only thing that matters in foreign affairs at the moment is to find some way of getting along with the military. That's what occupies my own mind all the time." Precisely the same feeling plagued him after he became prime minister, even though Arita was now in charge of the Foreign Ministry.

As a result of patient negotiations, the talks on the Soviet-Japanese fishing agreement, which was valid for eight years, at last reached a compromise, and a new agreement was ready for signing. Unfortunately, however, when the Soviet Union got wind of the moves to conclude an anti-Comintern pact, its attitude suddenly stiffened, and it refused to sign the agreement. Hirota and Arita worked hard trying to explain to the Soviet Union the true purpose of the pact, and the Russians finally accepted a provisional agreement to be renewed every year (the form that is still in effect today). Here again, the government had found itself obliged, in a broad sense, to clear up after the military.

Where China was concerned, however, the government decided to make positive attempts to place relations on a more normal footing, and as an essential preliminary tried to persuade the military to dissolve the autonomous governments they had set up in northern China. But the Kwantung Army, almost as though in deliberate mockery of such efforts by the Foreign Ministry, was already plotting to create yet another autonomous government, in Inner Mongolia. An uprising under the leadership of Colonel Tanaka Ryukichi and supported by Chief of Staff Itagaki took place with Prince Teh as its figurehead, but on November 4, 1936, the puppet army was decisively defeated by Chinese forces at Suiyuan.

The result was a new flaring-up of the anti-Japanese movement and a hardening of the Nationalist government's attitude. Once more, the Foreign Ministry's patient efforts went up in smoke.

In autumn that year, the new National Diet building was completed after nineteen years of work and vast expenditures of money. The huge white structure towering high above other government offices in the vicinity was a new symbol of parliamentary government, and Hirota, a man of humble origins, was the first prime minister to address the nation's representatives beneath its roof. But the dark shadows threatening parliamentary democracy as such were already creeping into the new building. In presenting to the Diet

157

the draft budget for the 1937 fiscal year, Hirota said: "I want you to debate carefully whether or not this is the best budget possible."

There were sniggers among the assembled Diet members, in whose ears Hirota's request sounded less like honesty than naïveté. Any draft budget presented by the government should naturally be "the best possible," and there was no need for the prime minister to be falsely humble about it.

Yet their laughter had missed the true point of Hirota's words. Almost half the national budget was accounted for by military appropriations which the emperor himself had instructed Hirota to accept. Hirota hesitated to describe as "the best possible" a budget submitted under such circumstances—which was precisely why he wanted the Diet to go over it carefully and be ready, at least, to revise it. He himself was willing if necessary to see it obstructed or even aborted.

But attack in the Diet was to come from another quarter. The final item in the Hirota government's "Seven Major Items of National Policy"—"the reorganization and improvement of the administrative machinery"—had been added at the last moment as the result of a strong request made by War Minister Terauchi. An overhaul of the administrative machinery, he claimed, was obviously necessary as a first step in any moves to domestic reform. Hirota had asked Terauchi at the time whether the army had any practical proposals on the matter, but Terauchi had given no immediate reply.

Several of the seven items had resulted from requests from the army. Hirota, having been warned by the emperor not to do anything that would cause an upheaval in the nation's finances, adopted deliberate go-slow tactics on such items, setting up special committees and commissions to study the questions involved at their leisure. His government, accordingly, was frequently criticized for inaction; but Saionji, for one, showed a correct appreciation of what Hirota was really up to: "Both Saito and Okada were accused of twiddling their thumbs," he said. "And I imagine Hirota will be criticized in the same way. But the real question is whether any of the 'reformist' crowd would be ready to do battle with the military. I'm sure that in fact none of them would have the courage. What we really need, of course, is a government that would be ready to take on the army, but that's more than one can hope for at the moment. So the only immediate alternative, I suppose, is to manage things as Hirota is doing. A head-on fight, in short, would mean that the Constitution would go out of the window. Half of it has, in fact, gone already, but it can't be helped; the only practical course is to take things a little at a time."

The army, however, was apparently spurred into showing its hand, and at the end of September, 1936, the war and navy ministers appeared together and presented Hirota with "a joint statement of opinion on the reform of the administrative machinery." This document, which had been drafted by Sato Kenryo, heading a War Ministry policy-making team, set forth a whole list of demands for drastic reforms, including the establishment of a unified agency for national policy, the amalgamation of the Foreign and Colonial Affairs Ministries, the amalgamation of the Ministry of Agriculture and Forestry and the Ministry of Commerce and Industry, and the reorganization of the Foreign Ministry. Its demands even extended to the legislative body itself, calling for reforms of the parliamentary system including revisions of the Diet Law and the Electoral Law.

This obvious attempt by the military to curtail the authority of the Diet came as a sharp shock to the political parties, and increasing criticism of the military was heard. It was in such an atmosphere that the Diet was reconvened on January 21, 1937. And one of the first speeches was a bitter attack on the military by representative Hamada Kunimatsu of the Seiyukai party, who all the while he spoke glared pointedly at War Minister Terauchi on the ministerial bench.

During the preceding session, not long after his appointment as war minister, Terauchi had been subjected to similar blistering accusations by a member of the Minseito party. On that occasion, Terauchi had suffered in silence, since the February 26 incident was still fresh in everybody's memory. But it had left him bearing a grudge against party politics as a whole.

By now, the army purges were over, and the time had come—in the army's view, at least—for the parties themselves to mend their ways. This time, therefore, Terauchi made a direct counterattack,

159

accusing Hamada of having insulted the military. His blustering tone only heightened the impression of a high-handed attempt to muzzle the military's opponents.

When Hamada demanded whether Terauchi was really sure that his remarks had constituted an insult, Terauchi was reduced to saying that "that, at least, was the impression he had received." Hamada thereupon charged him with irresponsible statements. He even offered, if the minutes showed that he had insulted the army, to disembowel himself, and suggested that Terauchi do the same if his own claim was not substantiated.

The argument was a clear defeat for Terauchi, but when Hirota tried to smooth things over, Terauchi demanded dissolution of the Diet on the grounds that the political parties did not show a proper appreciation of the seriousness of the situation. Otherwise, he threatened, he would resign as war minister. Hirota tried to reason with him, but he was adamant. Hirota, having no intention of carrying out a Diet dissolution for which he saw no justification, rejected Terauchi's repeated demands for dissolution, and in the end his government resigned on the grounds of internal disagreement.

As a result of the government's resignation, the bills before the Diet were left pending. Those providing for the placing of electric power under government control and the provision of grants to set local finances on their feet were both held over and put into effect under the following government. The bill extending the period of compulsory education was also shelved for the time being. One other result was that the national budget, with its emphasis on vast military appropriations, was not in the end put into effect by the Hirota government. "At any rate," as Hirota remarked ruefully to a friend, "it put paid to that budget."

The Hirota government's parting gift to the nation was the establishment of a system of awards for "cultural merit." At dinner one day while Hirota was talking with his children, Masao had said, "I wonder why decorations are only given to military men and government officials? There ought to be separate decorations for scholars and artists, too." Masao was sometimes known to make preposterous suggestions, but this time Hirota was impressed.

Decorations in the past had been a virtual monopoly of the armed forces, bureaucrats, and politicians. Moreover, the grading of decorations tended to suggest that they were yardsticks for measuring human worth. Military men would work behind the scenes in the hope of getting as good a medal as possible, and the same kind of thing was common—as Hirota knew from experience—in the bureaucratic world as well. The affair of Shidehara's award had been an outcome of precisely the same kind of atmosphere.

If decorations were awarded not only to officials and the military but to members of the scholastic and artistic worlds too, it might help a little, indirectly, to encourage ordinary people by checking the undue emphasis placed on the military. In the same way, the absence of any distinctions of grade within the "Order of Cultural Merit" would be a silent reproof to those who thought always in terms of decorations and rank.

Hirota gave the Bureau of Decorations instructions concerning the establishment of the new cultural award. Though criticized for dilatoriness in other matters, he showed remarkable promptness here, and visiting the palace explained his idea to the emperor in order to obtain his personal agreement before presenting the plan to the cabinet. The emperor willingly gave his assent. "I suppose I may express my opinion here," he said, "since it is not a political matter." He himself suggested that the projected cherry blossom design for the clasp of the ribbon should be changed to an orange blossom, since the cherry blossom was already much used by the military. He also pointed out that since art and culture were for all time, it was not appropriate to represent them by the cherry blossom, a symbol of fleeting beauty. In this way, a simple, clean-cut, orange blossom design came to be used for the Order of Cultural Merit. Unfortunately, the government's resignation before the day on which the new system was to be announced—February 11—deprived Hirota of the chance to make the announcement personally, but he was satisfied nonetheless.

Freed from the burdens of the premiership, Hirota made straight for his villa on the coast at Kugenuma, and from then on went to Tokyo only when important business made it absolutely necessary. The wind had dropped, and the windmill was ready this time for a lasting nap. . . . He hoped, as he had tried to do once before, to have a chance to view affairs from a distance, without being plagued by considerations of party, faction, or personal position. It did not matter whether people saw him henceforth as a distinguished patriot, a sage in retirement, or a masterless samurai—all he wanted was a life free of the burdens of office. One outcome of this attitude was his request that he be allowed to give up all titles and decorations and waive his right to a pension. When people asked how he would live without even this support, Hirota said in all seriousness, "If possible, I'd like to teach at a school in the country. If that's not possible, then I'll earn a living teaching calligraphy or something."

To live by teaching young children to write well, in the "shack" amidst the pines, might not have been a bad existence, at least compared with a life spent regretting being "born fifty years too early." But his request was rejected. Such behavior in a former prime minister, it was said, was inappropriate at such a time, and would only give rise to unnecessary speculation. So, in the end, Hirota resigned himself to spending his remaining years as a perfectly ordinary pensioner.

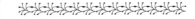

VII

As prime minister to succeed Hirota, the military favored Konoe; they behaved, in fact, as though no other candidate were even thinkable. On the surface at least, Konoe himself was ready and willing, declaring that one must obey the imperial command even at the risk of one's life. But in private he begged the two men who were in charge of the actual sounding-out of prospective candidates to let him be excused the task.

For reasons such as this, it was General Ugaki Kazushige who was in fact recommended to the emperor as the next premier. Ugaki had served as war minister under Hamaguchi and as governor-general of Korea. He was a skilled politician and was trusted at the higher levels of the political world as being relatively moderate for a military man. The military, however—and in particular staff officers in central positions such as Isogai (head of the Military Affairs Bureau), Sato (head of the policy section), and Nakajima (commander of the military police)—opposed Ugaki violently. The ostensible reason was Ugaki's failure during his period as war minister to punish severely those responsible for the "March plot" (the attempted coup d'état), which, they claimed, had had the effect of encouraging further such incidents. The underlying reason, however, was dislike of Ugaki because he had been responsible in 1925 for reducing the army's strength by four divisions and because he was an objectionable "political type" who, though a military man himself, toyed with ideas of disarmament.

As Ugaki was driving up to Tokyo from the country, a group headed by Isogai lay in wait for his car at Shinagawa and pressed Ugaki to refuse to form a government. Ugaki rejected their warning on the grounds that he had already received the imperial command. However, when he set about the task of forming a cabinet, he came up against a brick wall: the army refused to provide him with a war minister. It claimed that the three army leaders responsible had selected three candidates and negotiated with them, but that none of them had wanted the job. Ugaki named another possible candidate, but the army—taking advantage of the system of restricting war ministers to serving officers that Hirota and Terauchi had reintroduced only shortly before—rejected him because he was close to retirement.

Hearing of this, Hirota immediately sent a messenger to Ugaki to advise him that the prime minister was supposed to be able to choose his war minister freely, without depending on the recommendation of the army "Big Three." This forced Ugaki to pull himself together and, in a meeting with the imperial household minister, he requested him to arrange that the emperor should personally appoint the candidate that he himself chose or, if this was impossible, to personally approve his doubling as war minister himself.

The imperial household minister refused. There was no precedent for such a course, he said, and he did not feel justified in troubling the emperor over such a matter. Thus Ugaki found himself in the paradoxical position of being commanded to form a government by the emperor yet being prevented from doing so by the military, the emperor's own right-hand men.

Even the easygoing Konoe found it impossible this time to stand by in silence, and wrote a letter to Terauchi in which he said:

"Whatever one may feel about his policies, I find it highly inappropriate that a man in receipt of the imperial command should be prevented from fulfilling that command. I am not, of course, personally advocating the formation of an Ugaki government; I am merely, all such considerations apart, thinking in terms of the national polity and the nation's duty to respect and revere the imperial authority. Nothing is more important to the nation than to maintain correct relations between the emperor and his subjects. Anything that tended, however slightly, to undermine these principles would encourage a most deplorable disturbance of the proper order of things in society."

In practice, however, there was no realistic alternative under the circumstances but to have an army favorite form a government. Thus it was General Hayashi Senjuro who became the next prime minister. The Hayashi government was not merely a government headed by a military man; it was a government of the military. And the chief task it set itself was to deal a decisive blow to party politics, thereby fulfilling an ambition cherished by the military ever since Terauchi had become war minister in the previous cabinet.

As soon as the budget was passed, Hayashi dissolved the Diet. Dissolution always placed a great strain on the political parties. It had been carried out this time, moreover, with no time for preparation and for no apparent reason, so that the Seiyukai, Minseito, and other parties were thrown into turmoil.

The army in the meantime gave its overall backing to the Showakai as its official party, while Nakano Seigo, who came from the same district as Hirota, organized the Tohokai, whose stated aim was to "model itself on totalitarianism" and which launched itself into the fray against the existing parties with twenty officially recognized candidates, including some former Diet members.

During Hirota's period as prime minister, Nakano—who believed that Japan should not hesitate to send troops and intervene wherever she felt it was necessary in view of her sacred duty to "maintain the safety of East Asia and contribute to world peace"—frequently berated Hirota as "a typical case of subservience to Europe and America" who tended to run away from the realities of the emergency facing Japan. But the election gave Nakano approximately ten percent fewer votes than at the previous election (though he was the top vote-winner in his own constituency in Fukuoka), while his Tohokai managed to capture only eleven seats.

The Showakai, on which the military had pinned their hopes, won a meager twenty seats, while the Seiyukai and Minseito maintained approximately the same strengths with 170 and 190 seats respectively. On the other hand the social-democratic Shakai Taishuto, which was critical of the military, made a great stride forward with thirty-seven seats.

Thus the Hayashi government lost confidence in handling the

Diet, and after a short period in which it avoided any parliamentary clashes, submitted its resignation at the end of May.

There was now absolutely no candidate for the next prime minister —with the exception, that is, of Konoe. The military, of course, wanted him. Konoe had long had ideas of "national reform" as a way out of the difficulties facing Japan, and his advocacy of "positive policies" fitted in with the military's own views. He was, moreover, from one of the noblest families in Japan, and his height and good looks promised to make him a popular prime minister with the public. The military had high hopes that by having him appointed they could manipulate public opinion and carry through their own purposes more effectively. If Konoe proved impossible, the army hoped to appoint War Minister Sugiyama, since to choose someone other than a military man would create the impression, both at home and abroad, that the army had given in to the political parties as a result of the elections.

Should Sugiyama become prime minister, it would open the way to increasing dictatorship by the military, and the elder statesmen worked hard to persuade Konoe to accept. At first, Konoe continued to refuse, but he had already had his own way more than once before. It was he, moreover, who when Ugaki had failed to form a government had written so indignantly of the importance of obeying the imperial command. So, in the end, he found himself obliged to accept the premiership.

The army pledged its wholehearted support to Konoe, yet as soon as he started forming his government, objected to his choice of finance minister. The question developed into a kind of struggle between the candidate put forward by Konoe and the army candidate, till in the end both were dropped and Kaya Okinobu, a former Finance Ministry official, was appointed instead.

Particular interest was focused on the choice of foreign minister. Konoe's first idea had been to choose Nagai Ryutaro, but senior politicians were disturbed at the prospect of appointing someone whose capabilities as a statesman were still untested at a time when international relations were so delicate and when friction with the army was inevitable. Konoe also began to waver, and the opinion gained ground that the only man to whom foreign policy could safely be entrusted at the moment was Hirota.

Konoe, too, was gradually converted to this idea, and the view prevailed finally that Hirota was the only possible candidate. The task of persuading Hirota began. What finally induced him to accept was an argument put forward by Harada Kumao, speaking on behalf of elder statesman Saionji:

"Prince Saionji is extremely worried about foreign policy," he said, "and Prince Konoe is also, apparently, very keen that you should agree, so we hope you'll see fit to accept. Konoe is still young, and Prince Saionji would like you to help him carry his task through without incurring any untoward disgrace or committing any untoward mistake."

Hirota, who had hesitated lest his own age make things difficult for the younger man, finally yielded on hearing that Konoe himself was eager to have him in his government. Despite his having been a prime minister himself, he was a plain man who should be willing to accept if the country needed him, even though the post was inferior to his previous position and fraught with difficulties.

Around this period, when people asked him for a specimen of his calligraphy (it has long been the custom in Japan to ask famous men for a sample of their hand, to be framed and displayed in some prominent place), he often wrote the four characters signifying "adapt to whatever comes." It was in this spirit that he took the office of foreign minister for a third time. Little did he know that this final participation in government was to lay a fatal trap for him— nor, even if he had known, would it have stopped him from accepting the task.

Saionji was greatly pleased on hearing that Hirota was to join the government. As for the other posts, Konoe had a wide acquaintance throughout the political spectrum from left to right, and there was a rush of potential ministerial candidates recommended both by others and by themselves. Among them was Nakano Seigo who, having been on very close terms with Konoe, had high hopes of joining the cabinet. Konoe, however, made a number of unexpected choices—among them newcomers such as Otani Sonyu, a Buddhist priest, and Arima Yoriyasu, an aristocrat—but did not approach Nakano. What was worse, Konoe chose Kazami Akira as his chief cabinet secretary. Kazami—who had been born on the same day, month, and year as Nakano, was his contemporary at Waseda University, and, like Nakano again, was a former newspaper reporter —was considered a natural rival, and Nakano's disappointment was correspondingly great. Neither was he amused to find that Hirota, who had frequently been the target of his criticism, had been brought back as foreign minister. He considered it inappropriate that Hirota should serve in this capacity under a man such as Konoe, who had always advocated drastic steps to lift Japan out of her difficulties and of whom, he considered, the courage to break precedents was now required. With Hirota in office, he complained, the same old pattern of subservience to England and America would be maintained, with the same boring insistence on the "Three Principles on China Policy."

In fact, the situation was to develop more rapidly than Nakano could have foreseen, and to swallow up Hirota's foreign policies in the process.

Before dawn on July 8, 1937, Hirota was informed by a telephone call from the Foreign Ministry that a clash had occurred between the Japanese and Chinese armies at the Marco Polo Bridge on the outskirts of Peking. The incident, it was claimed, had been provoked when Chinese 29th Army forces had illegally fired on a unit of the Japanese forces stationed in China which was engaged in night maneuvers.

Hirota went to his office almost immediately.

Early that morning, he assembled Undersecretary Horinouchi, Togo, head of the Bureau of European and American Affairs, and Ishii, head of the Bureau of East Asian Affairs, to discuss what steps should be taken. They agreed that their guiding principle should be "to prevent the incident from spreading and to achieve a speedy local solution." The prevailing attitude at the Foreign Ministry was one of disgust at this new outrage committed by the military.

The leaders of the Japanese forces in China known as the Tientsin Garrison were relatively cool-headed, but there were many younger staff officers who dreamed of a second Manchurian Incident and the establishment of a second Manchukuo. This, together with incitement from the Kwantung Army and behind-the-scenes activities by the special service agencies and the so-called "Shina-ronin" made it necessary to keep a constant eye on North China. Disturbing rumors had reached Tokyo that a second Manchurian Incident would occur in North China "around the Festival of the Weaver" (July 7), and a high-ranking member of the Military Affairs Section of the War Ministry had just been secretly dispatched to sound out things on the spot.

At the same time, the major victory of Chinese forces in the Suiyuan incident in the autumn of the previous year had encouraged the Chinese in their resistance to Japan, while Chiang Kai-shek's conciliatory gestures toward the Communist party in the Sian incident* had stirred anti-Japanese elements, particularly among the students, into greater activity.

Under the Ho-Umezu pact and other agreements, Chinese central government forces had withdrawn south of Hopei province, and the 29th Army under Sung Che-yuan, a local warlord, was installed in the North China area; Sung was also head in Peking of the Hopei-Chahar Political Council, a kind of autonomous regime that maintained, in a sense, a midway position between Japan and Chiang Kai-shek. In Tungchow, right next to Peking, there was another anti-Communist autonomous government—the East Hopei regime—that was virtually a puppet of the Japanese army, and there was constant trouble between the two.

Although both governments were in theory pro-Japanese, their lower ranks were infiltrated by the movement to resist the Japanese, and since the beginning of the year there had been a succession of small incidents in various parts of North China, ranging from the confinement of a police officer with the Japanese consulate to five sep-

---

*The arrest and confinement of Chiang Kai-shek on December 12, 1936, by General Chang Hsueh-liang and his associates. This—and his subsequent release—played an important part in leading the Kuomintang and Communist forces to sign an agreement the following year, thus enabling them to cooperate in fighting the Japanese.

arate incidents of violence against Japanese citizens and six cases where Japanese army telephone wires had been cut.

The stationing of Japanese forces in China was carried out in accordance with the Boxer Protocol of 1901, whereby China recognized the garrisoning of troops by foreign powers. The strength of Japanese forces there had increased steadily, partly because of the need to protect Japanese citizens in China, of whom there were 2,200 in Peking alone.

On the Chinese side, however, there was growing dissatisfaction at a state of affairs in which foreign forces were stationed within China's borders while China's own government army was obliged to retreat to the south of Hopei. The Japanese army, moreover, behaved with consistent contempt for the Chinese forces. So volatile was the atmosphere that a Chinese soldier brushing against a Japanese army horse as units of the two armies passed each other was enough to lead to a shooting incident.

It was at such a juncture that the newly reinforced Japanese army embarked on strenuous night exercises under the very nose of the Chinese 29th Army. The purpose, admittedly, was to prepare for the regular inspection to which Japanese units were subject, but this was entirely a matter of Japanese convenience. In practice, the maneuvers were a further source of irritation to the Chinese and aggravated an already overheated situation. This being so, it would have been quite enough for anti-Japanese elements to let off firecrackers between the two forces to set both sides fighting under the illusion that they had heard gunfire.

It is still not clear whether the first shot fired at the Marco Polo Bridge was the result of a plot by anti-Japanese elements or a ruse carried out by the Japanese army. What is certain is that, sooner or later, such an incident was almost inevitable. Either way, the area of the Marco Polo Bridge, famous as a site for viewing the full moon, became in fact the birthplace of the wretched war that followed.

Around this time the Japanese army was flying planes to various parts of North China, without permission from the National Government, in the name of what was ostensibly a civilian airline, and China had given notice that flights must be stopped as an infringement of her sovereignty. At the same time, the Japanese Foreign Ministry had decided to inaugurate an air route between Fukuoka and Shanghai as a means to facilitating exchanges between the two countries, and had directed Counselor Hidaka in Nanking to begin negotiations on the question. For this purpose, it was necessary that flights by the army-controlled "airline" should first cease, and the ministry was making strong representations to the army on the matter. Hirota and others at the Foreign Ministry had been hoping to use the negotiations on the new air route as a means of restarting talks on the adjustment of relations between China and Japan, which had been broken off ever since the Suiyuan incident of the previous autumn. Now, the confrontation at the Marco Polo Bridge once more put paid to all such diplomatic efforts.

At an emergency cabinet meeting on July 9, War Minister Sugiyama proposed that three divisions be assembled in Japan and sent to reinforce Japanese troops in North China. Hirota, however, insisted on his policy of not allowing the incident to expand and of seeking a local solution; most other cabinet members supported him, and the proposal to send more troops was shelved.

Hirota promptly sent instructions to Japanese diplomatic agencies in Nanking, Peking, Shanghai, and elsewhere, and summoned the acting Chinese ambassador in Japan to explain the course Japan was taking and request that in line with this the National Government should do nothing to hinder a local solution.

The National Government was in a delicate position, especially as regards relations with the Communist party; if the question should come to involve the whole country, it might well find itself powerless. Similarly, should the Japanese military, and the Kwantung Army in particular, decide on a concerted move, the Japanese government would be unable to hold them in check. There was a danger that unless the question was localized and solved on the spot, things would get out of hand on both sides.

Contacts were proceeding between representatives of the two armies. A day went by, however, then another, with no news whatever of any progress to a solution. There was another minor clash on

171

July 10, and there were rumors that the army of the National Government was about to move northward. Fears were voiced for the safety of Japanese in the area and for the troops stationed there, who with reinforcements still numbered only five thousand, and public opinion at home began to harden. Amidst such an atmosphere, an emergency cabinet meeting was held on the eleventh. Before the meeting, Hirota held a conference with Horinouchi, Togo, and Ishii at the Foreign Ministry; it was confirmed that no new information had been received, and the four men agreed that the Foreign Ministry should continue to pursue the course it had already chosen.

At the morning meeting of the cabinet on the eleventh, War Minister Sugiyama once more put forward his proposal for mobilization. Not that it was mobilization in the strict sense—according to Sugiyama, plans for mobilizing the extra troops should be drawn up immediately, but they should only be put into effect if the situation took a turn for the worse. In other words, it would be a kind of "preparing for preparation." Hirota, on the other hand, stressed repeatedly that local negotiations were still continuing, and might by now even have reached a solution. It would therefore be better, he suggested, to postpone debate on the proposal for a while.

The meeting adjourned without reaching agreement. It reconvened in the afternoon, but still with no news from those on the spot. The war minister stated that he agreed with the basic principle of localization. But even supposing three divisions were sent from Japan, they would total only forty-five thousand men. On the other hand, as many as two hundred thousand Chinese troops could be expected to march north. It would be obvious from this discrepancy in strength, he insisted, that the troops sent were intended as a necessary minimum to ensure the safety of Japanese residents and Japanese interests, and not to enlarge the scope of the fighting or seek to crush the Chinese forces.

"We shall not let the incident spread," Sugiyama declared repeatedly. However—he pointed out—mobilization would take at least ten days, and even in an emergency troops could not be produced immediately at the issuing of an order. Unless the country was at least mentally prepared for mobilization, it would be no use when the time came. This, he insisted, hinting at the possibility of his own resignation, was a minimum requirement for the army, and unless it was agreed to he would be unable to carry out his duties as war minister.

The mood of the cabinet underwent a subtle change. Prime Minister Konoe himself, who at the meeting on the ninth had been all in favor of caution, began to waver. If the war minister resigned, the cabinet as a whole would be obliged to follow suit and it would be very difficult to find another prime minister willing to take on such a confused situation. If the government hesitated at such a crucial time, it would only invite Chinese scorn and possibly delay a solution.

Thus after long hours of debate, the cabinet finally agreed to the war minister's proposal, but only on two conditions: that this should involve no more than a preliminary blueprint for mobilization, or a "state of mental readiness" for mobilization, and that any dispatch of troops should be confined to a minimum necessary to guarantee the safety of Japanese residents in China. Any actual mobilization order would require further study by the cabinet; no specific action was indicated at the moment. In a sense, this was a compromise that sacrificed the name for the reality. It was hoped, too, that it would draw the cabinet closer together and appease not only the army but hawks in other walks of life as well.

In the early evening, a government statement was issued. It criticized China for its "premeditated military acts against Japan," and declared: "At today's cabinet meeting, the government, in a major resolve, decided to carry out necessary measures in relation to the dispatch of troops to North China." There was no indication in the text as it stood that the "necessary measures" were merely intended as a kind of preliminary bracing for mobilization. It represented, rather, an attempt to appease mounting hawkish sentiment toward China at home by taking a clear-cut, tough stand, and at the same time to give China a sharp shove in the direction of the negotiating table. Its real point lay in the concluding passage, which said: "The government has still not despaired of peaceful negotiations as a means of containing the situation, and hopes that prompt self-reflection on the Chinese side will lead to an amicable settlement."

That evening, Prime Minister Konoe assembled leading figures from the political, business, and intellectual worlds at his official residence and told them of the government's resolve, asking them for their understanding and support. Again, nothing was said about the measures being a mere "preparing for preparation." The emphasis was solely on the boldness of the decision, and there was stormy applause from all present. The general impression was that Konoe had shown an approach quite different from the halfhearted China policies of preceding prime ministers, including Hirota. Instead of passively clearing up in the army's wake as before, he had actually stolen a march on it. Konoe, a Hamlet type by day, thus emerged by night as the dashing military adventurer—an image due less to clever stage management on the part of Konoe's staff, than to his own aristocratic personality which included a fondness for playing to the gallery. And, as it happened, history was made that same night.

Around the same time that Konoe was holding forth at the prime minister's residence, the cease-fire talks in China reached agreement. The 29th Army had accepted almost all of Japan's demands, including the punishment of those responsible, measures to prevent further such incidents, the withdrawal of troops from the Marco Polo Bridge area, and the enforcement of legal restrictions on anti-Japanese organizations. The news of this breakthrough came within less than a day—indeed, within a few hours—of the Konoe government's tough declaration and the hawkish response it evoked in the press. The declaration, and specifically its mention of sending troops, infuriated the Chinese National Government just at a time when success in the negotiations promised to cool things down somewhat. As a result, the central army of the National Government began to march north in force.

Following the cabinet decision on the eleventh, Hirota on the same day sent cables to Foreign Ministry agencies in China emphasizing the need for localizing disputes and finding on-the-spot solutions. He also instructed them once more to request the National Government in Nanking not to hinder local solutions. Unlike the flashier Konoe, Hirota aimed to achieve his results through patiently

174

repeated negotiations carried out as swiftly as possible and by whatever means were at hand.

He had Japanese representatives start to negotiate for a halt to the central army's northward march, but the Chinese Foreign Ministry promptly demanded that the Japanese forces return to their original stations and that Japan refrain from any new increase in her forces. Hirota repeated the same instructions as before, and at the same time ordered officials at his own Foreign Ministry to draw up a plan for a solution centering on a halt to troop reinforcements by both sides. He first submitted this plan to the navy. Undersecretary Yamamoto Isoroku and other officials at the Navy Ministry, who were for localization of the conflict, accepted it. He next presented it to the army. The army at first agreed, but when the head of the Military Affairs Bureau returned to the War Ministry he was hastily sent back to withdraw his acceptance. His explanation was that the lower-ranking officers had insisted on it. And he brought a different plan, which the army itself had drawn up.

The new army proposals presented still stiffer conditions for a local solution, demanding—and specifying, moreover, a time limit for compliance—that the Chinese cease all military activity, without making any promises concerning the activities of the Japanese army. There was no longer even any pretense of studying the Foreign Ministry proposal that the undersecretaries and bureau chiefs of the three ministries had agreed on at one stage.

Since cease-fire negotiations affected military operations, the Foreign Ministry wondered whether its proposal had "infringed the independence of the supreme command." At the War Ministry, a few men including Ushiroku, head of the Military Affairs Bureau and the man responsible for dealings with the Foreign Ministry, were in favor of a cautious approach, but War Minister Sugiyama and almost all the staff officers were in favor of positive action.

The General Staff Office, on the other hand, though equally part of the army, tended to advocate prudence where China was concerned, since in its eyes the Soviet Union was the major foe; but though it was headed by a member of the imperial family, it was unable to win over the War Ministry to its views. And it was hardly likely that the Foreign Ministry would be successful in persuading the War Ministry when even the General Staff Office had failed.

So marked was the split within the army that it was sarcastically said that the "Nihon-gun" (Japanese army) was in reality the "nihon-gun" (two-branch army, written with different Chinese characters). Chiang Kai-shek is likewise said to have complained of the difficulty of knowing precisely with whom he should deal in the Japanese army, and one of his aides is reported to have replied jokingly that he couldn't go far wrong so long as the other man was only a colonel, a major, or a captain. There was a good deal of truth in this, since staff officers of the field grade were, in fact, taking things into their own hands.

Hirota in the meantime once again sent a telegram to Counselor Hidaka in Nanking, instructing him to explain the Japanese government's true intentions to the Chinese Foreign Ministry and to work to prevent the incident from spreading.

The Foreign Ministry in question was slow in reacting. Even within the government, the advocates of a tough policy toward Japan were gaining the ascendancy, while Chiang Kai-shek himself was away from Nanking, attending talks at Lushan. The timing, moreover, was bad. At the Lushan talks, which were being held in response to the oft-repeated request of the Communist party, one hundred and fifty prominent figures from political, business, and intellectual circles including the Communist party had gathered from all over China to meet for the first time under the same roof. The focal point of discussion was the recovery of China's national prestige, and Japan's continental policy, beginning with the partition of Manchuria, came in for bitter criticism.

The incident in North China, followed by the Japanese government's tough declaration with its mention of sending troops, raised anti-Japanese sentiment at the conference to fever pitch. Under such circumstances Chiang Kai-shek himself had no alternative but to deliver his "on the brink" speech, in which he declared that China had reached the brink of war in her relations with Japan. Thus—far from accepting the Japanese demands—the conference's conclusion was that the National Government should establish control over local governments, and it was even decided to dispatch the vice-chief of staff to give encouragement to the 29th Army under Sung Che-yuan.

The Foreign Ministry under Hirota was still clinging to the hope of localizing the conflict. At a cabinet meeting on the morning of July 20, a proposal by War Minister Sugiyama that troops should now be sent from Japan was shelved on account of opposition from Hirota and Navy Minister Yonai. That same afternoon, however, a report came saying that Chinese forces had again opened fire on Japanese troops, and at a cabinet meeting that evening approval was given to the preliminary mobilization plan—though on condition that any forces could be brought back in mid-journey if the situation improved.

In protest against this cabinet decision, Ishii, head of the Foreign Ministry's Bureau of East Asian Affairs, submitted to Hirota a letter of resignation which was also signed by the section chiefs under him. When Ishii began to complain about the decision to prepare for mobilization, the usually mild Hirota showed a flash of anger. "Be quiet!" he ordered. "You don't know enough about what goes on in cabinet meetings to talk like that." But he soon reverted to his usual gentle tone, and explained further: "The war minister has promised that even if mobilization is carried out no troops will be sent unless the situation is desperate. And since a lawful solution is not far off, I hope you will withdraw your resignation and wait a while to see what happens. I understand very well how you and your colleagues feel."

Ishii and his subordinates withdrew their resignations. More than any of them, in fact, Hirota himself had felt like resigning. His third son Masao, seeing Hirota's frustration after days of dealing with the military, said to him, "If you feel like that, why don't you resign?"

"I might," he replied, "if there were only myself to consider."

It was the same feeling that had made him persuade Ishii to stay on. Basically, Ishii was in the same line as Shidehara and Saburi; he was a proud, tough man who had clashed openly with the army during his days as consul general at Kirin and Shanghai. Hirota had considered him ideal as head of the East Asia Bureau on account of his knowledge of China and his ability to stand up to military pressure. All the more reason, therefore, that he should want him to suppress his own feelings and stay on the job to give him support.

On July 22, there was word from the chief of staff of the expeditionary force in China saying that the local situation had improved and that reinforcements from home were no longer necessary. War Minister Sugiyama, though disgruntled, had to agree, as he had promised the cabinet, to put off mobilizing the three divisions. Unfortunately, this was a lull before the storm rather than a real peace settlement, as was shown by the rapid move toward North China being made by the National Government's central army.

Prime Minister Konoe had calculated that a tough attitude of the kind indicated in the recent government declaration would bring the National Government to heel, but this assumption proved to be wide of the mark. On the contrary, the declaration merely served to stiffen resistance and to make the Chinese stand up to Japan—as, for instance, in Chiang's "on the brink" speech.

Konoe was dismayed and considered sending Hirota—or even going himself—to Nanking for talks with Chiang Kai-shek. He did not of course expect such top-level talks to produce any immediate solution. "I want a solution that's as politically far-reaching as possible," he said. "I want to let other countries know that Japan has no territorial ambitions and is not looking for opportunities to resort to armed force. If the demands made by whoever goes are reasonable, then even if it all comes to nothing it will at least have shown the great powers Japan's true position and intentions."

Hirota could not agree with this idea. As he saw it, the most important task then facing the prime minister was to get the military under control and by forcing them to make certain concessions establish a strong, broad-based policy of localizing any disputes. To go for talks with Chiang Kai-shek without first dealing with the hawks at home would probably mean that Chiang would take no notice at all. If Japan gave some pledge which it proved impossible later to observe, the only result would be to make Japan's international position more difficult than ever. The problem, in short, lay with the Japanese military. Konoe's only proper destination lay just a stone's throw away, at the War Ministry at Miyakezaka, rather than in distant Nanking. In the end Konoe decided to send Miyazaki Ryusuke to Nanking secretly as his personal envoy. Miyazaki, the son of Miyazaki Toten who had been active in the Chinese revolution as a supporter of Sun Yat-sen, was known and trusted in China. Konoe secretly contacted Nanking via the National Government's embassy in Tokyo, then sent Miyazaki off. However, the coded cable was intercepted by the army, and Miyazaki was arrested by military police as he was boarding a vessel at Kobe. This was the same army that, when Konoe was forming his government, had pledged its "wholehearted support."

Hirota continued to encourage Foreign Ministry representatives in China to persist in their efforts. Counselor Hidaka in Nanking met Kao Tsung-wu, head of the Chinese Foreign Ministry's Bureau of Asian Affairs, then had talks with Governor Chang Chun of Szechwan, who was a former head of the Foreign Ministry and a friend of Chiang Kai-shek's. There were three meetings, beginning on the twenty-fifth, as a result of which a tentative agreement was reached, providing for:

1. The enforcement of local agreements.
2. A declaration of the withdrawal of Japanese forces.
3. The beginning of the movement (withdrawal) to the south of the National Government's central army.
4. The beginning of the withdrawal of Japanese forces.

At just around this time, however, another incident occurred in North China. The withdrawal of the 29th Army from the neighborhood of Peking was still progressing slowly when, on the night of the twenty-fifth, Japanese troops engaged in repairing military telegraph lines at Langfeng were fired on by Chinese forces. Then, on the night of the twenty-sixth, a convoy of Japanese military trucks that tried to enter Peking's Kuangan Gate to protect local Japanese residents drew the fire of Chinese troops on the walls above.

As a result, the army in China issued a statement saying, "By now the maintenance of public order has broken down completely and the rights and property of Japanese residents are in constant peril.

179

The maintenance of peace and order in North China has always been a matter of the greatest interest for both Japan and Manchukuo. A situation has now been reached where no further possibilities for a peaceful solution remain and the only alternative is retribution. We regret this very deeply." And it embarked on hostilities with the Chinese forces. The 29th Army in turn called for an all-out battle of resistance, and asked the National Government for reinforcements. As a result of these developments, a cabinet meeting on the twenty-seventh finally gave orders for the mobilization of three divisions. The nation at home was already a hotbed of hawkish sentiment. Not only did the emergency Diet then in session approve, on the same day that it was presented, a bill providing for ninety-seven million yen in military appropriations, but it even passed a resolution expressing thanks to the expeditionary force in North China.

In North China itself, the fighting spread still further. The East Hopei government, a pro-Japanese puppet regime, had a security force under its wing, with barracks in Tungchow. This barracks was now bombed by mistake by airplanes of the Kwantung Army, the incident occurring at a time when anti-Japanese sentiment among the lower ranks of the security force was already fairly advanced. That night, the enraged troops attacked Japanese residents in Tungchow and killed 260 of them. Although this in fact represented a revolt by a puppet army, the Japanese side assumed that it had been instigated by the 29th Army, and stepped up hostilities still further throughout North China.

Even at this stage, Hirota still did not give up hope of a cease-fire. He assembled the bureau chiefs concerned in the Foreign, War, and Navy Ministries and again gave them instructions to draft a cease-fire agreement that might be acceptable to the Chinese. All of them consented, even the army men. The military themselves had begun to grow uneasy in case the war got out of hand, while a suggestion made by the emperor to Prime Minister Konoe, that the time had come for a settlement of the question by diplomatic negotiations, also had a restraining effect on the army's hawks.

The Foreign Ministry, thus, took the lead in drawing up an interim cease-fire agreement and a plan for the subsequent adjustment of relations between the two countries. Since these proposals were aimed, above all, at obtaining Chinese agreement as a means to a speedy armistice, they ignored opposition from the military and embodied considerable concessions on the Japanese side while asking very little from the Chinese. Hirota championed the proposals in the strongest terms, and, obtaining the approval of the war and navy ministers and Prime Minister Konoe on August 7, sent Funatsu Tatsuichiro, director of the Association of Spinning Industries in China, to Shanghai as special envoy bearing the two drafts. Funatsu, who had served for many years as a diplomat in China, had many acquaintances on the Chinese side. He arrived, however, at the same time that Ambassador Kawagoe, who had been on sick leave, returned to his post, so the actual negotiations were entrusted to the ambassador, partly at his own request.

The top-secret instructions to Kawagoe began with the following passage: "The aims of the dispatch of troops to North China are as laid down in the cabinet decision of July 11; however, although illegal acts by the 29th Army have rendered countermeasures necessary, the true Japanese aim is not, of course, unnecessary retribution." The word "retribution," which had appeared in the declaration by the forces in China, was constantly recurring in official Japanese statements and newspaper editorials at the time, and it is a measure of Hirota's feelings about the proposed agreement that he should have taken trouble at the very outset to cancel out the impression created by the word.

The principal conditions for a cease-fire were as follows:

1. The establishment of a demilitarized zone.
2. (a) The voluntary reduction of the strength of Japanese forces stationed in China.
    (b) The nullifying of the T'ang-ku truce,* the Chin-Doihara

---

*The agreement (May 31, 1933) ending the fighting that followed the invasion of Hopei province by Japanese troops in April and May, 1933. It provided for withdrawals by Chinese and Japanese forces and the setting-up of a demilitarized zone south of the Great Wall, and tacitly accepted Japanese occupation of Manchuria.

agreement, and the Ho-Umezu agreement.

(c) The dissolution of the East Hopei and Hopei-Chahar regimes, and the placing of those areas under the administration of the Nanking government.

The aim, in other words, was not merely an immediate cease-fire, but to do away with all the measures so far taken by the Japanese military that might serve to provoke anti-Japanese feeling. The documents made frequent use of the phrase "forgetting the past."

Where proposals for the adjustment of relations were concerned, the general tone matched that of the previous "Three Principles on China Policy" put forward by Hirota, and included considerable concessions by the Japanese side, such as a promise not to make any attempt to exclude the influence of Nanking from Inner Mongolia and the Suiyuan area, and a pledge to abolish unrestricted flights by Japanese aircraft.

This was a return to the policy of conciliation that had always underlain Hirota's thinking. His hope was to use the unhappy lesson of the latest clashes to effect a fundamental improvement in Sino-Japanese relations. However, he did not present the two plans as a package deal, but added detailed instructions saying that the proposals for the adjustment of relations could be dealt with later if it seemed they would hinder an agreement on a cease-fire. At all costs he wanted to arrange a cease-fire as soon as possible.

Ambassador Kawagoe invited Kao Tsung-wu, head of the Asia Bureau, to his official residence in Shanghai, and outlined to him the cable with Hirota's instructions. Kawagoe, who was something of an eccentric, with decided opinions of his own, had virtually usurped the task with which Hirota had entrusted Funatsu. The result was that Hirota's intentions were watered down, and that the conditions Japan was offering were presented in insufficiently concrete form. Even so, Kao was more or less satisfied, and replied that although he foresaw certain difficulties the conditions offered seemed to justify, at least, the holding of talks. He would return to Nanking immediately, confer with his superiors in the government, then call on the ambassador again to report the results.

He left in haste on the night train for Nanking. The date was August

10, 1937. Unfortunately, though, yet another complication had occurred the previous day. In the same city of Shanghai, an officer of the Japanese naval brigade had been killed by Chinese security forces. Chinese troops, moreover, had advanced into the demilitarized zone established under the cease-fire agreement concluded after the fighting in Shanghai in 1932. As a result, the navy hastily sent reinforcements for the naval brigade from Sasebo, which irritated the Chinese still further and prompted them to shell the Japanese residential area.

On the night of the twelfth, the prime minister and foreign, war, and navy ministers held a conference. On the morning of the thirteenth, there was an emergency cabinet meeting, which approved the sending to Shanghai of two divisions from Japan in order to protect Japanese residents in China.

At the same time, the National Government ordered a nationwide mobilization. Chinese army planes bombed Japanese naval vessels on the Yangtze River. Communications were cut between Nanking and Shanghai, and it was no longer possible for Kao to contact Shanghai. For this reason, Hirota cabled Hidaka in Nanking on the fifteenth, hoping to have him present the two plans directly to the Foreign Ministry of the National Government. But here too it was too late for Hidaka to make contact, since Japanese naval aircraft bombed Nanking and Nanchang, and it was decided to evacuate the embassy staff and all other Japanese residents.

After a cabinet meeting that lasted until 1:00 A.M. on the fifteenth, the government published a statement declaring that Japan had reached the limit of her patience and would have no alternative but to take resolute steps to punish the Chinese forces for their outrages as a means of inducing the Nanking government to reflect on its own actions. This was less than half a month after the Foreign Ministry put forward its proposals stating that Japan's real concern was not with retribution.

At a further cabinet meeting on the seventeenth, it was decided to "abandon the policy of localization." Hirota would seem to have been caught up in the prevailing mood of the cabinet, yet in fact he had still not given up all hope of a cease-fire leading to a peace agreement of some kind. Just before Counselor Hidaka, back home from Nanking, went to the palace to deliver a lecture to the emperor, Hirota went out of his way to advise Hidaka to talk to the emperor as though there were still hopes for peace. He also sent former foreign minister Arita, whom he personally trusted, as special envoy to Shanghai, hoping to have him stay there for a while and find some way of opening negotiations with the leaders of the National Government. But the hostilities prevented realization of his plan.

What had previously been referred to as the "North China Incident" now came to be called the "China Incident." No actual declaration of war was made, for fear of provoking an economic blockade by the Western powers, but in fact there already existed a state of war no longer amenable to "local solutions." For this reason, sentiment within the cabinet strongly favored holding an immediate imperial conference to decide on some firm national policy concerning the conduct of the war, but Hirota vehemently opposed any such move. His view was that the situation was constantly changing and that adequate contact had not yet been made with the National Government; it would be a mistake to destroy all chances of negotiation at a single blow.

As a result, an outline of measures to be taken was formulated, not in terms of an immutable "national policy," but in the form of an agreement between the four ministers. The aim of military action was to be "to make China abandon her belligerent attitude forthwith," and "the principal areas for the use of land forces" were to be Hopei, Chahar, and the Shanghai area. Where North China was concerned, the main goal was "to tidy up the political confusion and bring it under the central Chinese government." This reflected the Foreign Ministry's views, and left a basis still for localization.

Having moved, however, the army was not to be stopped. General Matsui Iwane was appointed to command the expeditionary force to central China, and Prime Minister Konoe and War Minister Sugiyama went to Tokyo Station to see him off. On this occasion, Matsui repeatedly urged Sugiyama to bring the whole army round to the idea of advancing as far as Nanking. He also pressed Konoe to accept the same idea, since he, personally, was determined to reach

Nanking. Konoe was taken aback. Despite all the talk of "retribution" and making China abandon her "belligerent attitude," the original aim of sending troops had been to protect Japanese residents there. All Japanese citizens had already been evacuated from Nanking, and to advance as far as that city would be to exceed the expeditionary force's original duties.

"Does the army really intend going as far as Nanking?" Konoe asked Sugiyama anxiously.

"That's what Matsui says," Sugiyama replied. "But he'll never get there. Only as far as Wuhu at the most."

The war minister underestimated the army, however. The expeditionary force to central China was to carry the attack not merely beyond Wuhu but beyond Nanking and still deeper into China, as far as Hankow.

Hirota was still hoping to find some way to peace. Now that the direct communication line with the National Government had been cut, there was no alternative but to look to some third country to bridge the gap. Obtaining the agreement of the prime minister and war and navy ministers, he contacted the ambassadors and ministers of various countries with this in mind. He also worked hard clearing up after the army wherever possible, so as to prevent the international climate from becoming any more unfavorable to Japan.

When a warning came from U.S. Ambassador Grew about the danger of foreign interests being damaged in the navy's bombings of Nanking, Hirota made repeated protests to the navy authorities, and had them take steps to ensure respect for international law. In mid-October, there was an incident in which the British ambassador to China, Sir Hughe Knatchbull-Hugessen came under fire in the outskirts of Shanghai from what was believed to be a Japanese army plane, and was seriously wounded. To prevent unpleasant complications, Hirota had Navy Undersecretary Yamamoto, Foreign Undersecretary Horinouchi, and other high-ranking officials from both ministries take all the necessary steps and make appropriate apologies, with the result that Sir Robert Craigie, British ambassador to Japan, was considerably mollified. Hirota also took the opportunity afforded by this contact to inform Craigie frankly of the Japanese government's intentions concerning a solution to the China Incident.

The League of Nations, in the meantime, set up a committee of investigation and asked Japan to participate, while the Brussels conference of the Nine-Power Treaty signatories sent a request for Japanese participation. After consultations in many different quarters, Hirota decided that Japan should decline to attend. One factor here was that Japan had already seceded from the League of Nations and was committed to having no part in any of its political activities. Another was that, as a result of moves by the National Government, preparations were more or less complete for the issuing of a resolution condemning Japan. It seemed likely, moreover, that the Brussels conference would be no more than an extension of the same political maneuverings, so that for Japan to take part would not only be pointless but might even increase friction unnecessarily. In mid-October, Hirota met individually with the ambassadors of Britain, the United States, France, Germany, and Italy, and explained the circumstances behind Japan's decision not to participate, then discussed the China question and emphasized that if any of them should be willing to act as a bridge in arranging negotiations, Japan would fall in with this at any time.

Of the five countries concerned, the two on which Hirota pinned most hopes, in view of the leverage they could bring to bear on China, were Britain and the United States. He had many meetings with American Ambassador Grew, in which he pointed out that Japan's terms for peace were not particularly stiff, but that they were likely to become stiffer as the fighting progressed; and he asked for American mediation in getting Chiang Kai-shek to join in talks as soon as possible. America replied, however, that it could not undertake mediation unless asked to do so by both sides. Thus Hirota was obliged to look to Britain. British Ambassador Craigie, who had only just taken up his post when he had to deal with the Knatchbull-Hugessen affair, had been impressed by the willingness of the Japanese side to make amends, and he now promised to do everything he could to help arrange peace talks.

Thus a route for communication with the National Government was opened via the British ambassador in China, and Hirota awaited the outcome eagerly, meeting Craigie on several occasions in order to find out what progress had been made. Once more, however, the army began its obstructionist tactics. The army hawks had considered all along that no foreign countries, least of all Britain and America, should be allowed to intervene in questions concerning China and Japan, and viewed British attempts at mediation as unwarranted interference in Japan's pursuit of her "holy war." They began open criticism of Foreign Minister Hirota for the moves he was making, referring to him as the "Minister of Harm" (a pun depending on two different Chinese characters meaning "foreign" and "harm" respectively, but with the same pronunciation). A Major Kagesa of the General Staff Office actually went around complaining that it was dangerously foolish of Hirota to let the Chinese know that Japan wanted peace, and asserting that "Hirota should be killed or arrested."

Simultaneously, right-wing organizations began to echo this with an anti-British campaign of their own. Britain, they declared, was the representative of the old order and as such was trying to keep "new" nations such as Japan and Germany under her thumb. In deliberately encouraging the anti-Japanese movement in China and giving generous aid to the Chiang Kai-shek regime, Britain was an enemy of the Japanese people. The mass communication media—and the textile industry, which saw Britain as a rival—also stepped up their activities, till the word "Britain" was on the way to becoming a synonym for all that was iniquitous.

Hirota, who deplored the spreading mood, invited prominent businessmen for an informal meeting on November 11 for the purpose of urging restraint. "No other nation is as suitable as Britain to bridge the gap to peace talks with China," he said. "The campaign you are carrying on at present places the government, diplomatically speaking, in a very awkward position."

However, another country besides England—Germany—was also attempting to play the mediator. German Ambassador Dirksen was on friendly terms with Hirota, having been stationed in Moscow during Hirota's own spell in the Soviet Union.

Pressed by the men at army headquarters, who tended to favor

Germany, Hirota went through the motions of asking Dirksen to arrange peace talks—though he did not believe that Germany, which did not have China's confidence, could act alone as mediator. In fact, however, the military had already started negotiations with Germany independently of Hirota. General Ott, military attaché to the German embassy in Japan, had even gone to Shanghai and conferred with Trautmann, German ambassador in China, who had come specially from Nanking on the far side of the fighting. Just as the Japanese military were two-faced in their diplomacy, so the German military in Japan, too, were acting without the knowledge of the German ambassador there.

Hirota judged that if talks were to succeed under such circumstances it might be better, rather than have Germany act on her own, to get Britain, the U.S., and Germany, or Britain and Germany alone, to cooperate in the role of mediators. To this end, he persuaded the British ambassador to sound out Dirksen on the score. The German side replied, however, that they would prefer to go ahead alone for the time being, since things were still at the stage of preliminary contacts, and Britain was obliged to withdraw. The stepping-up of the pro-German and anti-British mood fostered primarily by the military was another major factor in making England hold back.

Either way, the Japanese offer, in the form of "the Hirota proposals," was handed on by the two German ambassadors, Dirksen and Trautmann, and eventually delivered to Chiang Kai-shek in Nanking.

The proposals, thanks to the curb Hirota had put on the military in drawing them up, made an impression on Chiang. He told Trautmann in his reply that he was ready to agree to peace talks on the basis they afforded, provided that they were not treated as an ultimatum and Japan did not come to the talks as a victor. This reply passed through the hands of the two German ambassadors again and was finally delivered to Hirota on December 7.

The situation both at home and abroad had undergone a subtle change in the meantime. The two divisions of the Japanese army that had first landed in Shanghai ran into stiff opposition from the Chinese army, and a further three divisions were sent to reinforce them, but the stalemate continued. On November 5, therefore, another three divisions had landed at Hangchow Bay and by attacking the Chinese forces from the flank finally effected a breakthrough. Japanese troops were pressing on with tremendous impetus toward the capital, Nanking. The fighting had spread in North China also, and on October 28 an autonomous government was formed in Inner Mongolia with Prince Teh at its head, thus bringing into existence the puppet regime that Itagaki, Tanaka, and other officers of the Kwantung Army had envisioned when they provoked the Suiyuan incident.

As the fighting escalated, so a wartime atmosphere began to prevail at home. Prime Minister Konoe began to talk of a "campaign to mobilize the national spirit." At the same time, the trend toward putting the whole nation on a wartime footing was beginning; the National Federation of Labor Unions, for example, announced a ban on all strikes.

For all this, the picture that Konoe himself presented was less that of a wartime prime minister overflowing with confidence than of a vacillating, lonely, isolated aristocrat easily swayed by the words of those about him. The military, who had seemed to welcome Konoe's emergence, were not always as cooperative as they might have been, nor did the members of his government give him the close support that he had hoped for. At one stage, he even considered resigning. Nevertheless, late that autumn he began to recover his spirits a little. The first sign came when Konoe, in accordance with a suggestion from the minister of home affairs, Baba, instituted a system of cabinet councillors to back up the already existing cabinet. Eight men of ministerial level were selected from various fields of activity in order to deal with important political matters connected with the China Incident and to give advice to the cabinet. Including men such as General Ugaki and various hawks like General Araki, Admiral Suetsugu, and Matsuoka Yosuke, they formed a kind of second cabinet. Next, Konoe brought in his friend Kido Koichi as minister of education. Kido, who had experience of bureaucratic life, favored a practical approach that contrasted with Konoe's theoretical bent, and acted as a reassuringly stable confidant for Konoe within the cabinet.

His spirits recovered, Konoe considered the establishment of an "Imperial Headquarters" with the prime minister as one of its members. Since nothing could be done about the independence of the military, he aimed by creating such machinery to remove at least some of the division between government and military; however, both the army and navy were violently opposed to the prime minister's participation, and in the end it was decided that Imperial Headquarters should come into being not as Konoe had envisaged it but as a purely military agency for coordinating army and naval strategy.

Once again Konoe started threatening to resign—to the dismay of Kido, whom he had only just asked to join the government—and Kido's first task, as Konoe's friend, was to persuade the latter to change his mind. Konoe also alarmed Kido by declaring at one stage that he wanted to replace the whole of the present cabinet by the newly selected cabinet councillors. In order to calm Konoe down, the military set up a liaison council between Imperial Headquarters and the government. All important government business connected with military matters was to be placed before this council, which was to include the prime minister, foreign minister, war minister, and navy minister, together with other ministers as the occasion required.

Chiang Kai-shek's reply as transmitted by Dirksen was to have been put before a meeting of the council scheduled for December 14. However, on the thirteenth the Chinese capital of Nanking fell to Japanese forces, thus giving fresh encouragement to the advocates of hawkish policies. Cries of "banzai" were to be heard all over Tokyo, and the army, without a word to the government, set up an emergency Chinese government led by Wang Ko-min in Peking.

It looked as though all the efforts for peace made so far were in danger of being nullified at one stroke. At a meeting with U.S. Ambassador Grew a month or two previously, Hirota had urged him to get Chiang Kai-shek to the negotiating table as quickly as possible;

if the fighting reached the stage where Chiang was driven from Nanking, the army might well put forward still tougher terms. Now things had turned out precisely as he had feared. Hirota had little time to deplore this fact, however, since unfortunate incidents involving American and British nationals obliged him once again to rush around trying to counter the effects of the army's headstrong behavior.

On December 12, just before the fall of Nanking, Japanese naval aircraft bombed and sank the U.S. gunboat *Panay*, sailing down the Yangtze River with U.S. embassy staff on board, and also damaged three steamships carrying American refugees. Americans trying to swim to safety were raked by machine-gun fire from the aircraft, and were even fired on by an army boat; in their eagerness to chase the fleeing Chinese forces, the Japanese military were attacking everything indiscriminately. The incident infuriated American public opinion. Feeling toward Japan took such a turn for the worse that Ambassador Grew, anticipating the severing of diplomatic relations, actually began to think of packing for his return home.

It was Hirota's efforts that tided over the crisis. As soon as the news was received, he went personally to call on Grew, had the Japanese ambassador in Washington call on the American government, and ordered Japanese officials in China to contact U.S. officials there, all to express their profoundest apologies. He prodded Navy Undersecretary Yamamoto and other army and navy authorities into expressing appropriate regret. He also made it clear that in investigating the facts of the case there would be no artful attempts at evasion, but that blame would be frankly admitted where it existed, that proper amends would be made, and questions of compensation discussed.

On the same day, December 12, a regiment commanded by Colonel Hashimoto Kingoro fired on the British gunboat *Ladybird* and three other vessels at Wuhu. At first, the army claimed that it was a case of mistaken identity due to thick fog, but in fact it had ordered the attack knowing that the vessels were British. Hirota promptly called on Ambassador Craigie to express his apologies, and at the same time gave Japanese authorities on the spot instructions to obtain the cooperation of naval craft in effecting hospitalization and treatment of the wounded. Both Craigie and Grew joined in expressing satisfaction at the "speedy and commendable" reactions of the Japanese government. Officials of the two embassies in Tokyo were further mollified by the flood of letters of apology and inquiries after the well-being of the injured that arrived from all over the country; flowers and gifts of money were delivered to the embassies, and even hair that women had cut off as a mark of regret.

In other quarters, however, the incident was used as a pretext for stepping up attacks on Britain and America, on the grounds that the presence of vessels of those countries within the Japanese forces' field of operations was part of their attempt to aid Chiang Kai-shek and obstruct Japan's "holy war." The total effect, in fact, was to heighten, rather than diminish, anti-British and anti-American sentiment. It required nerve and determination for a foreign minister to apologize—and to get the army and navy to join him—at such a juncture. As Craigie pointed out in his *Behind the Japanese Mask*, it was a mark of considerable moral courage that Hirota, while aware of the inflamed emotions of Japan's extremists, should have taken the unusual step of visiting him personally to express his regrets.

It was amidst such turmoil that the Japanese authorities, in a series of meetings of the liaison council and the cabinet extending over approximately one week, studied Chiang Kai-shek's reply to the peace proposals. In drawing up his plan for a solution, Hirota had persuaded the army to make concessions by reserving the right to add new conditions should a fresh situation arise; he had, via Dirksen, informed the Chinese to this effect. It seemed likely, thus, that the army would insist on a certain number of new conditions now that it had occupied Nanking.

As feared, a string of new demands was put forward by the army and certain members of the cabinet, so that the proposals gradually became harsher. They insisted, for example, that military agreements such as the T'ang-ku truce should be retained, as well as the East Hopei and Hopei-Chahar regimes; that Japan should demand compensation, including compensation for military expenditure; and that the demilitarized zone in central China should cover not only Shanghai but the whole area occupied by Japanese forces. Navy Minister Yonai and Hirota began to express doubts that China could accept the terms.

The situation was further aggravated by the resignation of the minister of home affairs for reasons of ill health, which allowed Admiral Suetsugu to step up into the cabinet from the cabinet council. Suetsugu, who started attending meetings of the liaison council on the fourteenth, had always had a taste for politics and was known as one of the navy's bitterest foes of Britain. There was considerable comment on Konoe's action in making such a man minister of home affairs without consulting anybody, and even the emperor expressed concern at the appointment.

Almost immediately after his appointment, in fact, Suetsugu made use of his new position to brush aside the fears of those who believed the new conditions would be unacceptable to the Chinese. Any other terms, he asserted, would be unacceptable to the Japanese public and make it impossible for him, as home minister, to take responsibility for maintaining public peace and order. Even Konoe balked at this, and objected heatedly: the public's approval was irrelevant since the terms were unacceptable to China from the beginning.

In the streets of Tokyo, celebrations to mark the fall of Nanking were in full swing, with "banzai"-shouting, banner-waving parades by day and lantern processions by night. The occupied areas marked out by countless tiny Rising Sun flags on the map of China already enclosed more than two hundred million people—nearly half the population of China. Deprived of its capital, the National Government was little better than a provincial government. "So much for Chiang Kai-shek!" was the prevailing mood.

Backed up by such sentiment, the military could afford to ride high. "These terms represent an absolute minimum," declared War Minister Sugiyama. "The army has no intention of making any further concessions." If China did not agree to them, military action would proceed.

The argument involved many sessions and a great deal of time. In the end, it was decided to present China with the following four conditions in writing, and to have Hirota convey further details to Dirksen by word of mouth:

1. China must abandon her fellow-traveling, anti-Japanese and anti-Manchukuo policies, and cooperate with Japan and Manchukuo in fighting communism.

2. Demilitarized zones must be established in the necessary districts, and special administrative machinery set up in the areas affected.

3. Close economic relations must be established between Japan, Manchukuo, and China.

4. China must pay Japan appropriate reparations.

China was given until the end of the year in which to reply. Hirota met Ambassador Dirksen on the twenty-second, and asked him to transmit Japan's proposals to the National Government. Dirksen was dismayed; the terms seemed to offer little hope for agreement, and the time allowed for a reply was too short. Hirota himself was well aware of this, but the army was so adamant that he had no alternative for the present but to use the terms as a way of sounding out the ground. The only thing he could do on his own responsibility was to extend the time limit until the fifth or sixth of January.

The occupation of Nanking presented Hirota with another troublesome—and, in the long run, fatal—problem. This was, of course, the "Nanking Massacre." The general outlines of what had happened had been made known in a cable from the acting consul general, who entered Nanking shortly after its occupation. A copy of the cable was promptly handed to the War Ministry, and at a liaison conference of the three ministries concerned, the Foreign Ministry made a strong demand that the army take itself in hand. When Hirota heard the reports he was violently angry. He went to see War Minister Sugiyama to protest and to ask him to take immediate steps to tighten up discipline in the army. At the same time, Counselor Hidaka and others in Nanking visited local army leaders in order to urge them to do something. General Matsui, commander-in-chief, admitted that those under him seemed to have behaved outrageously. When Hidaka asked him whether perhaps the ordinary troops had not heard their superiors' orders, he muttered darkly that it seemed the superiors themselves were sometimes to blame.

Fearing what might happen if his troops poured into the city after such a prolonged struggle and with inadequate provisions, Matsui had ordered that only picked units should go in, and had issued strict warnings concerning the maintenance of military discipline, but his word was disregarded. Matsui was responsible only for directing strategy; the control of individual units was in the charge of the two army commanders below him—Imperial Prince Asaka and Major General Yanagawa Heisuke—and of the divisional commanders beneath them. Yanagawa had long been on bad terms with Matsui, and since landing in China had done everything possible to induce a warlike outlook in his troops, declaring that "every mountain and stream, every tree and blade of grass was an enemy." Some of the divisional commanders, again, were in a far from normal frame of mind; for example, Major General Nakajima, commander of the 16th Division and officer in charge of policing the fallen city, had himself been wounded and was in a rather excitable state.

Hidaka also called on Prince Asaka and urged him to take steps to tighten discipline, particularly since the behavior of the army in Nanking was attracting worldwide attention. In fact, the massacre had occurred less than ten days after Prince Asaka had taken up his command. The Japanese forces that entered Nanking, finding themselves with tens of thousands of prisoners on their hands, embarked on a process of wholesale slaughter, which touched off in turn a series of atrocities including murder, rape, looting, assault, and arson. The city itself was an almost deserted ruin, and two hundred thousand citizens who had been unable to get away had taken refuge in the foreign concession, where approximately thirty Americans and Germans had organized an International Committee for the Nanking Safety Zone. The atrocities took place in and around this district, and the foreigners who witnessed what went on set down detailed accounts, which they handed to Japanese authorities on the spot as well as making them public in other countries. The atrocities appalled the rest of the world, though there was no mention of them in Japanese newspapers.

With the arrival of more detailed reports, Hirota again protested to War Minister Sugiyama. At liaison meetings also, the Foreign Ministry made repeated protests to the War Ministry's Military Affairs Bureau and demanded that immediate action be taken. As a result, Lieutenant General Honma Masaharu, head of the Second Section at the General Staff Office, was sent to the scene at the end of January, and in February eighty staff officers including Commander-in-Chief Matsui and Prince Asaka were recalled to Japan (though this was not specifically referred to as a disciplinary measure). Prince Asaka called on Hirota at the Foreign Ministry especially to apologize to him, in the presence of Foreign Undersecretary Horinouchi, for "all the trouble that he had caused him."

In Nanking, meanwhile, military discipline had at last been re-established, and there were courts-martial. Nevertheless, the chief reason for the restoration of law and order was that the main units had passed on, leaving Nanking behind them. The fighting went on spreading toward the more distant parts of China. As each fresh position fell there were more cries of "banzai" and more Rising Sun flags fluttering in the breeze; and the hopes for a peaceful settlement receded still further into the distance.

Via Ambassador Dirksen, Hirota requested the National Government to expedite its reply, but on January 4, 1938, there was an interim report from Dirksen saying that so far he had received no answer either way. On January 11, an imperial conference was held, at which a "basic policy for dealing with the China Incident" was decided on. Hirota had long been opposed to laying down any immutable national policy, but the situation had reached a point where it was no longer possible to get by with temporary expedients.

Apart from a specific reference in the preamble to "respect for each other's sovereignty and territories," the "basic policy," in its calls for the eradication of the anti-Japanese movement, opposition to communism, economic cooperation and so on, differed little in its general outlines from what had gone before. In practical terms it stated that Japan would demand that the National Government accept a peace agreement based on Japan's conditions, otherwise "the

196

Empire [Japan] would henceforth abandon any hope of a solution to the Incident through dealings with that government, and would encourage the establishment of a new Chinese government with which it could come to an agreement on the adjustment of relations between the two countries, and with which it could cooperate in the construction of a new, reformed China."

Days went by, and still there was no reply from the National Government. There was increasing pressure not only from the military but from the political parties as well to break off negotiations, but Hirota got the cabinet to agree to wait until the fifteenth. In practice, though, the new, stiffer Japanese conditions left little room for hope. Ishii, head of the Bureau of East Asian Affairs, advised Hirota as follows:

"There is no real possibility of a favorable answer. There is no prospect of peace, for the time being at least. Japan has let the Incident run away with her, and until she wakes up there is no way out. That time will come eventually. Until then, the bit about having no dealings with the National Government will have to do; I will raise no objections." By now, the Foreign Ministry could only throw in the sponge.

In the course of a cabinet meeting on the fourteenth, word came saying that Dirksen was waiting to see Hirota. Anxiously wondering whether the message he brought was one of hope or despair, Hirota left the meeting and hurried to the Foreign Ministry.

His old acquaintance's expression was grim. The Chinese reply had stated merely that it wanted a more specific and detailed account of Japan's demands. But although the finer points had not been set down in writing, they had already been verbally transmitted in full detail, and there seemed little more that could be said. Dirksen himself had the impression that the National Government had had enough of mediation efforts and was inclined to go ahead with the war.

Hirota returned to the cabinet meeting, which came to the conclusion that the National Government's reply "lacked good faith" and must be taken as a delaying tactic.

At this stage, however, the General Staff Office suddenly became reluctant to give up the idea of peace talks. There had always been a faction there that believed that Japan, in order to be ready for a showdown with the Soviet Union, should avoid getting too deeply embroiled in China, and this faction's views had come to the fore.

The army, in short, was still a double-headed eagle. The War Ministry and the General Staff Office held different views: what was more, the latter, though it had agreed until recently to the stiffening of Japan's terms, now started suggesting that they should be amended. But nothing could be done about it when opinion was divided even within the military and the government's policy, moreover, had already been laid down at an imperial conference.

When the chief of army general staff, Imperial Prince Kan'in, went to the palace and once more started talking of the need to be armed against the Soviet Union, it was the emperor who said, with annoyance, "In that case, it would have been better not to get involved with China in the first place."

Thus on the sixteenth the government issued a declaration saying that "the imperial government would henceforth have no dealings with" the National Government—echoing the phraseology of the "basic policy for dealing with the China Incident." The Foreign Ministry had chosen the words "have no dealings with"—which it considered less definite than "not recognizing" or "severing relations with"—to signify that the National Government would be ignored for the time being. Konoe, however, was led on by the general mood into explaining that "it indicated a firm resolve, stronger than non-recognition." And when he was asked "whether the Japanese government would deal with Chiang Kai-shek if he should ask for peace talks now that the declaration had been issued," Konoe, without giving the slow-moving Hirota a chance to speak, replied, "Absolutely not."

Hopes for peace talks, thus, had vanished. Exultantly, the army pressed on in triumph toward Canton in the south and toward Hankow, deep in the heart of China. It was the beginning of the inevitable decline and fall of the Japanese Empire.

Though events were sweeping headlong down a course which

Hirota could not condone, he still retained some faint hope; for example, he sent instructions to Ambassador Yoshida Shigeru in England, telling him to try to get the British government to do something. But Yoshida made no reply at all. Two months later, though, he sent a letter to his father-in-law Makino, and via Makino to Saionji, saying that the British government was willing to make efforts to bring the dispute to an end, and requesting the Japanese government to take immediate steps. As a result, the foreign minister was criticized in some quarters for doing nothing.

Men such as Saionji and Makino loomed so large in Yoshida's world that by now he seemed to have little time for old acquaintances such as Hirota. Relations with Britain and America, thanks to Hirota's prompt response to the shelling incidents, had been tending, if anything, to improve. U.S. Ambassador Grew, too, had said he would do whatever was in his power to help. There were no particular problems where the Soviet Union was concerned, either. In that sense at least, the wind had dropped, and it was time for the windmill to rest. Hirota felt that his role had finished.

In February, while the Diet was in session, in one of the innumerable rooms of the great Diet building, Hirota tendered his resignation to Prime Minister Konoe. The war and navy ministers were also present. Konoe, however, refused to accept the resignation. "Wait, at any rate, until I reshuffle the cabinet," he said.

"Then be sure you let me resign at that time," insisted Hirota.

The huge white building lay chill and quiet. When Hirota had come to it as the first prime minister to take his seat there after its completion, he had not foreseen a situation like the present. Even then, though, he had believed that the military were the diplomat's most formidable antagonist, and he was still being made painfully aware of the truth of that belief.

In the Diet, debate had begun on the National Mobilization Bill. The bill imposed serious restrictions on the rights and freedoms of the people, and there was considerable opposition to it as "ignoring the Constitution." Konoe countered by recognizing that the bill was controversial in many ways, but insisted painstakingly and repeatedly that the bill was necessary in order to cope with a fluid war

199

situation. And to get it passed properly by the Diet and established as law, even if only in its general outlines, would be more in line with the spirit of constitutionalism. Thus the bill moved on toward becoming law.

During the debate, Major Sato Kenryo, a member of the Military Affairs Section of the War Ministry, created a stir by yelling "Shut up!" at a member who asked him a question about the bill. Outside the Diet, there were demonstrations by rightists and others calling for the dissolution of the political parties. Constitutional government as such had already begun to totter. The same creeping rot began to undermine the foundations of the Foreign Ministry, too. The military and other forces who had long been directing slanderous statements and criticisms against Hirota, the "Minister of Harm," now began scheming to weaken the Foreign Ministry structurally with a plan for the establishment of a "China Bureau."

The army had promised the Foreign Ministry all along that it would not set up military rule in the occupied areas of China. In theory, it was committed to respecting Chinese sovereignty and not making it a "second Manchukuo." Local pro-Japanese regimes provided what administrative machinery there was, but as the occupied areas expanded, the question arose of how to coordinate them as a whole. It was on the grounds that this was something that the existing machinery of the Foreign Ministry was not qualified to cope with that the Cabinet Planning Board now proposed to establish a "China Board," or "China Bureau," as a central agency for handling the Chinese question under the direct control of the prime minister. The scheme had the support of Prime Minister Konoe, and backing for it grew in the Diet. In the Foreign Ministry, on the other hand, the plan met opposition on the grounds that it would disrupt the integrity of Japan's foreign policy. Hirota, in line with this view, opposed the project head-on; to counter it, he put forward a Foreign Ministry proposal for the creation of a China Economic Affairs Bureau as an external agency of the Foreign Ministry to deal strictly with economic development. The army around this time was creating large state policy corporations as a means of promoting development on its own, and Hirota's plan would also have served to see that these were kept under Foreign Ministry supervision. As a result of this resistance from Hirota, establishment of the China Bureau was shelved for the time being.

In the meantime, an increasing number of young men—primarily those who had come under the influence of Matsuoka and Shiratori—were beginning to call for "reform" within the Foreign Ministry itself. Occasionally they would come in a body to the minister's room. He would take them on and let them have their say before presenting the opposite side of the case. Their chief complaint was that Hirota lacked a "positive" approach—a similar view to that of War Minister Sugiyama, who had accused him of "shilly-shallying." Such right-leaning views found a ready listener in Konoe, who fretted over what seemed to be Hirota's low reputation within the ministry and at one stage even considered bringing Matsuoka into the cabinet instead.

Konoe was also dissatisfied with Hirota because, he complained, he failed to provide sufficient information and personal views at cabinet meetings and the like, so that it was difficult to discuss things with him. There was a reason for this, however. Konoe's immediate entourage included many outsiders ranging politically from right to left, and Konoe frequently divulged secrets to them. Hirota complained privately to his more intimate subordinates that one had to be careful talking about anything important at cabinet meetings, since "the Soviet ambassador would know all about it in no time." War Minister Sugiyama was dissatisfied on the same score, and tended to be reticent "because all kinds of things leaked out via those around Konoe." To Konoe, however, it looked as though two of his most important ministers were holding back on the truth with him. Even among the members of the cabinet, there were some who put indiscreet questions with no real idea of the requirements of foreign policy, and when on top of this Matsuoka and other advisers joined in, there was little hope from the start of keeping official secrets.

Hirota was still waiting for a chance to resign. Konoe himself, however, was ill from time to time and periodically considered resignation only to be dissuaded by the senior statesmen. Whenever Konoe was laid up the other ministers trooped in to inquire after his health, the only exceptions being Hirota and Navy Minister Yonai.

In late May, 1938, there was a cabinet reshuffle. A large number of men were replaced, including the ministers of war, foreign affairs, finance, education, and commerce and industry; Hirota's successor was General Ugaki, one reason for the choice being that he "knew where the army was vulnerable." "The most important thing for the new minister," observed Hirota, "is to retain, in the Chinese question as in everything else, the confidence of Britain and the United States. Whatever else happens, I hope he will keep that in mind. Where China is concerned, there is no alternative but to collaborate with those nations. Although I'm quitting, the situation is serious; I shall be keeping a careful watch on developments."

It was Konoe's intention to apply for imperial permission to accord Hirota the privileges appropriate to a man who had served as prime minister and, in three cabinets, as foreign minister with deputy prime minister rank. Hirota was obviously qualified for this. Saionji also agreed with Konoe, but Lord Privy Seal Yuasa refused to pass on the request to the emperor. "Since the post he's quitting is that of foreign minister, minister-of-state privileges will suffice," was his rather doubtful reasoning. He also insisted that Hirota's term as prime minister had been too short.

Although part of the trouble was that Yuasa and Konoe were on bad terms around this time, there was also a strong implication that Hirota was not suitable for admission to the "aristocratic" world of those who were honored as former prime ministers. Hirota himself, of course, was quite indifferent to this exchange. A "plain man" once more, he retired to his unpretentious villa on the coast at Kugenuma.

VIII

Shortly after Ugaki became foreign minister, Yoshida Shigeru was relieved of his post as ambassador in England and returned to Japan. Yoshida himself had been anticipating the change, but the stay of over two years in England which had begun when Hirota had appointed him had made him more of an anglophile than ever. Despite the anti-British campaign at home, both government and private circles in England were still on the whole well disposed toward Japan. This British attitude was, no doubt, not entirely disinterested, but Yoshida, at least, saw in it the large-mindedness of a great nation, and the feeling cast an appropriate glow over the last months of his life as a diplomat. He was all the more disgusted with Japan, therefore, when he arrived home and found how high anti-British and anti-American sentiment was running there.

Hirota, in the meantime, was leading a life of study and reflection, spending most of his time at Kugenuma. Although he had membership of the House of Peers by imperial appointment, in practice he stood virtually outside public life. When the Hiranuma cabinet, which took over from the Konoe administration for something over a year, submitted its resignation, Hirota's name was put forward once again as first candidate for recommendation to the emperor as prime minister. The windmill's sails were threatening to turn yet again—but fierce opposition from the military blocked the formation of a second Hirota government, and General Abe Nobuyuki took over instead. Abe himself retired after four months and Yonai, former navy minister, created a new government in which Hirota agreed to act as cabinet councillor. He was persuaded to do so by his long-standing acquaintance with Yonai, who had indirectly supported the Foreign Ministry's position in the days of the Konoe government.

The cabinet council by now had in fact become little more than a body of extra-governmental advisers, without the air of a "second cabinet" that it had had when Konoe first established it. Hirota himself did little more than recommend, at the time the war broke out in Europe, Japanese neutrality and an early peace settlement with China.

With the fall of the Yonai government in July, 1940, Hirota found himself, as a member of the conference of senior statesmen, in a position to help select the next prime minister. The decision to transfer the task of choosing the new premier to a council of senior statesmen was a result of a long-standing wish of Saionji's; the council on this occasion, which was made up of former prime ministers Wakatsuki, Okada, Hirota, Hayashi, Konoe, and Hiranuma, together with president Hara of the Privy Council and Lord Privy Seal Kido, recommended to the emperor that Konoe should once more be called on to form a government.

After the conference, Hirota had a talk with Konoe in a separate room. Hirota was worried by a rumor that Matsuoka Yosuke would be appointed foreign minister, and warned Konoe that such a choice would be dangerous. He himself would have preferred some man such as Togo Shigenori (ambassador in Russia). Konoe equivocated. He had, in fact, already summoned Matsuoka and obtained his private agreement to serve as foreign minister should Konoe himself be obliged to form another government. Konoe and Matsuoka had both accompanied the Japanese delegation to the Paris Peace Conference and—unlike Yoshida, who had also attended the conference—were well attuned to each other ideologically.

Konoe himself, in his article "A Protest against 'Pacifism' Which Serves the Interests of Britain and the U.S.," had attacked the conciliatory approach to foreign policy in strong terms: "The attitude that allows itself to be deluded by a pacifism which serves principally the interests of Britain and the United States and looks up to the League of Nations as though it were divinely ordained represents the height of servility and is to be despised from any moral point of view." He had long had his eye on Matsuoka, who had also later played a leading role in Japan's secession from the League of Nations; during Konoe's first term as prime minister, he had even considered having Matsuoka replace Hirota, and consequently was not disposed to heed Hirota's warning. On the contrary, following the formation of his government he went so far as to laud Matsuoka in the following terms: "Some people, it seems, are dissatisfied with Matsuoka, but in fact he is a born leader, a national hero. If a man is ninety percent great, one should ignore the remaining ten percent. To do so is in the best interests of both the people and the state. . . . A man who promises to develop major stature should be cherished and his qualities encouraged. A man of such promise as this will not be found again easily."

Thus Matsuoka found himself back in the Foreign Ministry for the first time in nineteen years. He was sixty years old. In a speech on taking up his appointment, he appealed for unity within the Foreign Ministry—a preparatory move for the far-reaching personnel changes that he had privately already decided on. He issued recall orders for forty diplomats serving abroad, including Horinouchi Kensuke, ambassador to the United States, and Togo Shigenori, ambassador to the Soviet Union, and in most cases either retired them or placed them on the waiting list. At the same time, he gave office to a large number of younger members of the "reformist" faction within the ministry, and appointed Shiratori as adviser. Even admitted that the aim was a thorough overhaul, Matsuoka's methods were rather drastic and high-handed. Earlier in his career, he had started his term as president of the South Manchurian Railway by carrying out, similarly, a major reshuffle of personnel. The Foreign Ministry, however, was different from a business enterprise—it called for the experience and wisdom of long years, and for a relationship of trust with other countries. To replace almost all of its upper echelons at one swoop was going too far. Neither were the reasons for some of the new appointments at all clear. There was resistance among the diplomats concerned. Togo, for example, refused to submit his resignation as a sign of protest against Matsuoka's order.

Horinouchi was a man of moderate outlook who as undersecretary had worked closely with Hirota during his period as foreign minister, while Togo's dispassionate, sincere nature had made him one of Hirota's most trusted subordinates. When, under Foreign Minister Hirota, Togo had found himself a rival to Shigemitsu Mamoru—one year his senior at the Foreign Ministry—for the post of ambassador to the Soviet Union, Hirota had had a talk with Togo, and Shigemitsu had been given priority for the posting. Then, when Shigemitsu went to London to take over from Yoshida, Togo was given the embassy in Moscow he had coveted.

Matsuoka, therefore, worked to get rid of Hirota's influence at the Foreign Ministry. At his first press conference, he called for the establishment of a "Greater East Asia Co-prosperity Sphere." The same day, he launched out on his own individual course, and calling on the German ambassador, General Ott, began sounding him out concerning the conclusion of a tripartite pact between Japan, Germany, and Italy. Where Hirota was a "dallier," Matsuoka was a "doer"; where Hirota applied himself disinterestedly to whatever came along, Matsuoka was burning with ambition. Before long Matsuoka, overcoming the qualms of the emperor and leading members of the political world, concluded—in September, 1940—the tripartite pact he had hoped for, and also signed a neutrality pact with the Soviet Union in April, 1941.

As though to put a brake on these frantic activities, Konoe tried to get negotiations going between Japan and the U.S. This caused a clash between the two men and was eventually, in July, 1941, to lead to the fall of the second Konoe government. Since the government's resignation was largely a move designed to make it possible to get rid of Matsuoka, Konoe was once more recommended to lead the next government. During this third term of office, he privately intended to bring Japan and America to the negotiating table. As foreign minister he chose Toyoda Teijiro, a former naval undersecretary who had also served as minister of commerce and industry, hoping thereby to gain the cooperation of the navy in resolving the situation. But the advocates of Japan's push into Southeast Asia—among whom the navy itself had been prominent—were all the while effecting an advance into southern French Indochina. Those responsible hoped thereby to secure supplies of strategic materials and also, by making the first move and striking into part of the ring encircling Japan, to deprive the other side of the will to fight. In his own mind, of course, Konoe had little confidence in the viability of this judgment, and he had also begun to feel uneasy concerning future developments in the international situation as a whole.

His appointment of Matsuoka, leading as it did to a "Matsuoka whirlwind," had alienated Hirota and other leading figures in the diplomatic world. Thus he employed an intermediary to approach Shidehara, in the desperate hope that this veteran of the world of foreign policy, who was well versed in British and American affairs, might have at least some help to offer in finding a way out of the situation. Shidehara was sixty-nine at the time, and had already been in disapproving retirement for nearly ten years. Hearing that a transport convoy had set sail for southern French Indochina two days previously, he pressed Konoe to get imperial permission to recall it immediately. This was impossible, said Konoe; besides, the troops on board were only intended to be garrisoned there. But Shidehara would not change his stand: "If you send in occupation troops, we shall have a major war. Under such circumstances, there's little point in attempting negotiations with the United States."

The warning had the same effect on Konoe as if it had come from the Americans themselves, and he left badly shaken.

The situation, in fact, began to develop more or less along the lines that Shidehara had predicted. Konoe sought direct talks with President Roosevelt as a means of finding some way to a solution. His thinking here was much the same as at the time of the outbreak of the China Incident, when he had conceived the idea of direct talks with Chiang Kai-shek. This time, however, Konoe was resigned to a degree of personal danger to himself, and resolved to throw himself wholeheartedly into the attempt rather than stand by as a kind of commentator. Shidehara, when consulted, was opposed to the idea; such moves, he said, should be made through normal diplomatic channels. President Roosevelt showed some slight interest, but opposition from the State Department and other quarters finally put paid to the plan.

Here again, the real "enemy" with which Japanese diplomats should have concerned themselves was, as Hirota had more than once pointed out, the army. The realization of Japan-U.S. negotiations depended on whether or not the Japanese army would accept the demand for a withdrawal from China. In fact, it was resolutely opposed to any such measure. As a result, Konoe lost confidence in his ability to bring the situation under control, and threw in the sponge after three months.

At 1:00 P.M. on October 17, 1941, a conference of senior statesmen was held at the imperial palace to pick a candidate for recommendation as the new prime minister. Konoe himself was absent on the grounds of ill health. On the other hand, the presence of former prime minister Kiyoura, who was ninety-one by now, was a sign of the importance attached this time to the choice of premier. In practice, though, the situation had reached a point where the choice of candidates was not so much limited as virtually nonexistent.

The hope expressed by the senior statesmen was for some man who would be able to exert control over the army and navy so as to leave some chance for negotiations. This task was already beyond the powers of anybody save a member of the imperial family, and Prince Higashikuni's name came up for consideration, but it was finally decided that if he were brought in at such a critical time, and if war with the West should break out, it would burden the imperial family with excessive responsibility; thus this idea, in its turn, was dropped.

Finally, Kido mentioned the name of War Minister Tojo. Nobody opposed it; opposition would have meant that no government was possible at all. Among Kido's reasons for suggesting Tojo were the hope that he would be able to reconcile conflicting views within the military; the fact that Tojo had already been inside the government and was well aware of what had been going on at home and abroad; and the hope that he would be amenable to suggestions from Kido himself.

Returning home that day following the conference, Hirota said to his sons Hiroo and Masao: "I don't know much about Tojo as a man; however, it seems that he listens to what the lord privy seal has to say." Then he added, as though looking back over his own past, "By now, a pure figurehead would only do more harm. The army will have to take responsibility itself. If he's put in a position where he has no choice but to get the army to agree to holding diplomatic negotiations, Tojo isn't likely to do anything too rash."

After an interview with the emperor, Kido requested the new prime minister "to reappraise the situation without feeling bound by the decisions of the imperial conference in September, and to strive to get the situation in hand." The imperial conference of September 6, 1941, had resolved that: "(1) preparations for war should be completed by the last third of October; (2) in any diplomatic exchanges with Britain and America, Japan should insist on realization of her minimum demands; (3) Japan should be resolved to commence hostilities immediately should her demands not be met by the last part of October." Following this, however, the emperor without warning had quoted a poem by the emperor Meiji:

> "Inasmuch as all
> The seas in all directions
> Seem twins of one birth,
> How often must the winds and
> The waves clash in noisiness"

thus indicating indirectly his desire for peace. The emperor's feelings had not changed in the interim, and he was now telling them once more, via Kido, not to feel committed by the decisions of that conference.

Togo was selected as foreign minister in the Tojo cabinet. The military were hoping that Togo, a former ambassador to the Soviet Union, would be useful in trying to avoid war with that country. They also made a show of enthusiasm for diplomatic negotiations between Japan and the United States. But in practice Togo found himself isolated, bound hand and foot within the government. He felt compelled to submit his resignation, but it was turned down on the grounds that the situation was too serious to permit it. Thus events hastened unchecked toward disaster. The emperor, dissatisfied with the judgment of the government and Imperial Headquarters alone, suggested that the views of the senior statesmen be sought. Prime Minister Tojo replied guardedly that it was the responsibility of the government and supreme command, not the senior statesmen, to advise the emperor on affairs of state. There was no need, therefore, to debate formally with these men; he had no objection, however, to an informal exchange of views with them.

At 9:30 A.M. on November 29, the government met with the senior. statesmen at the palace to discuss negotiations with America. Following the government's account of the present state of affairs, Hirota and the other former prime ministers put their own questions. These stretched on until after 1:00 P.M., so there was a break for lunch, after which each of the statesmen in turn expressed his views to the emperor. First came Wakatsuki, then Okada, Hiranuma, and Konoe. Yonai said quite simply that he hoped the nation "would not jump out of the frying pan into the fire." He was followed by Hirota. Hirota, while strongly deploring the situation that had come about, clearly stated that he did not believe America would go to war with Japan over the China question. A diplomatic crisis should not be thought of as a single occasion, but as something that might occur three or four times before the two sides eventually reached understanding. A single impasse in talks did not mean that there should be immediate resort to war; and even if war did break out, the emphasis should be less on the pursuit of military advantage than on seeking peace talks at the earliest opportunity.

Everything Hirota said was a distillation of his long years of experience and observation as an international statesman. The *Panay* and *Ladybird* incidents had also been "crises," but they had been overcome by the obvious good faith of the response Japan had made, and direct clashes with America and Britain had been avoided. The attempt to bring about peace in China had been a bitter lesson. With quiet persistence, Hirota had seized every opportunity for negotiations, and had created others himself, but the army's insistence on "retribution" had always won the day; negotiation had always taken second place to belligerence. For Hirota, the chances thus missed were a source of intolerable frustration. Foreign Minister Togo, a younger man, must have shared the same feelings, but being locked up, as it were, within a government that was united in its determination to fight, he could do nothing. To rescue Togo would have been to rescue Japan, but Prime Minister Tojo ignored the views of Hirota and his like, and insisted simply that war by now was inevitable. The result was the commencement of hostilities on December 8 (Japan time).

The beginning of the war brought, for a while, a stream of optimistic reports of Japanese victories, and the streets resounded to cries of "banzai." One day around this time, Hirota brought a postcard he had just received and with a discouraged expression showed it to his son Masao. The postcard was from Yamamoto Isoroku, commander-in-chief of the Combined Fleet. After the conventional apologies for not having written earlier, Yamamoto—who was skeptical concerning the final outcome of the war—had added, "The cherry blossom, you might say, is just at its best now."

This attitude, in Hirota's view, was irresponsible. "You'd think it was some gambling game," he said scornfully (Yamamoto was known for his love of gambling). "It may amuse Yamamoto, but what about the nation? The important thing for a nation is survival, not brief glory."

Hirota was on friendly terms with Yamamoto, who together with other navy men also well versed in British and American affairs, had sought throughout to localize disputes and keep the situation in hand. When Yamamoto had been undersecretary to Navy Minister Yonai, the two men had cooperated with Foreign Minister Hirota in resisting the army. The postcard, therefore, came as something of a shock. Yamamoto, in fact, is said to have declared that he "could manage things up to Pearl Harbor, but would not be responsible for what happened after that." Hirota could not go along with this attitude— with the feeling, apparent in the postcard, that a military man's job was to obey orders and go to his death without questioning the worth of the sacrifice. What was to become of the country as a whole? Why hadn't the navy opposed the war before things had reached this pass? If the navy had only stuck to its opposition in the imperial conferences, the outbreak of hostilities might well have been averted.

Hirota and the others were "senior statesmen" in name alone.

Even concerning such a vital national concern as the opening of hostilities, the only chance of "discussion" they were given was the one meeting on November 29—and even that on the understanding that it was not a formal "debate." All the more, therefore, was Hirota dissatisfied with the men who were an integral part of the decision-making machinery. Kido, for example, was lord keeper of the privy seal; would it not have been possible, seeing that the emperor himself did not want war, for him to have refused, as an exceptional measure, to set the seal on the imperial edict declaring war? Via a mutual acquaintance, Hirota made a suggestion to Kido. The emperor's entourage, he proposed, should include not only Kido but other veterans from various fields—men such as Makino (foreign affairs), Ikeda (finance), Ugaki (army), Okada (navy), as well as Wakatsuki, Hiranuma, Konoe, and others—in case it should ever become necessary to make a fundamental change in the nation's organization. "While everything should be done to avoid such an eventuality," he said, "the time may come when we will be obliged to take decisive steps to put a rapid end to the war. I believe it essential that prominent specialists on various subjects be made advisers to the emperor so that it would be possible to put this into effect at any time." Not only was there no response, but word reached Hirota, via others, that Kido was displeased with him. Thus the court for Hirota became an even remoter place than before. Even apart from this, interference from Tojo was making it difficult for senior statesmen to gain access to the emperor; this was true even of Konoe. So long as Tojo's dictatorship continued, the senior statesmen would be obliged to languish in obscurity.

From then on, Hirota stayed outside the mainstream of events (apart from one visit to Siam in 1944, as special envoy at the request of the foreign minister). Most of his time he spent in the villa at Kugenuma, meeting whoever came to visit him, gathering as much information as possible, and keeping an eye on the development of the war with the idea of going to Foreign Minister Togo's aid should any opportunity for negotiation present itself. Eventually, however, Togo left the scene, and leadership of the Foreign Ministry went first to Tani Masayuki, then to Shigemitsu Mamoru. Thus the Foreign

Ministry, like the court, became in its turn a remote place for Hirota.

Hirota, of course, was a man temperamentally suited to the solitary life, and he had taken a liking to his lonely, placid routine in the country by the sea. But things were very different with some of his contemporaries or near-contemporaries. Yoshida Shigeru, for example, was busy calling on Kido and Konoe. Having heard reports of the failure of the Midway operation, he startled Konoe by suggesting that he should go to Switzerland and stay there for a while to sound out the possibility of peace moves. His idea, of course, remained precisely that and no more. Matsuoka Yosuke, on the other hand, was confined to bed with pulmonary tuberculosis. Disease and disappointment had wasted him and he sometimes wept openly before those who came to call on him, lamenting that the tripartite pact, the true aim of which had been to prevent American participation, had in the end only served as an incitement to war.

Hirota was already in his mid-sixties, but his health was robust. As ever, he rose early and did his "judo dance" exercises, then followed more or less the same routine every day, ending with his reading of the *Analects* before retiring. He often walked to the beach and stood there gazing out at the sea. The sea's moods changed with the season and the weather; but in Hirota's eyes, its colors were more somber than before. Whether it lay calm or was ruffled with white breakers advancing on the shore, it had become a symbol of sorrow. Far away across its waters, fierce fighting was in progress even now. Still farther away lay America—a country where he, Shidehara, and Saburi had once been stationed and where Matsuoka had worked to put himself through college, a country that now lay beyond all possibility of communication. His eldest son Hiroo had gone from the Specie Bank to Peking. With Hirota at home were Shizuko, two of his daughters, and his third son Masao and Masao's wife. Where, early that spring, the family had gone out together to dig up truffles at the foot of the pine trees, now they were busy cultivating sweet potatoes in the garden.

The diamond ring that Hirota had bought for Shizuko in Holland had gone—surrendered in response to a government appeal for gold, silver, and diamonds.

By 1943, with the withdrawal of Japanese troops from Guadalcanal and other setbacks, the signs of eventual defeat were growing steadily more apparent. At such a time, the death of Yamamoto Isoroku, commander-in-chief of the Combined Fleet, who was shot down in a plane over Bougainville in the South Pacific, came as a severe shock. Yamamoto was given an imposing state funeral amidst nationwide mourning. Hirota was invited to the funeral, but in the end did not attend.

Nor was the war situation the only cause for gloom. Domestic politics, too, were passing through some of their darkest days. By depriving the nation successively of the freedoms of speech, publication, assembly, and association, Prime Minister Tojo had established a kind of autocratic government by military police. He also formed an "Imperial Rule Assistance Association" which absorbed existing parties and factions and provided Diet candidates of its own recommendation with political funds from the emergency military account. This was not so much interference in elections as out-and-out dictatorship.

It was Hirota and another man from his home town—Nakano Seigo—who showed the only signs of resistance. Nakano, who had formerly criticized "pusillanimous" foreign policies of the type favored by Hirota, and who on the day war broke out issued a statement approving the war in highly jingoistic terms, had been provoked by Tojo's repressive measures into a characteristic display of resistance. He refused to let his own Tohokai group join the Imperial Rule Assistance Association, as a result of which it failed miserably in the elections; but he still continued to attack the Tojo government covertly in the press and elsewhere. He also exerted pressure on Konoe in an attempt to overturn the Tojo government. As he saw it, if Tojo had originally been appointed by the collective will of the senior statesmen, that same collective will could now induce him to resign. Konoe too, who seemed to have reached some kind of decision, agreed. Around the same time, however, Tojo—partly as a means of countering unfavorable opinion—suddenly started to invite the senior statesmen for discussions with him.

At one of these discussions, Hirota proposed that Allied prisoners at camps in Japan should be repatriated to their own countries. The differences between Japanese and Western customs, he said, caused unnecessary misunderstanding and suspicion of ill-treatment. To send them home, moreover, would show the Allies that Japan's morale was still good enough to permit her to make such gestures.

Tojo and the other ministers listened in silence, but a few days after the meeting two military policemen with swords at their sides suddenly turned up at Hirota's house. Standing in the entrance hall, they surveyed him in domineering fashion and requested him in tones of menacing politeness to desist from saying such things in future. Even so, he made a proposal of a similar nature at the next meeting as well. Japan had still not completed payments for the Chinese Eastern Railway, whose sale Hirota had taken so much trouble to negotiate, and he now urged that Japan should pay up.

"The Soviet Union can hardly feel pleased about the delay," he said. "There's a danger that it may be prompted into doing something disadvantageous to Japan. Besides, not to pay will further damage international trust in this country." Tojo listened with a sour expression.

For all this, none of the other senior statesmen made any proposal for peace talks. The situation, on the surface at least, had still not reached that point, but Hirota's suggestions had been made with an eye to the negotiations that would surely take place some day, and to help pave the way for them.

Several of these meetings had taken place when Konoe, at the instigation of Nakano Seigo, tried to stage Tojo's removal from power. The idea was for the senior statesmen to invite Tojo to lunch at the Peers Club, ostensibly out of gratitude for the chances he had given them to meet him, and then to exert pressure on him to resign. Tojo, however, almost as though he had sensed their design, brought four ministers with him—Foreign Minister Shigemitsu, Finance Minister Kaya, Navy Minister Shimada, and president Suzuki of the Cabinet Planning Board. This upset Konoe's plan. He found himself unable to bring up the subject of resignation, and the occasion passed off as a perfectly ordinary luncheon gathering.

From the very start, the senior statesmen had not been united in any firm determination to oust Tojo, nor had they discussed their plan thoroughly. Some of them, in fact, had hesitated to take part in what they considered a piece of double-dealing by Nakano. Tojo had taken skillful advantage of this disunity. His opponents had been too optimistic, and the situation was not yet ripe for ousting him.

As a result of this episode, Nakano suffered increasingly under Tojo's displeasure and began to feel that he was reaching the end of the line. One day in September, an old friend from Kyushu came to call on him. Nakano criticized Tojo and expressed his fears for the future of Japan. Then he added, almost as an afterthought, "There's one thing I'd like to ask you to do. I'd like you to tell Hirota that I misjudged him before, but that now I sincerely respect him."

The friend called on Hirota and told him what Nakano had said. Hirota nodded thoughtfully and expressed surprise that someone who normally disliked any show of weakness should have said such a thing. Hirota at this period was spending more of his time at the house in Harajuku, and one day Nakano himself arrived on horseback, having decided that it would be better to come to see Hirota himself. In the presence of Masao, he told Hirota that his objections to his foreign policies in the past had been mistaken, and apologized for the trouble he had caused him. He was a quite different man from the spirited Nakano of old.

A few days later, Nakano was arrested and taken first to Metropolitan Police Headquarters, then to the headquarters of the military police. On the evening of the day he was sent home, he committed hara-kiri.

Undercover moves by Konoe and other senior statesmen continued even after this. Tojo conceived the idea of taking some of them into the cabinet as a means of dividing their ranks and strengthening his own government. He approached first Yonai and Abe, then Hirota. Not only did all three refuse, but the statesmen agreed among themselves that they would not cooperate with the Tojo government. This open expression of non-confidence finally drove Tojo to resign.

At the ministerial conference convened to recommend a new candidate for prime minister, Hirota called for the formation of a national government centering around some member of the imperial family.

As he put it, a situation might arise "where it was necessary to risk everything." In short, he foresaw an end to the war and considered that only such a government could tide Japan over the chaos that would ensue.

Most of the ministers at the conference, however, favored an army man as the next premier, and in the end they decided on a coalition government with General Koiso Kuniaki as prime minister, backed up by Yonai as navy minister. On this occasion, Hirota urged Koiso to choose his war minister for himself, without waiting for a unanimous recommendation from the army "Big Three." In the event, Sugiyama was appointed war minister again, and Shigemitsu was retained as foreign minister.

As foreign minister, Shigemitsu had also been aware for some time of the possibility of an end to the war, and was looking to the Soviet Union as a possible mediator. For this purpose, he had proposed to the Soviet government in the summer of 1943 that "an important figure directly representing the Japanese government" should be dispatched to the Soviet Union for discussions and also visit various other European countries. The proposal was rejected, however, on the grounds that the purpose of sending this official envoy was not clear. A similar proposal was made in March, 1944, and was again rejected.

Following the formation of the Koiso government, there were further calls for peace talks, this time from the army and the General Staff Office in particular, so Shigemitsu once again suggested to the Soviet Union that Japan should send an envoy.

It was Shigemitsu's idea this time that Hirota should go, and he twice urged Hirota to accept the task. Hirota, in fact, as had been shown by his proposal earlier for payment of the money for acquiring the Chinese Eastern Railway, had been keeping an eye on the Soviet Union's behavior and was convinced of the need, in the interests of Japan's overtures for peace, for getting negotiations with the Soviet Union going before the Soviet-Japanese treaty of neutrality expired. He had in fact expressed these views in a private audience with the emperor.

Hirota agreed to Shigemitsu's request and resigned himself to visiting the Soviet Union as special envoy. Again, though, all such moves fell through in the end, since the Soviet Union refused to accept the envoy on the grounds that contact with a messenger from Japan without any obvious new problem to occasion it would only invite misunderstanding in other countries.

The war situation deteriorated, and in April, 1945, partly as a result of disagreement within the army, the Koiso government submitted its resignation. A conference of senior statesmen was held at the imperial palace at 5:00 P.M. on April 5. Since Tojo was present, the choice of the next premier was carried out on the superficial assumption that Japan would fight through to final victory; there were no calls for peace talks, whatever individuals present may have been thinking.

On this occasion Hirota suggested that it might be possible to have Makino (Yoshida's father-in-law) participate in such conferences. Makino was considered to be one of the leaders of the pro-Western faction, and the army had always singled him out for special attack. Hirota also insisted that the next prime minister should be "a man who could exert his leadership over the army and navy" and proposed that, as an emergency measure, the emperor should appoint individual ministers directly without first obtaining the agreement of those concerned.

He considered it likely that the war would end during the next government's term of office, and felt that important posts such as that of foreign minister should be filled with men of corresponding ability and resolution. As the only man who was likely to be able to lead the army and navy yet had nothing against him in his past, the ministerial conference finally decided to recommend Suzuki Kantaro, president of the Privy Council, who was also an admiral.

The only objection came from Tojo, who demanded that emphasis should be on the army, and that the candidate should be a serving army officer. If such a man were not chosen, he hinted menacingly, the army would go its own way. Kido took him up on this and pressed him to say whether there were in fact any signs of this happening. When Tojo replied equivocally that there were some, Kido retorted that public opinion against the army was growing, and that it might well be the people that would go their own way. On this note, the meeting ended.

In view of the nature of the new government, the most important ministerial post was naturally that of foreign minister. Any candidate must have a distinguished record and be interested in bringing about peace; he must be acceptable to other countries—and prepared for the worst. The obvious candidate was Hirota, and as soon as Suzuki started forming his government he called on Hirota and requested him to take the post.

Although Hirota had himself called for the direct appointment of ministers without giving them freedom to accept or reject the post, he considered the request misplaced. In fact, his advocacy of such a system had been partly motivated by the fact that he himself had in mind a candidate for the post of foreign minister, a man whom he wished to see installed in the post whoever might become prime minister. He considered this man—Togo Shigenori—essential if Japan was to obtain a satisfactory peace settlement, and he did not want to give him the chance to refuse. Thus he recommended Togo as strongly as possible to Suzuki.

Togo had had experience as ambassador to the Soviet Union, and his ability and other qualifications all ranked with Hirota's own. Togo, moreover, had come to the Foreign Ministry six years later than Hirota; he was still in his prime, and until recently had been the real power at the ministry. By comparison, Hirota considered himself too old, too far removed from his present successors there.

Suzuki fell in with Hirota's views, and summoning Togo put the case to him. Hirota also met Togo and tried to persuade him. Togo himself, in fact, had a strong motive for accepting: earlier, as foreign minister in the Tojo government, he had taken part—against his own will—in the launching of hostilities, and he felt a desire to help now in bringing the war to a close.

Determined to sound out Suzuki's true views concerning the outlook for peace negotiations, he asked him how long he considered the war would continue. Suzuki's reply—"Two or three years"—conflicted with Togo's personal estimate of less than one year, but in the end Suzuki gave in; it was agreed that everything should be left to

Togo, who thereupon agreed to accept the post.

Contacts with the Soviet Union had reached an awkward stage. On the very day that the ministerial conference had recommended Suzuki, the Soviet Union had notified Japan of its desire to allow the neutrality pact to lapse. Nevertheless, since both the army and navy wanted negotiations, Togo decided to have Hirota go ahead with them. The most pressing task if the Soviet Union was to act as intermediary in peace negotiations was to prevent its entry into the Asian war and ensure that it was favorably disposed toward Japan. Thus preliminary contacts with the Russians began.

Around the same time, Yoshida, in league with Konoe, was making his own peace overtures. Yoshida and Konoe alike were inspired by the fear that unless the war ended soon Japan would be forced to change her national polity and would gradually be dragged into communist revolution. Ever since the fall of the Tojo government, senior statesmen had had free access to the emperor. Yoshida, accordingly, was hoping to embody his fears in a memorial to the throne, thereby enlisting the emperor's power in restraining the army and making it possible by the same move to open negotiations for peace. Unfortunately, Yoshida had long been under observation as a man of dangerously pro-Western sympathies. The authorities got wind of what he was up to, and in April, 1945, he was arrested by the military police.

Being on friendly terms with Prime Minister Suzuki and War Minister Anami, Yoshida was not unduly perturbed. The military police in fact handled him with circumspection, though their questioning as such was rigorous. As a result, Yoshida took the whole affair lightly at first, declaring that "a taste of prison life might be an interesting experience."

Hearing of Yoshida's arrest, Hirota's wife Shizuko suggested anxiously that he ought to be got out somehow. "Don't worry," Hirota told her, shaking his head and smiling. "He won't come to much harm. If anything, it'll be a nice medal on his chest." Shizuko looked puzzled, so he added, "Yoshida's got himself a nice little certificate." Just what kind of certificate he meant was to become clear after the end of the war.

In fact, Yoshida's period of detention was unexpectedly prolonged, and after two weeks at the Military Police Headquarters at Kudan, he was transferred to the army jail in Yoyogi. Here he found himself free from questioning, in relatively clean surroundings and able to have food sent in from outside. Thanks to this, he had enough food to share out among the other prisoners and the guards, and became something of a "boss." The only hardship for this proclaimed liberal was the lack of personal freedom.

Hirota's home in Harajuku was only a stone's throw from the prison holding Yoshida. The raids on Tokyo were getting fiercer, and more and more of Hirota's acquaintances were taking refuge in the country. Hirota, however, stayed in Harajuku, and seemed reluctant even to go down to Kugenuma. When friends urged him to get out of Tokyo, he would often reply, "Ordinary people are hanging on in Tokyo; the emperor himself hasn't taken refuge anywhere, so how could I, as one of his former ministers, leave?"

He left his pictures, furniture, and personal belongings where they were. To fellow members of his neighborhood association, however, he would say, "Anybody who can get out should do so as soon as possible." He also advised them that once an air raid started they should take care of themselves first. There was no use, he said, in trying to fight the fires by bucket relays as the authorities urged.

In the great raid of May 25, Hirota's house was itself swallowed up in a sea of flames. He escaped with only what he stood up in, and took refuge in the Outer Garden of the Meiji Shrine, where he found huge crowds of people similarly driven there by the flames. Oddly enough, among them was Yoshida, who had arrived there from the army jail with a military policeman still in attendance. The two men, of course, did not meet. Both separately watched the capital going up in flames, standing there jostled by the throng of refugees, dodging the falling sparks and choking on billows of smoke, unaware of each other's presence.

One week after the night of the great raid, Hirota appeared at an acquaintance's villa in Gora, a hot-spring resort. He had been burned out, he announced, and had come to ask for shelter. Soviet Ambassador Malik happened to be staying close by at the Gora Hotel, and Hirota took the opportunity when he went out for a walk to drop in and pay his respects. The next day, Malik invited Hirota to dinner. . . .

The whole thing, of course, had been planned, but to all outward appearances the Hirota-Malik talks began in the most casual manner. There were two further sessions at the end of June. Hirota expressed Japan's strong desire for an improvement in Soviet-Japanese relations, and even tried to persuade the other man by suggesting concrete conditions such as the neutralization of Manchukuo, the annulment of fishing rights, and the supply of Soviet oil to Japan. It was just around this time, however, that the Soviet government leaders finally determined to declare war on Japan. There was no response from the Soviet side, and despite repeated urging from Hirota the talks were discontinued.

Togo, therefore, proposed that Konoe should be sent as special envoy to the Soviet Union, but once again the Soviet side refused on the grounds that the nature of the mission was vague. Shortly after this the Soviet Union came into the war. And eventually, with Japan's acceptance of the Potsdam Declaration, all hostilities came to an end.

The decision to end the war was made on August 10. On that day, Hirota, among other senior statesmen, had an audience with the emperor in which he expressed his views, and from around that time a threatening atmosphere enveloped his house in Kugenuma. Radical army elements were reportedly planning to attack his home because he had taken part in the moves for peace. The guard on his house increased to nearly ten policemen and detectives, but there were rumors that they too included possible radical elements. Someone was said to have been seen walking in the vicinity with a machine gun, and a gun was in fact found hidden in the pine grove. A navy plane circled Hirota's house not long after this. It flew over the house at a low altitude with a terrifying roar, and shortly afterward a machine-gun bullet was found embedded in a post on the second floor.

Increasing numbers of people had taken refuge here from the cities, and houses were springing up all around. Hirota's residence no longer stood in isolation among the pines, and he was urged by the police to move somewhere else if possible so as to avoid bringing trouble on his neighbors. With his home in Harajuku burned to the ground, there was nowhere to go. Finally, however, he located an acquaintance in Nerima, in Tokyo, and got him to put them up.

Lack of a truck to carry their belongings threatened to hold up the move, but the local firemen came to the rescue. The neighborhood was only too glad to see the last of this bird of ill omen. Thus Hirota and his family promptly boarded the firemen's truck together with a few necessary belongings and set off for Tokyo. Whenever they passed an army vehicle on the way, the other members of the family shrank back and urged him to hide his face. But Hirota remained unperturbed, and sat gazing around at the interminable procession of burned-out ruins.

 **IX**

The end of the war brought down a chill blast of change on the heads of Japan's long-time leaders. On September 11, an order was issued for the arrest of thirty-nine individuals suspected of war crimes, including Prime Minister Tojo, members of his government, and others.

Tojo attempted suicide with a pistol, failed, and was admitted to a U.S. army field hospital. On the twelfth, Hirota's old adversary, former war minister Sugiyama, killed himself by pumping four pistol bullets into his chest. He was followed by former welfare minister Koizumi, who committed hara-kiri, and former education minister Hashida Kunihiko, who poisoned himself. No one had any idea how far the net was likely to be cast, and whether it would affect the emperor himself or not. SCAP's next moves were awaited with undisguised anxiety.

Amidst all this there was one man who embarked on a new burst of activity, like a fish returned to water: Yoshida Shigeru, now armed with the "certificate" conferred on him by detention by the military police. In mid-September, Foreign Minister Shigemitsu was declared to be unsuitable as a member of the Higashikuni government that had come into power to tide over the immediate postwar period, and Yoshida took over the office. Under the Occupation, the post of foreign minister offered the greatest promise of power, since it brought its holder into direct contact with SCAP.

The ordinary Japanese at the time had difficulty in finding enough food to keep them going, and fears were even expressed that the whole nation might starve to death. But Yoshida invariably went to meet MacArthur with one of the expensive cigars he had saved throughout the war stuck in his mouth; the smoke that enveloped the general was Yoshida's own aristocratic gesture toward another man of aristocratic bent. He was soon given free access to MacArthur without the intermediacy of any underlings, and found himself almost overnight the most powerful figure in the postwar political world.

Within twenty days of Yoshida's becoming foreign minister, the Higashikuni government resigned. As next prime minister, mention was made of Konoe, Kido, or possibly Yoshida, but Yoshida himself strongly recommended Shidehara Kijuro. Yoshida, in fact, had foreseen this day even before the end of the war. In June, on ending his forty days in jail, he had hunted up Shidehara, who was living on a farm by the Tamagawa River, and had maintained contact ever since. The name of "Baron Shidehara" was already familiar to the American and British leaders. As Yoshida saw it, to push this venerable exponent of peace and conciliation to the fore was necessary for Japan's future international reputation—and for his own reputation as well.

As a diplomat, Yoshida had tended to criticize Shidehara for weakness in his foreign policies; he himself had advocated a positive policy toward Manchuria, and had gone along with Tanaka Giichi's armed diplomacy. Now, however, by bringing out Shidehara in this way, he successfully erased his own former image and replaced it with one of himself as the perfect heir to Shidehara and the apostle of a pro-Western, peaceful foreign policy. Shidehara was seventy-three by now and growing decrepit, with shaking hands. Since the end of the war he had had few visitors and, partly out of sheer loneliness, was considering retiring to Kamakura. He accepted the premiership. The appearance of extreme old age which he gave caused some consternation at SCAP, while many Japanese were astonished, even, to find that he was still alive.

The two men worked as a pair, playing the main role now that the military had collapsed. Yoshida was relatively young and vigorous; even Shidehara seemed to recover some of his own energy under the younger man's influence. He also became head of the former War and Navy Ministries—which at MacArthur's order had become the

First and Second Demobilization Ministries—in order to look after the welfare of demobilized servicemen.

On November 19, Generals Araki, Matsui, Koiso and eight others were officially named as war criminals. The list included the name of one man described as a former secretary of the Black Dragon Society. It seemed obvious that in America and Britain the designation of this group carried unexpectedly sinister overtones suggestive of a bellicose, ultrarightist organization. Although MacArthur himself knew nothing of the May 15 or February 26 incidents, he remembered the name "Black Dragon." At a meeting with Konoe, he confounded the latter by inquiring what the Black Dragon Society—which even in wartime had carried little weight in Japan—was doing nowadays. The Genyosha, with which Hirota had been associated, was another organization related to the Black Dragon Society.

Also on the list were the names of former foreign minister Matsuoka and former ambassador to Italy Shiratori, who had been responsible for swinging the Foreign Ministry to the right. On December 2, another order was issued, for the arrest of Prince Nashimoto and fifty-eight other suspected war criminals. Hirota was among them. The list, which also included former prime minister Hiranuma, was far-ranging, extending to lawyers and leaders of the business world. The arrest of Prince Nashimoto was apparently occasioned by his having been chief priest of the Grand Shrines of Ise.

The criteria determining which men should be singled out as war criminals were beyond the comprehension of the Japanese. Those so designated would search around for possible reasons, which they then found convincing or unconvincing as the case might be. When he heard that he was on the list, Hirota merely nodded and said nothing. A cold had proved stubborn and his heart was a little weak, so that the notification found him—unusually, for him—in bed at his temporary residence in Nerima. He was supposed to present himself to the Occupation authorities by December 12, so he applied to have the date deferred.

Four days after the announcement, orders were issued for the arrest of another nine men, including Konoe and Kido. Early on the morning of the sixteenth, when he was due to surrender himself, Konoe, finding it "intolerable that I should be tried as a war criminal in an American court," committed suicide by poisoning. Hirota showed unusual signs of emotion on hearing of this further suicide; he seemed to be uncertain as to how Konoe's death should be seen in relation to the war crimes trials about to begin.

The New Year brought no relief from the prevailing somber mood. On January 15, 1946, Hirota left for Sugamo prison. That morning, he and Shizuko worshiped together before the family Buddhist altar, then he held her briefly in his arms. "I shall go with my mind at peace," he said before leaving the house to board a police car that had come to fetch him. "But don't assume things are going to be easy."

An endless succession of bomb sites still pitted with craters, then the grimy gray walls of Sugamo prison loomed ahead. Once inside, he was made to strip and don a shapeless white garment. Photographs and fingerprints were taken. Next, an American army doctor measured his height and weight and subjected him to a rigorous inspection extending from nose and ears to the genitals and rectum. Finally, he was given shots against infectious diseases and sprayed all over with DDT powder.

A guard took him along innumerable corridors until they reached a distant block, where he was put in one of a row of cells whose iron doors lined the passageway. Generals Araki and Mazaki were in the same block, and so were a number of B- and C-class war criminals, officers and NCOs accused of crimes such as the maltreatment of prisoners. Hirota's own cellmate was a former colonel who had been commandant of a POW camp in Osaka. The three walls were of grubby concrete, and the cell was bitterly cold at night.

Life in Sugamo was to begin every day at six for Hirota, though the guards were sometimes as much as twenty minutes late in coming to rouse the prisoners. They would go round the cells switching on the lights and calling in loud voices. The prisoners rose, washed at the basins in the cells, then swept the cells and polished the metalwork with brass polish. There followed a brief free period during which some did *zazen*, others did exercises, and Hirota did his "judo dance."

Breakfast at 7:30 was heralded by the guards calling "Chow!" and opening the cell doors. Many of the guards were under twenty and rough in their language and behavior. The prisoners—prince and minister, general and NCO, all together—lined up in front of their cells holding their food trays. Four or five of them at a time would be detailed to serve the food. They used large ladles to dish it out into each man's aluminum tray. After the meal, they would line up again with their trays and march to the canteen, where they washed them.

There followed a free period during which many of them read newspapers, magazines, and books, or, if they were sharing a cell, played *go*, *shogi*, or cards. Hirota occupied himself reading Buddhist works or Chinese classics. Sometimes, he would watch others playing *go*, but never once joined in. In the afternoon, the prisoners took their exercise. They were divided into a number of groups, all of which followed the same course. Conversation was unrestricted, and once every three days they were allowed to take a bath in groups of two or three.

Hirota came across many old acquaintances. Among them, he found almost all of those who in the past had been chiefly responsible for thwarting his plans or causing him unpleasantness in one way or another. At first, the other man would often demand in surprise, "What on earth are *you* doing here?" Obliged to answer something, Hirota would say, "I'm not sure myself. I wonder if it might be my connections with the Genyosha."

He was aware that an old friend, businessman Shindo Kazuma, had been arrested simply because he was nominally head of the Genyosha. Hirota himself, however, was not a formal member of the organization. Moreover, by the time that the young Hirota had begun to frequent its judo hall, the Genyosha had already ceased to be a political organization and had turned into a body devoted to moral education, occupied with such activities as teaching judo to local children and erecting memorials to local sons who had distinguished themselves in the service of the country. Furthermore, since Shindo had become president, its chief activities had been giving classes in Chinese and Malay or looking after students who came to Japan from various other parts of Asia.

Among the general public, however, the name Genyosha still had strong associations with the political society with radically nationalistic leanings that had once perpetrated such outrages as the bomb attack on Meiji statesman Okuma Shigenobu. Moreover, the Black Dragon Society—which had attracted even MacArthur's attention —was first formed by a member of the Genyosha; although its administration was separate from that of the latter, the two were sister organizations in the public mind. Hirota, of course, had no connection whatsoever with the Black Dragon Society. But it seemed as though the prosecutors were going to fall in with the popular misconception and cast suspicion on him. . . .

As Hirota had told his wife at their parting, he did not imagine the trial would go easily for him. Even when people said, "There must be some mistake. I'm sure you'll be out in no time," he would dismiss it with an uninterested "We shall see." He kept himself to himself, replying when spoken to but never addressing anyone of his own accord.

Matsuoka, who had been named as a war criminal before Hirota, entered prison somewhat later than him on account of illness. He was a shadow of his former self—pale and drawn, and unsteady on his feet. Even when they went out to take exercise, he would often do no more than squat still on the ground. On their daily walk, some of the prisoners would stride along with shoulders back, still in their military uniforms; quite a few others would drift about vaguely, with downcast countenance. Some were jocular, some glum and silent, some full of complaints. And all the while they were repeating their daily routine, the B- and C-class prisoners were going off, first one then another, to be executed.

The prosecuting team had finally arrived—a party of nearly forty, including secretaries, headed by Joseph B. Keenan, a ruddy-faced, sturdy man—and preliminary hearings had begun for the A-class criminals also. The attitude of the prosecutors was courteous. The content of their questions seemed in many cases naïve and hard to grasp, almost as though they themselves were seeking advice. As a result, the optimistic view gained ground that Tojo would probably be the only one to receive a death sentence.

This, however, was a deliberate trap set by the prosecutors. The nineteen-member group included not only men such as Keenan with careers as public prosecutors, but others who were associated with the FBI. The chief and vice-chief respectively of the prosecuting team's research division were both FBI veterans. They had decided that during the hearings they would employ FBI methods such as instilling a sense of superiority in the accused so as to trip them up, or planting spies among them or others close to them. As they saw it, a war crime was essentially the same as a murder case: crime was crime, and the same attitude toward it would do in either case. Their experience with Chicago gangs, the Mafia, and so on gave them confidence that they could deal equally well with Japan's "international political gangsters."

When they actually set to work, however, they found that they were dealing with a very different breed of men. Lacking preliminary background knowledge not only of Japanese history but even of the Japanese political structure, they could not help most of their questions being naïve, whether intentionally so or not. In the end, they often found themselves asking the defendants for information.

They were obliged, of course, to seek something to go on in pinning suspicion on the accused, since this was their job. In finding it, any casual train of thought, any snippet of information garnered from any source would do. In Hirota's own case, he was—as he had expected—first questioned persistently about the Genyosha. Even the fact that his wife Shizuko was the daughter of one of the Genyosha's more ardent patriots suggested, in the eyes of the prosecutors, something more than a mere human relationship. They also accused him insistently of being "a secret member of the Black Dragon Society." They similarly picked on the fact that Hirota had been asked, following Toyama Mitsuru's death, to serve as head of the funeral committee. According to Western thinking, it seemed, the man who served in such a role was obviously one of the deceased's chief spiritual heirs.

Toyama had been an older man from the same city, and Hirota, ever since his days at the First Higher School, had occasionally visited him to ask advice about his own future. The acquaintance had persisted on a fairly personal basis. Toyama, however, had never forced his own views on Hirota, nor had Hirota ever sought his advice concerning affairs of state; their relationship had been, quite simply, that of old acquaintances.

It was true that all kinds of people would turn up at Hirota's house bearing Toyama's outsize visiting card by way of introduction. For Toyama's sake, Hirota would at least meet them, but Toyama—a typical touch—would invariably have inscribed on the back of the card "one minute," or "three minutes," as an indication of how long the interview should last, and nothing more was ever required.

Hirota's agreeing to serve as chairman of the funeral committee was motivated simply by a feeling that he had been asked in his capacity as former prime minister, and that to assume the duty was a natural mark of respect toward an older man and long-standing acquaintance from his own home town. It was quite unconnected with any political affiliations.

"We have investigated all kinds of other people, but none of them seems likely to have been responsible for the war," he was told at one stage. "We begin to suspect it was you who were managing everybody from behind the scenes." The prosecutors, it seemed—in whose own countries the politician always took priority; the army being directed and controlled by civilian officials—simply could not understand a system under which the military, in the name of the independence of the supreme command, could take things into their own hands and drag politics and foreign policy in their wake.

To this kind of question, Hirota always replied with a minimal "Yes" or "No." Not only did it seem useless to try to explain, but he sensed the danger of letting too much slip if he talked. He invariably responded with the utmost calm, aware that the prosecutors were spreading a net for him.

Not all of the prosecutors' queries, of course, were wide of the mark. Occasionally they put questions that startled him by their appositeness, probing him concerning matters of which they should have had no knowledge. Hirota, however, had some inkling of what lay behind this. Late the preceding year a strategic bombing survey team had come from America and summoned for questioning Konoe and more than 150 other important figures from all walks of life. When Hirota himself was questioned, he had had the impression that people before him had already talked in detail concerning the secrets of Japanese politics and diplomacy; he was shocked at times by the team's knowledge of matters with which only senior statesmen had been acquainted.

Throughout his interrogation, Hirota used words sparingly and cautiously. He had no intention at this stage of changing his long-held philosophy of "never actively seeking to advance himself," even though the trial was one that could well mean life or death to him. When a man talks a lot, an element of self-justification invariably creeps in, and the result is invariably disadvantageous to somebody else. Knowing that the investigators were lying in wait for precisely this, Hirota decided that he himself would say nothing at all.

One might argue that there is always value in bringing the truth to light at a trial, but it was very doubtful whether the military tribunal as such could be called a "trial." "Trial" implies appeal to the law; yet no law stated that war in itself was a crime. A trial where there was no law was no longer a trial, but a form of "politics"; if so, there was even less reason for him to talk.

The prosecutors had a difficult time with Hirota. Chief Prosecutor Keenan's second-in-command, Nathan, reported to the effect that, if given an intelligence test, Japan's "international political gangsters" would, with two exceptions, prove inferior to American gangsters. With those two exceptions, they had all fallen foul of the prosecutors' leading questions. Asked who these two formidable individuals were, Nathan replied, "Tojo and Hirota. Neither of them has kept a diary. A diary assumes continuity; the man who is prepared to die does not keep one. Neither of them will tell you anything unless you ask him, which means that unless one knows what it is they're hiding it's impossible to get it out of them."

It was understandable that Tojo should have been resigned to death and difficult to handle. But why should it have been so with Hirota? Keenan was at a loss. So far as he was concerned, there seemed to be no reason why Hirota should more or less ask for the death penalty, nor did he know enough about Oriental psychology to understand Hirota's philosophy of "selflessness."

The prosecutors were fairly rigorous in their questioning of suspects who had not yet been arrested. Those who remained free were inclined to cooperate with the prosecutors, out of fear that they might otherwise be arrested themselves. There were some, in fact, who voluntarily became informers and spies. Major General Tanaka Ryukichi, a staff officer of the defunct Kwantung Army, was one of them. The prosecutors were also supplied with information by war crimes suspects already in Sugamo. The prime example here was Kido Koichi's diary: extending from January 1,1930, to December 15, 1945, it provided a concise and painstaking account of the events of every single day of the period of Kido's career from the time when he first gained access to the court as chief secretary to the lord privy seal, through his period as a minister in the Konoe cabinet, and on through his own term as lord privy seal. Whereas the imperial household minister was, in a sense, no more than a kind of secretary-general to the imperial family, the lord privy seal was adviser and assistant to the emperor on affairs of state. He was both witness to and agent of imperial government, and his actual influence was such that eighty percent of the decision concerning who should be next prime minister was attributed to the lord privy seal's views.

Written as it was by a man in such a position, the diary spotlighted the process whereby decisions concerning matters of highest policy were made at the palace, as well as providing a record of the behavior of important figures who attended meetings there. At first, Kido had been in two minds whether he should submit it to the Occupation authorities or not. What finally persuaded him was word from an acquaintance well versed in GHQ affairs, reporting the American view that, even if Kido took the blame and was convicted, there was no guarantee that the emperor would be absolved, whereas if Kido was pronounced innocent, the emperor would be pronounced innocent also. In his diary Kido saw the emperor essentially as a pacifist, and presented a picture of himself, too, as a man who despite a certain amount of sidetracking had behaved by and large as a peacemaker in line with the emperor's wishes (a diary, moreover, is rarely written in a way that would be disadvantageous to its author). The idea that this lengthy diary might serve as proof not only of his own but of the emperor's innocence made the gamble a tempting one for its author.

One thing at least was certain about the gamble: the diary would provide a vital point of departure for the prosecutors, who were perplexed as to where to begin looking for proof of responsibility for the war. That in itself would doubtless tend to dispose the prosecution in Kido's favor. In submitting the diary, however, Kido made no hint of any possible quid pro quo—a fact which drew admiring comments on his wisdom from the investigators, and was to prove a valuable invisible asset later.

Kido, who was brought to the prison in a car normally reserved for the imperial family, was from the outset an isolated figure among the war criminals. Indeed, a man who had been born the grandson of Kido Takayoshi—who was partly responsible for the restoration of the emperor in 1868—and had served as steward to the imperial family must have felt more affinity with the emperor himself than with the men he found about him now. Five days before going to jail, Kido had in fact been invited to dinner by the emperor. He had at first declined on the grounds that he was under suspicion as a war criminal, but the emperor commented, "In American eyes he may be a criminal, but here he is a devoted servant of his country. If he is reluctant to come, have the food sent to him." Much moved, Kido presented himself at the palace and dined with His Majesty. In the course of the meal, the emperor offered his sympathy over Kido's present position and told him to take care of his health. "Now that we have talked together," he said, "and you are fully acquainted with how I feel, I hope you will explain my position in detail." To mark the occasion, he gave Kido an inkstone that he had used in signing official documents, and the empress gave him some cakes that she had made herself.

Between this aristocrat par excellence and Hirota, "the man in an ordinary suit," there had been no personal contact. Yoshida Shigeru had been a frequent visitor at the Kidos', partly because of his family connections with Makino Nobuaki, but Hirota's character would have deterred him from visiting Kido of his own accord. Their one connection was a friend of Kido's, a member of the House of Peers, who lived next door to Hirota and often talked to Kido about him. On one occasion, he reported a remark by Hirota to the effect that since Kido, as lord privy seal, had been in charge of the imperial seal, he could at least have refrained from setting it on the imperial declaration of war. Kido—the friend reported back to Hirota—had indignantly rejected the possibility of such an impropriety. When Hirota suggested that the lord privy seal's responsibilities were too much for one man and that he should be backed up by a body of advisers drawn from among other ministers and elder statesmen, Kido demanded to know—again via an intermediary—whether he was proposing a vote of non-confidence in the lord privy seal and his men.

For reasons such as these, Kido had tended to shun Hirota during the latter part of Hirota's life. It followed naturally that Hirota could hardly look to the Kido diary for shades of meaning likely to be favorable to himself. (Later, the diary was presented in court as testimony concerning the views of the senior statesmen as submitted to the emperor in the period leading to the outbreak of war. Although it contained careful summaries of the views of the various men concerned, the first half of Hirota's statement—to the effect that America had no intention of going to war with Japan over the China question—was not recorded. The omission was, for Hirota, a rather serious one, but when he taxed Kido with it the latter told him to tell the court himself on the witness stand. It was already clear, however, that Hirota had no intention of testifying in person.)

Kido was a small man of unprepossessing appearance, with round spectacles, but there was something forbidding about his expression; this, together with an ability to hide what he was really thinking, led to his being generally regarded as a man to be wary of, and he was nicknamed "little badger"—the same nickname as was later given to Foreign Minister Togo. The even tenor of the war criminals' life was beginning to be disturbed. Where at first they had been linked by the common experience of sudden imprisonment, the progress of the trials was to give rise to suspicion and wariness.

Toward the end of February, the general outlines of the International Military Tribunal for the Far East finally became clear. The judges represented eleven different countries, and MacArthur appointed Sir William Webb to head them as president of the tribunal. A judge from a provincial court in Australia, he was an old acquaintance of MacArthur's, and had been investigating cases of atrocities by Japanese forces on the island of New Britain. Where the site of the trials was concerned, work was going on day and night to refurbish the assembly hall of the former Military Academy at Ichigaya, which had been selected for the purpose.

The war criminal suspects, via personal connections, now set about finding lawyers to represent them. Hirota, however, insisted that he did not want one. It was only when people pointed out that this would make any proper trial impossible and cause trouble to others that he finally agreed. A lawyer called Hanai Tadashi, who was impressed by Hirota's character as a man, offered to represent him. Two lawyers connected with the Foreign Ministry, named Ando and Morishima, were also appointed. Morishima, like Hirota, came from Fukuoka; their homes were close, and Morishima's elder brother had been with Hirota at middle school, higher school and college. Morishima had served in the Foreign Ministry as minister to the Soviet Union among other posts, and had been one of Hirota's most trusted subordinates.

"This trial may well mark a new start for Japanese society," he told Hirota when he accepted the case. "I intend to unmask the military and make it clear that the Foreign Ministry was in the right, even though it may have been weak. That would be the main line of my defense. Will you leave things to me?"

Hirota nodded. "I'm sure it will be important to use Foreign Ministry sources in getting at the facts, so please work on that," he said. Then he added, "Don't ask me to speak out for myself, though. If I talk, I'll be obliged to say who insisted on this and who did that, which will just play into their hands. Their aim is to get us to accuse each other, and I'm not having any of it."

If he was halfhearted about his defense, it was not because he was optimistic about the outcome of the trial. The prospects, in fact, suggested the reverse. The further the hearings proceeded, the more the truth of his warning to Shizuko against easy optimism was brought home to him. Time and again, the prosecution put the same question to him: "We have investigated a lot of military men, but none of them seems to fill the bill. Who do *you* think was the central figure?" Several times, too, they posed the rhetorical question, "Do you mean to say that a war on this scale was entirely the responsibility of the military?" Hirota sensed that the prosecution was looking for someone on the civilian side to take the blame, and that the arrow of vengeance was pointed at himself, a former prime minister who had served three terms as foreign minister. Hiranuma was also a civilian who had once been prime minister, but though he was, ideologically speaking, a fairly militant nationalist, his term of office had lasted only eight months, and he had never served as foreign minister.

One other major figure on the civilian side who came in for attention was Kido. Both Hirota and Kido felt that with their own persons they should defend the emperor against involvement. However, where Kido believed that proof of his own innocence would show that the emperor, too, was innocent, and voluntarily submitted his own diary to the tribunal, Hirota's idea was to absolve the emperor of responsibility by taking it on himself and being judged guilty.

"It seems I'll have to resign myself to being a 'central figure,' " he muttered with a rueful smile to family members who came to visit him. "All the people who matter have done away with themselves, you see. Irresponsible crowd!" Then he added, almost as though he were talking of a stranger, "If someone on the civilian side has to be killed as a result of this trial, it looks as though I shall have to fill the role."

On April 13, Prince Nashimoto and Goko Kiyoshi (former president of Mitsubishi Heavy Industries) were released from Sugamo. With his upcurling moustache, the wooden clogs that he wore with a Western suit, and his habit of addressing all and sundry—"I've just been representing the imperial family. Some representative!"—the prince won considerable popularity with the mass media. His release inspired hopes that it would be followed by others. What happened in practice was just the reverse.

The next day, the Soviet judges and prosecutors made a belated arrival, and the suspects were obliged to undergo a rigorous examination all over again. The outcome, moreover, was that former foreign minister Shigemitsu and General Umezu were sent to Sugamo. The date was Monday, April 29—the emperor's birthday. It was an ill-omened day for Shigemitsu: it was on the same day, fourteen years earlier, that he had lost a leg in a terrorist attack in Shanghai.

Following the usual thorough physical examination, Shigemitsu, covered all over with DDT powder, limped through the prison corridors on his one leg. He was shown to a shared cell on the third floor of Block 4, and the iron door slammed shut behind him. The other occupant of his cell was a sergeant major accused of maltreating prisoners. The footsteps of the patrolling guard receded into the distance. The air was dank and chill. Someone came along the corridor, and the footsteps halted momentarily outside the door. "Shigemitsu, Shigemitsu!" came a voice. Shigemitsu gave a start of recognition. "It's me, Hirota. See you again later." The footsteps receded into the distance again. Hirota must have been on his way back from his walk. The encounter was a small thing, yet it helped lift Shigemitsu out of his depression.

After the evening meal, the A-class war criminals, including Shigemitsu, were assembled in a room in the basement. A military police officer called their names in alphabetical order, and handed to each a large envelope containing a statement of the charges against him. The number of those charged was twenty-eight. In the first category, "crimes against peace," the counts against them included conspiring to wage, planning, preparing for, initiating, and waging a war of aggression—thirty-six counts in all.

The second category, "crimes of murder and conspiracy to murder," included counts thirty-seven to fifty-two, which treated the attack on Pearl Harbor and other activities immediately preceding the declaration of war, together with the slaughter of ordinary

238

civilians, as acts of murder.

The third category, covering counts fifty-three to fifty-five, included "other conventional war crimes and crimes against humanity." Of the fifty-five counts, forty-eight were considered to apply to Hirota.

Even though they were resigned to whatever might come, the accused were taken aback by the charge of "conspiracy." Twenty-five of the charges were considered to apply to all the defendants, and in most of them the word "conspiracy" occurred. The impression it gave was that all the accused had got together, of one accord and on frequent occasions, to arrange everything from the planning of a war of aggression to the murder of ordinary civilians.

Some of the accused were not so much angry as wryly amused at this gross "overestimation" of Japan. In the case of Nazi Germany, one could no doubt speak of a "unified national purpose and organization," and of conspiracy both in the pursuit of the war and the murder of the Jews. But in Japan's case the military had taken things into their own hands in the name of the independence of the supreme command, manipulating foreign policy and domestic government at will, and sometimes even ignoring them completely. Even within the military, the army and navy were frequently at loggerheads; so, within the army itself, were the General Staff Office and the War Ministry. There had been plenty of conferences—cabinet meetings, liaison conferences, imperial conferences, and so on—but the emphasis had always been less on any definite "conspiracy" than on attempts to settle differences of opinion on a makeshift basis (though it still remains true, of course, that the net result was in fact a war of aggression). Even more was it inconceivable that civilian ministers should have "conspired" to commit atrocities at the front.

It was announced that hearings would start on May 3. In accordance with British and American legal practice, the proceedings were to begin with the defendants' pleas of "guilty" or "not guilty." When Hirota's lawyer Hanai told him to reply "not guilty"—a necessary step if he was to have any case to discuss—Hirota shook his head. "I do have responsibility where the war is concerned," he said. "You couldn't call me 'innocent.' " However much Hanai insisted that it was purely a formality, Hirota still objected; if it was absolutely necessary, Hanai must do it for him.

"But," argued Hanai, "this is something the accused has to answer to himself. His counsel can't do it for him."

"Surely it can be managed somehow?"

"You'll have to say it; it doesn't take a moment."

Hirota was at a loss. He was unwilling to pronounce the words "not guilty," even as a pure formality. Nor was this in any sense a pose. He keenly felt his own responsibility in failing to prevent the war, whatever mitigating circumstances there might have been. In that respect, he was clearly to blame. He had come to feel increasingly strongly, moreover, that by being shown guilty he could fulfill the task still remaining to him. Repeatedly, Hanai pressed his point, but Hirota merely muttered obstinately and refused to give his assent.

On Friday, May 3, the courtroom in Ichigaya was ablaze with arc lights; President Webb even joked that it would be hard to find anywhere so bright outside Hollywood. For the Japanese reporters and public present, many of whom were still living in temporary shacks or air-raid shelters, with no electric light at night because of power cuts, the brightness was painfully dazzling. For the defendants, it was a punishment in itself.

The flags of eleven countries formed a backdrop for the judges. The defendants sat in two rows facing the judges, with counsel and clerks in between. Hirota sat in the front row, somewhat to the right facing the bench, amongst generals such as Doihara, Hata, and Minami. Most of the accused were in military uniform or wartime civilian garb (*kokuminfuku*), but Hirota wore a suit. His face was rather drawn, but his expression was impassive.

Of all the defendants, it was Matsuoka Yosuke whose appearance was most pitiful. His face was ashen and puffy beneath his shaven head, his eyes were sunken, and his stooping frame, clothed in drab *kokuminfuku*, was supported with difficulty by a bamboo stick. Another who attracted attention was ultranationalist Okawa Shumei. An odd figure in light blue pajamas with wooden clogs on his bare feet, he could not sit still and was constantly either pressing his hands together as though in prayer, muttering to himself, or playing practical jokes on the other defendants.

After President Webb's opening address, the court adjourned until the afternoon, when the prosecution read the charges. In the course of the reading Okawa twice slapped Tojo, who was sitting in front of him, on his bald head, and was ordered to leave the courtroom. Those present looked with disapproval at such grossly irrational behavior in a man known for his vehement nationalism (Okawa was subsequently sent for psychological tests, and was diagnosed as a case of "psychosis with syphilitic meningo-encephalitis." He was treated at various hospitals until finally, in April, 1947, he was pronounced unfit to stand trial despite rumors that his symptoms were feigned).

May 4 was also devoted to reading the charges. On the sixth came the arraignments. Just before this, Kiyose Ichiro, second-in-command of the defense, moved that President Webb should be challenged on the grounds that he had worked uncovering Japanese army atrocities during the war, and that a man responsible for investigating a case should not also sit in judgment on it.

There was uproar in the courtroom; Webb was furious, the chief of counsel tried hastily to seize the microphone from the stand, and proceedings were temporarily suspended. When the court reopened, the motion—without reason, again, as befitted a political trial—was rejected. Webb returned to his seat, and the court proceeded to hear the arraignments. A number of army men gave their reply of "not guilty" in a casual voice, others spoke in contemptuous or ringing tones; some of the accused replied politely, some barely audibly, others as though it were a matter of indifference to them. Matsuoka alone replied in English, haltingly and in a hoarse voice: "I plead . . . not guilty . . . on each . . . and every account." It was a typical last gesture from a man who was conscious, even at his last gasp, of the eyes of the world upon him.

Hirota allayed the fears of his counsel by replying simply and calmly "not guilty." All the defendants had made their pleas within nine minutes, and the stage was set for the legal struggle proper.

All this while, the Japanese government led by Yoshida and Shidehara had been paying scarcely any attention either to the war criminals in Sugamo or to the proceedings at Ichigaya. One reason was that the wave of purges from public office initiated by SCAP left politicians and bureaucrats little time to think about anything else. Another was the pressing need to find some way out of the food crisis. Shidehara personally, moreover, was facing the major task of drawing up the draft of a new Constitution.

It was decided that the aim of this draft should be an ideal Constitution founded on a firmly democratic and pacific basis, and that Japan's relinquishment of the right to arm herself should be set down clearly in writing. This was partly a result of a recommendation from MacArthur, but it accorded well with the personal feelings of Shidehara, who had suffered so long from the high-handed ways of the army. Shidehara repeatedly stated that the clause renouncing war represented his own conviction. "Halfhearted armament is as good as none," he declared on one occasion. "Provided the nation acts in the belief that it is in the right, it has nothing to fear even if it goes without weapon in hand."

At last he could proclaim, for all to hear, his underlying belief that a peaceful foreign policy was the only possible one for Japan. Unfortunately, however, Shidehara was in a position to do no more than draw up the first draft. His government was essentially suprapartisan and transitional; the Constitution was to be enacted and put into effect by a new government based on a parliamentary majority elected by the people.

At the general election held on April 10, the Liberal party won 141 seats, the Progressive party 94, and the Socialists 93. Thus the Shidehara government, which had come into being in order to supervise the holding of elections, might seem to have fulfilled its function. Shidehara, however, refused to relinquish office on the grounds that there was no stable political force commanding an absolute majority. He set to work to persuade the Progressive party and others to join forces with the government, thereby incurring violent opposition from the remaining parties.

It had always been Shidehara's rule to stay outside politics, but now he found himself faced with the necessity of joining a party if he was to lead a government in this new age of parliamentary politics. Many people had been surprised to learn that Shidehara was still alive, yet once he became prime minister he showed a vigor and toughness that belied his age. Throwing overboard his cherished convictions, he moved to join the Progressive party, and the Progressives, whose fortunes were flagging at the time, took him in as their president. However, there was so much criticism within the party at this move that on April 22 he and his government submitted their resignation.

It was a period of transition. Many of the elder statesmen who should have chosen the next prime minister were in jail at Sugamo. Shidehara, therefore, set about selecting a candidate from a list of his own which included himself. First of all, he considered a coalition of the Progressive, Liberal, and Socialist parties, but the attempt failed. Next, he put forward other plans, including one for a Liberal-Socialist coalition, but in the end he was obliged to ask the majority party, the Liberal party, to form a government on its own.

On May 3, the same day that the Tokyo trials began, Shidehara called on the emperor and recommended that Hatoyama Ichiro, president of the Liberal party, become the next prime minister. The following day, the emperor was to have summoned Hatoyama and entrusted him with the task of forming a government, but a few hours earlier Hatoyama was purged from public life by SCAP. Hatoyama was indignant, but in the interests of the party went to see Yoshida at the foreign minister's official residence, and asked him to take on the post of president of the Liberal party.

The newly formed political parties had not yet produced any commanding figures. No one knew, moreover, when men who had been in leading positions before the war might be purged. It was difficult even to find a suitable party president. Hatoyama's calculation was that Yoshida, who was virtually Shidehara's vice-premier and was on close terms with MacArthur, would be acceptable as president at such a time.

Yoshida took advantage of this to make Hatoyama agree to a rather demanding set of conditions whereby Hatoyama would take care of all party matters, including finances, leaving cabinet appointments to Yoshida, who would be free to quit whenever he felt like it. Yoshida had always had a taste for politics, and now the path to the premiership lay open before him at last—ten years later than Hirota, his contemporary in the Foreign Ministry. But the path facing Hirota, whose creed had always been to deny self-interest, was one that led, via a political trial, to the scaffold.

While these two so widely contrasting prospects were opening up before the two contemporaries, Matsuoka, two years their senior at the same Foreign Ministry, was drawing close to the end of life's road itself. Conditions in Sugamo had proved too much for a man seriously ill with pulmonary tuberculosis, and his appearances in court had aggravated his state still further. If anything, it was Matsuoka rather than Okawa who required hospitalization, but President Webb ignored the entreaties of his counsel and dragged Matsuoka into court for days on end. Matsuoka grew rapidly more debilitated, and finally it became so obvious that he was dying that, on May 9, he was admitted to the American army hospital at Ryogoku. Despite the gravity of his condition, Matsuoka seemed more himself once he was settled on the hospital bed, and even exchanged jokes in English, in a hoarse voice, with the army doctors.

When the court reconvened on May 13, two figures—the pajama-clad Okawa and Matsuoka in his civilian uniform—were absent from the defendants' dock. On this day, the defense launched a sharp challenge to the judges and the prosecution concerning the court's jurisdiction. Whereas the prosecution had had ample time to prepare its case, with huge numbers of personnel, a huge investigation network, ample funds, and all the authority it needed, the defense was in poor shape. At that time, immediately after the war, it was difficult to muster enough Japanese lawyers, and some of them were obliged to represent two defendants simultaneously. Moreover, having neither investigative personnel nor any authority, they were obliged to rely on tentative personal contacts to find material for their defense. On top of this, they were given inadequate time to prepare their case, and had few funds at their disposal. The Foreign Ministry and those associated with the former War and Navy Ministries did their best to help, but the defendants could not afford to pay their counsel adequate fees.

The American lawyers for the defense were, similarly, an ill-assorted collection of men drummed up out of the Occupation forces, together with others assembled from different parts of the States, and though there were first-rate lawyers among them, there were others who were hopelessly elderly or incompetent. None of them, moreover, was well versed in Japanese affairs or had had time to overcome this disability by study. Despite such unfavorable conditions, there were, nevertheless, a number of lawyers, both American and Japanese, who transcended national boundaries in a valiant fight to secure legal justice.

Right at the outset, counsel Kiyose (representing Tojo and Sato), a short, stocky figure in military boots, raised an objection. Rushing headlong into the fray, banging on his table for emphasis when necessary, he set forth his argument along the following lines: unlike Germany, Japan had surrendered not unconditionally, but conditionally, i.e. in the form of acceptance of the Potsdam Declaration. Although the declaration contained a provision for the punishment of war criminals, the accepted definition of war criminals at the time of the declaration had been those who contravened the rules of war by, for example, maltreating prisoners. It was unreasonable to extend the definition to crimes against peace and humanity, in the same way as with Germany, which had surrendered unconditionally.

The Potsdam Declaration, moreover, was concerned with the termination of the Pacific War, and it was odd to charge people with responsibility for crimes dating back to the Manchurian Incident. When Chief Prosecutor Keenan and Comyns-Carr of England objected to these arguments, defense counsel Blakeney put forward the additional argument that it was inappropriate for a victor to turn plaintiff and pass judgment on the vanquished. He also argued that if the attack on Pearl Harbor was to be considered murder rather than war, the same was surely true of the dropping of atomic bombs on Hiroshima and Nagasaki.

The defense's arguments, in short, concerned the fundamental question of the Far East Military Tribunal's right to pronounce judgments on such matters. Their motions received further support from other defense lawyers on the fourteenth and fifteenth. However, on the morning of the seventeenth, President Webb—again in a manner more appropriate to a political trial—dismissed all the motions outright. They would be notified of the reasons, he said, sometime in the future. No further business was conducted that day, and the court was adjourned until June 3.

That morning, two of Hirota's daughters, who were invariably present in the public gallery on days when the court was in session, had brought their brother Masao with them. Proceedings were over in a bare five minutes, however, and finding themselves at a loose end, they went back to their temporary home in Nerima, where Shizuko, Hirota's wife, was waiting. When they told her that the court was adjourned for over two weeks, she suddenly announced that she was going to Kugenuma. At this stage, prisoners at Sugamo were allowed visitors only once or twice a month, and only one at a time. A few days earlier, after the hearing on the fourteenth, Shizuko had visited the jail and met Hirota there for the first time. Since no further visits would be allowed for some time, and the court too was in recess, there was no point in staying in Nerima. The villa at Kugenuma, which was still shut up with no one to look after it, offered the chance of a brief rest. Since it seemed natural, too, that Shizuko should remember life at the villa with affection, Masao and the rest of the family saw nothing out of the ordinary in their going there.

In fact, though, Shizuko had made up her mind to commit suicide, and had chosen to die, not in their temporary home where she would cause trouble to strangers, but at her own home in Kugenuma that harbored so many memories of life with her husband.

The house at Kugenuma felt desolate and empty. One reason was that a short while earlier all their most valuable belongings had been impounded as the property of a war criminal. The young officials who had come at the time had carried out a thorough check of everything. Then they had said to Masao—whether in disgust or in an attempt at sympathy was not clear—"To think that this is the home of a former prime minister! . . . You should've got your father to leave you a bit more property. Things will be hard going from now on."

Desolate though the house was, however, it was good for Shizuko to be home among her memories. For dinner that evening, she made one of the family's favorites. Her conversation, with her two daughters and Masao and his wife, was more animated than for many a day; she even rejoined them for more talk after her bath instead of going straight to bed.

One of the remarks she made that evening was, "We've always enjoyed life together, so one shouldn't look for anything more, surely?" She also said—cryptically at the time—that there was "one way to set her husband's mind at rest." Something turned the conversation to the suicide of General Nogi and his wife,* then to the wife of former war minister Sugiyama, who had followed her husband into death, and they discussed whether it was better for a wife to die before or after her husband.

"I'd want to die first," she told them quite clearly. And early the following morning they found her, true to her word, dead in bed. There was no farewell note. She was sixty-one years old.

Born into a poor family, daughter of one of the leaders of the Genyosha, Shizuko had never been terrified by the thought of death. She had been troubled by the idea that her husband's association with the Genyosha had been a factor in his arrest. Moreover, the two of them had lived happily as husband and wife right up into old age, and the thought of the man who had made her happy living such a life in Sugamo must have been intolerable to her. The outlook for the trial offered little hope, and she knew that Hirota himself was resigned to death. No doubt she felt that, if she went ahead of him, it would make him a little less reluctant to say good-bye to life if the worst came to the worst. It was the only thing that she, as his wife, could do for him.

Another probable factor was that she had never been very strong, and did not want to be an added burden to their children. As the officials had predicted, the family would almost certainly be facing

*The general who, believing that he had failed in his duty to the emperor during the Russo-Japanese War of 1904–1905, committed suicide upon hearing of Emperor Meiji's death in 1912, thereby following his lord into death and atoning for his earlier error. His suicide was preceded by that of his wife.

247

hard times financially. By themselves, though, the children could probably manage. The eldest boy, Hiroo, had just returned with his family from Peking, where they had been in detention. Two of the girls, who showed no signs of finding husbands yet, were something of a worry, but once the trial had reached some kind of conclusion things would probably be easier. Besides, the youngest boy, Masao, and his wife were with them. . . .

As ambassador's wife, foreign minister's wife, prime minister's wife, Shizuko had always stayed inconspicuous in the background. As she faced death, it would not have been like her to leave anything so pretentious as a farewell note. Her life, true to her name, had been "quiet," and her end was the same.

The death—"of the wife of a former prime minister, from angina pectoris"—was given a discreet two or three lines in the papers. It was not until seven years later that the truth of her suicide was made public.

An American officer informed Hirota, briefly, of what had happened. At first, he reacted to the news with utter despondency, but eventually he pulled himself together. He had already been resigned to saying good-bye to her, and her death had not been entirely unforeseen. Nor was it the first time that he had suffered this kind of shock: his mother Take had virtually starved herself to death, and his second son Tadao had killed himself. Now, it was Shizuko's turn. . . .

On the seventh day after her death, Masao visited Hirota and told him the details. Hirota nodded vigorously as his son spoke, but said not a word. Only at the end, when he heard that Masao and the others were going to take Shizuko's ashes to be laid to rest at the Shofukuji temple in Fukuoka, did he break his silence in order to ask Masao to have the priest decide on a posthumous name for himself at the same time.

The name that was eventually delivered to him, written in the temple priest's hand, consisted of a full eleven Chinese characters suggesting the extraordinary achievements and virtues of the deceased's earthly life. Hirota smiled wryly when he saw it. It was too good for him. . . . But such posthumous names had always been pompous and long-winded; unlike official titles and decorations, they were scarcely worth the trouble of refusing. He resigned himself to the inevitable.

His single gesture against it was that, even after this, the letters that he sent from jail to his family continued to be addressed to Shizuko, and he continued to address her as though she were still alive. To facilitate translation for the censor, Hirota wrote his letters in the simple *katakana* script—which creates much the same effect as writing an English letter in block capitals. Thus even his wife's name became SHIZUKO. For him, she would not really die until there was no one to write SHIZUKO—until, in other words, he died too. In such ways, he refused to draw a clear line between this world and the next.

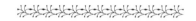 X

Five days after Hirota lost his wife, a new government came into being with Yoshida Shigeru at its head. Former prime minister Shidehara, their senior and mentor, joined the government as a minister of state. The government itself took the form of a coalition with the Progressive party.

Yoshida, as we have seen, had secured an agreement from Hatoyama that the formation of the government should be left to himself while Hatoyama took care of the party. For this reason, although in theory it was a party government, in practice it reflected Yoshida's own taste, with a minimum of party men and a large number of bureaucrats and scholars. Yoshida retained for himself the important post of foreign minister, combining it with that of prime minister. Like its predecessor, the new government was obliged to devote all its energies to attempts to solve the food shortage, and paid no attention whatsoever to the Tokyo trials.

On June 4, Chief Prosecutor Keenan delivered his opening statement, and on the same day Matsuoka Yosuke, whose condition had deteriorated steadily, was transferred at the urgent request of his counsel from the American army hospital to the Department of Internal Medicine of Tokyo University at Sakaguchi, so that he could be close to his family. By now, he had no strength left even for jokes.

On June 11, a typical monsoon day of misty rain, the twenty-six A-class war criminals who remained now that Matsuoka and Okawa had gone were transferred from Block 4 to Block 6. The prosecution had already been in Japan for half a year. After giving his opening address, Keenan returned to the States, partly to take home leave and partly in order to report to the leaders of the American government. At the same time a number of the best American lawyers under him resigned and returned home due to dissatisfaction concerning their salaries and other matters.

Such things had a vaguely unsettling effect on the accused. Rumors went the rounds of Sugamo that Keenan was quitting, and that President Webb was being dismissed. On the fourteenth, the prosecution began reading the details of each defendant's career, and this was followed by an outline of the "conspiracy to wage a war of aggression." On the seventeenth, the first witness took the stand. A major attached to SCAP who had been a teacher of English in Wakayama prefecture before the war, he testified concerning the militaristic education that had produced such a fanatical patriotism and blind subservience to authority in the Japanese.

The hearings proceeded. First, the prosecution would attempt to demonstrate the truth of the charges by producing documentary evidence and witnesses, then counsel for the defense would seek to undermine their evidence by cross-examination. Evidence on militarism in education was followed by evidence on the nationalist movement. A succession of politicians, government officials, writers and journalists, and men associated with the right were summoned and gave evidence. On June 25, former prime minister Shidehara Kijuro took the stand. As a minister of state in the Yoshida government, he was the first serving minister to appear in court. It was many years since Hirota had seen him, but Shidehara scarcely glanced at the seats where the accused sat. In his testimony, Shidehara gave an account of the attack on Prime Minister Hamaguchi at Tokyo Station. The incident had taken place just when Shidehara, as foreign minister, had come to see off Hirota, who was leaving to take up his post as ambassador to the Soviet Union. The scene must have presented itself vividly to Hirota's mind once more; at the time, he had been fifty-two and still in the prime of life. He and Shidehara had parted amidst an atmosphere of turmoil, both of them acutely aware of the dark times that lay ahead. Neither had dreamed that sixteen years later they would reencounter each other as defendant and witness for the prosecution.

Despite his distinguished past and his present position in the government, the fact remained that Shidehara was seventy-three. He seemed to be growing distinctly decrepit; for example, when asked the name of the man who had served as finance minister in the Hamaguchi government in which he himself was foreign minister, he replied, "I've forgotten his name, but it was the fellow who was assassinated later." Then shortly afterward, he stirred the courtroom to inappropriate laughter by suddenly recalling the name and giving it in the middle of another, completely different exchange.

Shidehara's testimony continued the following day, throwing light on the government's lack of control over the army, the government's policy of localization in the Manchurian Incident, and the way the army on the spot had ignored it and gradually taken affairs into its own hands. In a way, the experiences he described were precisely the same as those encountered by Hirota as foreign minister during the China Incident. Yet Shidehara related his story on the witness stand, while Hirota listened from the prisoner's dock.

As Shidehara wound up his testimony at Ichigaya, another former foreign minister, Matsuoka, was nearing the end of his life not far away at Tokyo University Hospital. That afternoon, Matsuoka's condition became critical, and in the early hours of June 27 he died, at the age of sixty-six. While his body was still warm, a woman doctor baptized him into the Catholic church, believing that this would have been his wish. His farewell verse was, "With no regrets, / Bearing no grudges, / I go to the realm beyond."

When the hearing opened on the twenty-seventh, the Japanese counsel representing Matsuoka, under direction from the president of the court, made a brief announcement of Matsuoka's death, then withdrew from the court together with Matsuoka's American counsel. It seemed to mark the end of a stage in the proceedings.

By the end of June the court had held twenty-one hearings. From July 1, it started hearing evidence on the Manchurian Incident.

The charred ruins of Tokyo were sweltering under the hottest summer in seventy years; but the windows of the military bus that took the defendants to and from the court were pasted over with paper. Through the cracks, they could see little but a reddish-brown waste, its somberness relieved only by the occasional sunflower trembling in the waves of heat rising from the ground.

To make matters worse, the courtroom was still subject to the brilliant "Hollywood-style" lighting of which President Webb had boasted. Japanese and foreigners alike, Webb himself among them, wilted visibly. The proceedings seemed to have entered on a slack period, but the general somnolence was rudely shattered on July 5 when Major General Tanaka Ryukichi began to give his evidence. Formerly a staff officer of the Kwantung Army, Tanaka had been head of the Military Service Bureau under War Minister Tojo. The head of the Military Affairs Bureau at the time had been Muto Akira, a protégé of Tojo's. Tanaka had clashed with Tojo concerning Tojo's and Muto's methods, which he criticized as interference by the army in politics. When local women's organizations throughout Japan were amalgamated into the Greater Japan Women's Association, Muto had obstructed the originally planned appointment of Hatoyama Kaoruko as vice-president and had Tojo's wife Katsuko named instead. On that occasion Tanaka had shown his disapproval by advising Mrs. Tojo that "she had better not throw her weight about too much." Things such as these had led to his being shunted off onto a siding; he had suffered a kind of nervous breakdown, and had been living a life of semi-retirement. When the war ended and a summons came from SCAP, Tanaka expected to be arrested, but in fact he was asked to cooperate with the prosecution. His career and personal standing made him the ideal witness for their case: a man on the inside who could be made, in FBI style, to inform on his associates.

Partly to ensure his personal safety, Tanaka was lodged in top-grade U.S. housing facilities, where he was supplied with the same food as the American forces, and was even able to summon his mistress, a former geisha, to live with him. Yet Tanaka's behavior was not simply an apostasy dictated by gratitude for favorable treatment, or by a personal grudge against Tojo. His discussions with the prosecution had convinced him that the best thing was to see that heavy punishment, so far as possible, was meted out to a small group of the accused, thus saving the majority and preventing the emperor from being charged with responsibility. This was one further reason why Tanaka went to court determined to make a thorough exposé of the "outrages" perpetrated by Tojo and other military men among the A-class war criminals.

Some of the army defendants, unaware of this, greeted Tanaka with smiles as an old friend, but the smiles soon froze on their faces. Tanaka's testimony, which extended over many days and many sessions, covered a wide range: from the machinations of the Japanese army in China, including the bomb attack on Chang Tso-lin and the blowing-up of the South Manchurian Railway near Mukden, to the behind-the-scenes moves at home that led to the attempted coups d'état of the early thirties, and even to trends within the highest echelons of the military at the time of the outbreak of war with America.

Not content with clearly enunciating the name of whoever was responsible for a particular incident, Tanaka would point to him in the dock and declare, "That's the man, there." The first to fall victim to his accusations were Itagaki, who had once given Tanaka promotion, and Hashimoto Kingoro. The same fate befell the two generals sitting on either side of Hirota—the elderly Minami and the younger Doihara. Next came Umezu. Tojo and Muto, of course, were a foregone conclusion.

Dismay, not to say alarm, overtook the military defendants. The entry in Itagaki's diary for that day, in which the reference to Tanaka is marked with a double circle, says, "Enter Tanaka, a creature with the face of a man and the heart of a dog. The word treason is too good for his behavior."

The prosecution had scored a stunning victory. When the defense opened its cross-examination, Tanaka's revelations only became the more sensational. It was, of course, the truth strictly as Tanaka remembered it; most of the documents to which he referred no longer existed, and most of the men from whom he said he had obtained his information were already dead. The military defendants grew excited and embarked on a mudslinging match within their own ranks.

Throughout these exchanges, Hirota sat listening in silence, his body upright, his eyes half closed. Both those being accused and their accuser were men who had caused Hirota trouble in the past. In particular, the Suiyuan incident in Inner Mongolia in late autumn, 1936, which Itagaki had supported and Tanaka directed from behind the scenes, had dealt a fatal blow to Prime Minister Hirota and Foreign Minister Arita in their attempts to set Sino-Japanese relations to rights. Bitter memories of those days came welling up. He himself, if anybody, should be out there accusing the lot of them. Instead, he sat with them in the same dock. . . . But still he had no inclination to defend himself. In fact, the sight of the military men falling out among themselves only diminished still further his enthusiasm for a court struggle. A poem that former foreign minister Shigemitsu, who was so far untouched by the trials, wrote in his diary at the time ran:

> The curses of those
> Calling for retribution
> And the panic of those
> Trying to escape—
> Fools, all of them!

Another question that was raised at this stage in the proceedings was the handling of the so-called Tanaka Memorial. The document in question was a lengthy one, supposedly submitted personally to the emperor by Prime Minister Tanaka Giichi and outlining Japan's plans for aggression on the continent. According to this, Japan would first occupy Manchuria and Mongolia, then use them as bases for gaining control of China proper and her valuable resources. China would then be made a starting-point for the subjugation of India and the South Pacific, to be followed eventually by Asia Minor and, finally, Europe. The prosecution was relying on the document as one of the most important proofs of the existence of a conspiracy to wage a war of aggression.

In court, however, the defense's cross-examination soon cast doubt on the genuineness of the document itself. Neither the original nor anyone who had seen it existed. Even a witness from the Chinese side had seen it only in Chinese translation. Moreover, it contained a number of elementary errors that no Japanese could have made, such as attributing membership of the imperial family to rank outsiders, and quoting remarks supposedly made by persons already deceased at the time in question. Some witnesses, too, concluded that it was a Chinese forgery, and in the end it lost most of its force as evidence.

For Hirota, however, the dismissal of the Tanaka Memorial as a fake was to have, if anything, unfortunate results, since the prosecution, thwarted in its energetic efforts to prove a conspiracy, was obliged to find a substitute, and was to light instead on the "Bases of National Policy" that was drawn up under the Hirota government.

Toward the end of July, work on the courtroom's air-conditioning system was completed, and a cool breeze began to waft over those assembled. Possibly because they were not used to air-conditioning, many of the defendants developed upset stomachs, and Hiranuma and Shiratori were taken to hospital; Hiranuma, who was seventy-eight, had only just recovered from a spell in hospital with pneumonia. Yet the new comfort of the courtroom contrasted strangely with the gruesome testimony, which went on until the middle of August, concerning atrocities committed by the Japanese army in Nanking and elsewhere.

During his term as foreign minister, Hirota had received reports on some aspects of the affair, and had protested several times to War Minister Sugiyama, but now he found himself accused of having a hand in "conspiracy to murder" and charged with negligence in efforts to prevent such incidents.

A middle-aged Chinese official of some charitable organization took the stand:

"I saw bodies lying all over the place, some of them slashed to ribbons. They were just left there where they'd been killed. Some of the corpses lay hunched up, others spread-eagled. All these deeds were done by Japanese troops; I saw them at work myself. I began counting the bodies on one of the main streets, but after I'd counted about five hundred on both sides of the street, I gave it up."

An American missionary testified as follows:

"Rape was a commonplace, and large numbers of women and children were killed. If a woman refused or resisted, she was killed on the spot. I took photographs and movies myself of women with their heads cut off, or with their bodies covered with stab wounds."

A professor of Nanking University appeared in court:

"About fifty thousand Japanese troops robbed the refugees of their bedding, cooking utensils, and food. For six weeks after the occupation, almost every building in the town was invaded by these wandering bands of soldiers. In some cases, the looting was well organized, involving large numbers of military trucks and directed by officers. . . ."

The court listened in hushed silence. Shigemitsu wrote in his diary: "One wants to plug one's ears, so horrifying are the accounts. Has the spirit of Japan gone to rot?" And in his entry for the following day: "The accounts are appalling. Alas for the 'holy war'!"

Witness followed witness, the large number of affidavits and documentary evidence showing clearly how much importance the prosecution attached to the incident. In the meantime, B- and C-class war criminals in the same prison, who were accused simply of maltreating prisoners, were being executed in steady succession. Executions were also proceeding at a rapid pace in areas formerly occupied by the Japanese army. In the circumstances, it was obvious that the only punishment possible for such a great massacre was the death penalty.

Whether fortunately or otherwise, Matsui Iwane, commander-in-chief of the Japanese forces in central China, was in hospital with stomach trouble at the time, and did not hear the horrifying evidence that was to have a decisive influence on his fate. As a result, the only defendant in court on whom the evidence had an immediate bearing was Hirota. Hirota, of course, had no direct connection either with the actual murders or with any "conspiracy to murder." The charge against him was that he had failed to do what he could to prevent it. Yet under a system in which the supreme command was independent, what could he, a civilian minister, have done? It was quite clear, nevertheless, that the prosecution was setting its sights on him. And it was equally clear that Hirota had no desire to speak up in his own defense. He was not without some inkling of what would be the outcome.

257

On days when the court was in session, Hirota's two daughters always attended. When the chief of the court guards, a kindhearted man, noticed this, he began to keep two seats for them in the very front of the press section. Even so, there was of course no chance to exchange any conversation. As he entered the court, Hirota's gaze would meet that of his daughters. And as the session came to an end and he stood up, they would again greet each other in silence; that was all.

Unlike the newsmen around them, the girls had no particular interest in the historical facts being brought to light, or in the legal struggle as such. For them, it was quite simply a chance to be, if only for a short while, beneath the same roof as their father; just to be able to watch him was a relief. It was as though the spirit of their dead mother were there too, with her husband and daughters.

In the latter part of August, when the *higurashi* cicadas, heralds of summer's end, were already singing busily outside, the courtroom took on new life. P'u-yi, former puppet emperor of Manchukuo, had been sent to Japan from the Soviet Union, and took the stand. Suddenly, the seats reserved for distinguished visitors and the press were full to overflowing.

The dethroned emperor began his account with details of his own early life. Partly under the influence of the prosecution, this developed, from around the point where he was made the token emperor of Manchukuo, into a bitter attack on Japan. He claimed, among other things, that his consort had been poisoned, and that he had been forced to embrace the Shinto religion. He himself had had private ideas of leading an independence movement, he said, and had done his best to resist, but constant repression and the threat of death had obliged him to live as a servant of the Kwantung Army, to which he attributed the entire burden of responsibility.

His eyebrows twitched nervously as he spoke, and his body jerked continuously. At times, he would bang hysterically on the witness stand. He was, in fact, terrified lest he be hauled back to face trial as a war criminal in the Soviet Union or China. Under cross-examination by the defense, his accounts of the poisoning of his consort and of his compulsory conversion to Shinto began to seem doubtful, and it also gradually became clear that it was he himself who had wanted to be made emperor rather than regent. But whenever the argument took a turn unfavorable to himself, he would say "I don't know," or "I've forgotten." He seemed shifty, with none of the dignity one might have expected in a former emperor.

Eventually, President Webb had had enough. "I'm reluctant to say this," he began, "but though the witness talks a great deal of the danger to his life, the threat of death is no excuse for, say, a soldier who flees the battlefield. Since this morning, the witness appears to have been doing nothing but make excuses for collaborating with the Japanese army, and I feel we don't need to hear any more."

In mid-September, General Matsui left hospital and returned to Sugamo looking somewhat fatter than before. Again he could be heard reading aloud the Kannon Sutra as he had done every day before. Unaware of the shocking testimony that had been given concerning the rape of Nanking, he allowed himself to be soothed with suggestions that, for instance, he would be transferred to China where, after a purely formal trial, he would he invited to become military adviser to the National Government.

On October 10, when the first evidence was given from the Soviet side, the Soviet prosecutor presented a copy of a memorandum that was to prove unfavorable evidence for Hirota. The memorandum, which had been made by Major Kasahara, military attaché at the Japanese embassy in the Soviet Union, summed up a conversation between Hirota, then ambassador, and a member of the General Staff Office who came on a tour of inspection. According to this document, Hirota had asserted that "Japan should take a tough policy toward the Soviet Union, even if it meant war."

Any summing-up of a conversation is liable, of course, to be influenced by the writer's subjective impressions and preconceptions. Moreover, the fact that the memorandum was background material for a report to the General Staff Office rendered it still more suspect as an account of what Hirota had said.

In their cross-examination of Kasahara, the defense suggested that Hirota had spoken thus in a deliberate attempt to sound out the military's intentions. They also found it odd that there should be a copy of only one page of the memorandum, without the rest. Evidence, nevertheless, was evidence, and the court was duly impressed by the grim perseverance shown by the Soviet prosecutors in hunting out the paper. The question still remained of how accurately it reflected what Hirota had said, and what he had really had in mind. Only Hirota himself could provide the answers. And so long as he refused to give evidence, there was no doubt that the Kasahara memorandum would be held against him.

Evidence from the Soviet side completed, the prosecution turned to general preparations for war in the economic and financial fields, then called witnesses from the British, American, Dutch, and Philippine sides. During the evidence concerning economic preparations for war, Hirota's foreign counsel Smythe probed a witness from SCAP's Economic and Scientific Section, obliging him to admit that it was to some extent inevitable that Japan's economic policies should have been put on a quasi-wartime footing, and that the same kind of thing could have happened in countries other than Japan.

Smythe, who was a devout Quaker and had twenty years' experience as a lawyer, was conspicuous among the other American counsel—a cheerful, happy-go-lucky group—for his quietness and air of cynical reserve. In this respect, he had something in common with Hirota himself. As a lawyer, moreover, he was able, conscientious, and did his homework well, so that Hirota was impressed and satisfied.

As part of the evidence from the American side, the prosecution produced an affidavit from former ambassador Grew. This document was, if anything, advantageous to Hirota, since Grew ranked Hirota and Shigemitsu highly as champions of peace, and deplored the fact that their efforts in this direction had been thwarted by the military. For this reason the counsel for the defense was anxious that Grew should come to Japan to give evidence before the court, foreseeing that he could be looked to for still further evidence favorable to Hirota. But Grew, unfortunately, was ill, and the plan could not be realized.

On September 30, at the Nuremberg trials, judgment was passed on the German A-class war criminals. Of the twenty-two accused, twelve were sentenced to be hanged, but three were actually pronounced not guilty. The news was received by the accused in Sugamo with comparative impassivity. Unlike Japan, there had obviously been a conspiracy in Germany to embark on war, and a conspiracy to exterminate the Jews had resulted in mass murder. To some extent, it had been foreseeable that there would be a large number of death sentences. This being so, it was the three verdicts of not guilty that attracted most attention, and there was even a wave of mild optimism. It was at this stage that rumors began to reach Hirota's ears that diplomats would be found not guilty, or that he and Shigemitsu would soon be released. Hirota told Shigemitsu of the rumors immediately, but he himself gave them no credence.

The Nuremburg trials subsequently had other, unexpected repercussions in Sugamo. Goering, under sentence of death, had committed suicide by taking poison he had concealed on his person. The result was a sudden tightening-up of surveillance and body checks. Before the accused left for court and after they returned, they were stripped, their spectacles and false teeth removed, and they were even made to go on all fours for a rectal inspection. They were made to change cells repeatedly, and their personal belongings were subjected to frequent and thorough examination. At one time they had been allowed to take exercise in a spacious garden, with trees and grass, but now they were thrust back into a narrow area surrounded by wire netting. The number of young men of eighteen or nineteen in the guard increased, and treatment of the prisoners became correspondingly rougher. On clear, sunny autumn days, it was a common sight to see elderly prisoners, hustled along by young soldiers, carrying their bedding out to be aired or bringing it in again over their shoulders in the late afternoon.

Autumn advanced steadily; on one occasion, the prisoners were pleased to find a few chestnuts on each of their meal trays. The call of the shrike was often to be heard outside. On November 3, the new Constitution was promulgated. Reading the report in a newspaper in the anteroom of the court, Shigemitsu said:

"Things should be all right from now on."

"Yes, I agree," replied Kido. "Today I feel the struggle's over at last."

Hirota shared their feelings. The new Constitution drawn up by Shidehara—his predecessor as an exponent of peaceful foreign policies—was not merely designed to keep the army in check, but denied its very existence. It was as though a new and reassuring era had dawned for Japan. The greatest responsibility for the war had lain, in a sense, less with individuals than with a political structure that had given independence to the supreme command. Hirota's fear that "the Meiji Constitution will be the ruin of Japan" had proved amply justified. The cost to Japan of this lesson had been exorbitantly high; indeed, it was still to cost her something yet. . . .

On another day in the same anteroom, Hashimoto Kingoro, on some trivial provocation, struck fellow defendant Shiratori smartly with his fist and sent Shiratori's spectacles flying. The American troops present watched in disgust, while the other defendants shrank into themselves in embarrassment. "No wonder that Japan got herself into such a mess," muttered Kido to Shigemitsu.

The central heating had been on since the end of October in the courtroom at Ichigaya; finally, in December, it came on in Sugamo too. The strain of trying to make both ends meet began to show itself on the faces of the prisoners' families when they came to visit. Prices were shooting up, and they were obliged to sell off clothing and possessions one by one to make a little money.

Masao was visiting Hirota one day, when they heard another prisoner saying to a member of his family nearby, "You've still got that diamond, haven't you? You ought to be able to get quite a bit for it." Hirota and Masao could scarcely believe their ears. The prisoner in question had been a member of the Tojo government, the same government that during the war had demanded that the public hand over its diamonds and precious metals. At that time Hirota had unhesitatingly surrendered Shizuko's one and only jewel—the diamond ring, for so long a symbol of their affection, that he had brought back from Holland to replace the original shell ring. . . .
He would also hear other defendants and their relatives making re-

marks such as, "It's no good without money," or "It's a case of the pot calling the kettle black. The prosecution and the defense are both acting a part." They might have been living in a different world from Hirota and his family.

Finally, 1946 drew to an end. On New Year's Eve, they had macaroni for supper at Sugamo, "presumably a substitute for the traditional New Year's Eve noodles," wrote Itagaki in his diary. "The reaction of the defendants as a whole could be summed up in two words: 'complete indifference.' "

He went on to sum up the past year in the following fashion: "Probably the two major news items of the last twelve months were the food shortage and the establishment of the new Constitution. Society these days is, quite simply, in a state of chaos. Somehow it seems to have got by as far as food is concerned, but there is the housing shortage, inflation, a rampant black market, a fashion for strikes, and an increase in serious crimes. Shortages of coal and the like are promising to bring crisis in 1947. Domestic government and the morale of the public are not yet able to cope with reconstruction without outside aid. The struggle in China between Nationalists and Communists seems likely to go on for some time, and the Communists appear to be firmly established in Manchuria, North China, and northern Korea."

Scarcely had the New Year begun when the number of defendants decreased again. On January 3, former fleet admiral Nagano Osami entered hospital with acute pneumonia, and died two days later, at the age of sixty-six.

On January 24, the prosecution finished presenting evidence in support of its case, for which it had summoned a total of 104 witnesses. The court had already sat 159 times. Following this, the defense presented a motion urging dismissal of the case on the grounds that the prosecution had presented insufficient evidence. This would normally have been considered a purely formal procedure, but Smythe, Hirota's counsel, ignored the president's directions and submitted a whole succession of motions claiming, for example, that the hearings themselves were improper, and that there was no basis for the establishment of the court. He clashed violently with Webb, who dismissed all his motions. Following this, Smythe and the other American lawyers each submitted an individual motion on behalf of the man he was defending.

Finally, Smythe once more submitted a general motion on behalf of all the defendants, claiming that there was no evidence of a conspiracy, that the prosecution's evidence was insufficient to establish the fifty-five different charges, and that the case should therefore be dismissed.

Two members of the prosecution argued against the motion. One of them was British lawyer Comyns-Carr, who delivered a scathing address which included a personal attack on each of the defendants and reserved a special venom for Tojo and Smythe's client Hirota. Hirota, he declared in terms that might almost have suggested he bore him some private grudge, had been the aggressor from start to finish; the difference between his public and private words and deeds was evidence of a special brand of cunning. Carr's arguments against most of the defendants were relatively mild, or qualified in various ways, but against Hirota he unleashed all his fury. Hirota himself heard all this unperturbed. As with his games of patience, he showed neither surprise nor alarm, whatever cards fate chose to deal him.

Counsel Smythe had a typically Quaker uprightness and sense of justice. A short while before, the Japanese defense had invited their American colleagues to a restaurant and given them a dinner, attended by Prince Takamatsu, to thank them for their work. Throughout the meal, Smythe had touched neither the food nor the drink, insisting that he could not accept it when ordinary Japanese were half starving. He was keen on his work and brimming with confidence in his court battles. In his eyes, prosecution and judges alike, including President Webb, were no more than a collection of second- and third-rate legal men from various countries, and the trial itself had a strong political flavor.

Personally, he was less concerned with defending Hirota, whose brief he held, than with the desire to see that legal justice prevailed; to do so, he assumed rather largely, would be best for Hirota too in the long run. Although this was, in a way, heartening for the man he was defending, in another sense it was a disturbingly risky gamble. For a defendant who had no concern for his own personal welfare to be represented by a counsel who was preoccupied with larger questions of "legal justice" was almost asking for disaster.

Sure enough, about a month later Smythe clashed once more with President Webb. On March 5, the defense summoned political writers and other witnesses in an effort to demonstrate that, since in the twenty years preceding the war there had been seventeen changes of government with a correspondingly large turnover of ministers, circumstances had not been such as to permit any "conspiracy."

The president, however, frequently interrupted the testimony, ordering some parts of it to be cut and seeking to obstruct others. As a result, Smythe became impatient, and rose to complain that the judge's behavior constituted "improper interference." Furious, Webb demanded that he either apologize for his use of the expression or leave the court. Smythe insisted that he had frequently used the expression during his twenty years as an attorney; since he had intended no contempt of court, there was no call for him to apologize. Webb continued to insist he withdraw the term, and Smythe was equally adamant in his refusal.

Webb accordingly recessed the court for a while, then after a debate among the judges announced that Smythe would be excluded from hearings until such time as he withdrew his remark and apologized. Smythe retorted heatedly that he saw no reason to, and had no intention of changing his position; and he withdrew from the defense counsel's bench.

Some of the military defendants were highly delighted by Smythe's attitude, which they said was "as good as a tonic." It was decided that George Yamaoka, who held the brief for Togo, should take over as American counsel for Hirota as well. Smythe continued to watch the proceedings from the section reserved for the press, and gave advice to Yamaoka, but there was no denying the fact that Hirota's defense had been weakened considerably.

Life was grim in Sugamo as their second winter there drew to a close. A steady stream of B- and C-class war criminals who had been tried in Yokohama and condemned to death were housed temporarily on the floor above Hirota and the rest; some of them attempted suicide, and others went out of their minds and could be heard shouting at the top of their voices. Surveillance of the A-class war criminals was stepped up at the same time. Even their letters reached them in the form of photostat copies. Lights were left blazing at night to prevent any attempt at suicide, and they were forced to sleep with their cell doors open, their pillows projecting into the corridor, and their heads well out of the blankets. The inevitable result was frequent colds.

After an adjournment of three weeks for preparation, the defense's counteroffensive began with an opening address by counsel Kiyose (defense lawyer for Tojo). It was preceded, however, by something of a disturbance among the defendants and their counsel. The line due to be taken by the military defendants was that the war was provoked by the other side and had been inevitable in the interests of self-defense. Hirota, however, took the attitude that war, even in self-defense, could not be justified, and that he was responsible for having failed to prevent hostilities. Thus he refused to put his name to Kiyose's address.

The belief that there was no good war and no bad peace, and that the diplomat's and statesman's aim should be to prevent war as such, had been a tradition at the Foreign Ministry from the time of Komura Jutaro to that of Shidehara. The statement Hirota had made while he was foreign minister—that there would be no war during his term of office—was a declaration of his sense of responsibility. Nevertheless, during his last term as foreign minister, under Konoe, the war with China had broken out. He felt like proclaiming aloud, for all to hear: "On that score, whatever the other defendants may think, I cannot escape responsibility. I am the man responsible."

The defense's statement of its case and presentation of evidence proceeded, dealing in turn with relations with China, the Soviet Union, and Britain and America. Counsel began their case by dealing with points common to the defendants concerned, and sought to prove their arguments by submitting evidence and questioning witnesses. This also served, incidentally, as defense for individual defendants. Hirota, however, continued to show so little enthusiasm for the proceedings that his counsel made almost no effort to elicit evidence that would help him. Shigemitsu fretted because he felt the defense's concern for Hirota was inadequate, but it did not even occur to Hirota, who had little taste for self-justification from the start, to put up any individual defense at the stage of general rebuttal evidence. Individual defenses would come later; if his counsel's job required that they should give rebuttal evidence for Hirota, it would be enough for them to do it at the appropriate time. Even at this stage, situations had already occurred in court where evidence advantageous to defendant A had proved disadvantageous to defendant B. Such cases made Hirota feel still more distaste for testimony that benefitted only himself.

President Webb, on his side, was in a hurry to get the proceedings over as soon as possible, in accordance with a wish expressed by MacArthur. Thus he frequently cut defense counsel off in midstream —which several times led to acrimonious exchanges—and, while admitting many of the prosecution's objections, dismissed a large number of the documents submitted by the defense. In particular, he refused almost all documentary evidence associated with the Soviet and Chinese Communist parties.

The tiresome proceedings dragged on. For the defendants, though, the visits to Ichigaya were a welcome relief. Their "homes" in Sugamo consisted of cells each the size of three tatami mats—about five square meters. Each had two tatami, the remaining one-mat space being occupied by a washbasin that also served as a desk, and a toilet that also did duty as a seat. There were a few blankets and a thin underquilt. Once a week, this humble home was ransacked— even the tatami were turned up—in a hunt for concealed objects. The journey to Ichigaya, on the other hand, afforded a view— through cracks in the paper pasted over the windows—of the streets of Tokyo with their rows of hastily erected shacks. Conversation in the bus was unrestricted. In the anteroom of the court, they were sometimes given special allowances of American cigarettes and chocolate, and were occasionally allowed surreptitious meetings with their counsel or family members.

By now, spring had come round for the second time since they became war criminals. They were allowed again to take walks on the grass, and would sometimes sit there and talk to each other. Hirota, however, remained aloof and rarely joined these little gatherings. In an adjoining exercise area, surrounded by barbed wire, young B- and C-class war criminals dressed in POW uniforms walked in pairs, handcuffed together and barefooted—pointless exercise that merely helped fill the time till they were executed.

Another execution of which they received news was that of Lieutenant General Hase, former commander of the 6th Division, who had been charged with responsibility for the Nanking Massacre in a Chinese court and put to death at the end of April on the outskirts of Nanking, before a large crowd of Chinese citizens. The news could not help having a personal significance for Matsui, who alone among the defendants wore Chinese dress, and for Hirota, who was charged with a related crime.

Also around the end of April, Japanese society beyond the prison walls saw the holding of a general election. Yoshida, who had intended to stand from his constituency in Kanagawa prefecture, was warned by Yamazaki Takeshi, speaker of the House of Representatives, that a man like himself who took so little pains to ingratiate himself with the electorate might get elected once, but would never be reelected. Yoshida therefore switched to Kochi prefecture and was duly elected, but the Liberal party itself yielded pride of place, by a matter of ten seats, to the Socialist party.

Shidehara, who had stood for the Democratic party (the former Progressive party) was elected in Osaka prefecture with a record 75,000 votes, thanks to the new fame which had suddenly descended on him following the war. The party itself, however, dropped to third place because a number of its members were purged from public office just before the election.

The outcome was that a Socialist government headed by Katayama Tetsu was formed with the cooperation of Ashida Hitoshi and other Democratic party members, who joined the cabinet. Both Yoshida and Shidehara were confident that a Socialist government could not last long, but movements were afoot in both their parties, particularly among long-established party members, to have them either put out to pasture or expelled. For such reasons, both men were almost completely indifferent to the progress of the Tokyo war crimes trials.

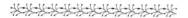 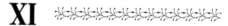

Summer came; the prisoners were grateful for the green shade of the cryptomerias at Sugamo, and at Ichigaya for the cool breeze from the air conditioners. The general rebuttal evidence for the defendants went on, though a number of the judges were absent on leave. President Webb continued as ever to favor the objections of the prosecution, and defense counsel's evidence ran into heavy weather. Antagonism surfaced, moreover, within the ranks of the defense itself. In particular, counsel representing Togo made a thoroughgoing vindication of him where U.S.-Japanese relations were concerned, despite the fact that the court was still at the stage of general rebuttal evidence; this drew violent protests and objections from counsel representing the military defendants, and Togo's lawyer was obliged to retract part of the testimony and proofs he had submitted.

Throughout all this, Hirota's Japanese counsel and Hirota himself maintained strict silence. As a result even Sasakawa Ryoichi, who had not yet been indicted and who had never exchanged a word with Hirota before, felt compelled to address him urgently: "I imagine that at least two or three of those already charged will be found innocent and acquitted, and I see you and Shigemitsu as likely candidates. Either way, I'm sure there's not much against you, so why don't you take the stand of your own accord and let everybody know your own position and convictions? I myself was found guilty in the past at the second hearing of another trial, and at the time I regretted terribly the things I hadn't spoken up about. If one has said everything one wants to say, then however severe the verdict one feels satisfied in one's heart, but you'll only feel more bitter if you get an unexpectedly severe sentence without having expressed anything at all."

But Hirota's attitude did not change.

On September 5, just as the general rebuttal evidence was drawing to a close, Hirota's counsel Smythe, who had been excluded from the hearings, appeared before the bar for the first time in six months and expressed regret for the remarks he had made earlier—qualifying this, however, by saying that "differences between American and Australian courts" had led to misunderstanding. The apology was made on the assumption that President Webb would permit him to attend the court, but Justice Mei of China persuaded Webb to have Smythe repeat his apology, which he said was inadequate. As a result, Webb asked Smythe to apologize again the next time the court sat, on the grounds that all the judges were not present that day. Angered, Smythe declared that he could not tolerate such treatment any longer, and, formally resigning his position as counsel, he returned to America.

Amidst such developments, the court turned to the defense of individual defendants. Hirota's own defense began on September 25. The opening argument was presented by counsel George Yamaoka, then ten witnesses took the stand over a period of a week. Seven of them were connected with the Foreign Ministry,. in accordance with Hirota's expressed desire that evidence associated with the ministry should be used to make clear what its actions had been. The first witness (Kameyama Kazuji), a former counselor at the Japanese embassy in Moscow, testified that the sale of the Chinese Eastern Railway had been made at the Soviet Union's request, and described how Hirota had worked enthusiastically and patiently, despite all kinds of difficulties, until a final agreement was reached. To back this up, defense counsel subsequently submitted evidence in the form of cables exchanged between Hirota and Soviet Foreign Minister Litvinov, together with passages from a book by Litvinov, and the evidence was accepted. In the book, the Soviet official was quoted as having said to a Japanese reporter: "Due to various obstacles, the negotiations took approximately two years, but the overcoming of the difficulties must be attributed in large measure to Foreign Minister Hirota, who took an active part in the negotiations at every stage of their progress." Also submitted and accepted as evidence were various speeches and answers made by Hirota in the Diet; among them was the statement, "In handling relations with foreign nations, my ideal is world peace, and I intend to devote all my energies to achieving the realization of our policies by diplomatic means." On the other hand, unfortunately, the excerpts from Grew's diary that were considered such important evidence were in many cases dismissed as the personal opinions of the author; the prosecution raised persistent objections, which President Webb more often than not admitted.

The second witness was Kuwashima Kazue, who had been head of the East Asia Bureau at the Foreign Ministry while Hirota was foreign minister. In his testimony, he described in concrete detail how the switch from Uchida to Hirota had marked a start to improved relations with China, which had been virtually suspended until then. As a result, the Nationalist government's attitude became much more favorable, and a new, more friendly trend developed, as witnessed by the elevation of the countries' legations to the status of embassies. At the same time, he recalled how the clashes provoked by the Kwantung Army and other Japanese forces in China, and their setting up of puppet regimes, had seemed deliberately aimed to pour cold water on these new developments, and he described the Foreign Ministry's protests and other efforts to counter such moves.

Itagaki, Doihara, and the other men who had frustrated Hirota so frequently at that time were all together in the dock; it was ironical to see Hirota, the victim of their moves, sitting amongst them, a defendant himself. Most men would have been angered by the situation; but Hirota sat there looking as placid as ever, ready for whatever might come.

On the third day, Carr began his cross-examination concerning Hirota.

"Is it not true that he had the army issue all kinds of threats or ultimatums in order to achieve the demands he made in negotiations?"

"No, absolutely not."

"Is it not true that Hirota was preparing to resort to armed force by the army and navy at some suitable time in order to impose his policies on China should the pressure of threats prove insufficient?"

Under pressure from Carr, Hirota's counsel rose loyally to his defense:

"He made no such preparations whatsoever. I might add as evidence that Hirota's negotiations were invariably carried out via diplomatic channels."

On the same day, the speech by Hirota in the House of Peers in which he stated his belief that foreign affairs should be conducted with the idea of enhancing friendly relations with all countries, as well as cables showing that Chiang Kai-shek had welcomed Hirota's "Three Principles on China Policy," were submitted as evidence and accepted.

On the afternoon of the fourth day, former foreign undersecretary Horinouchi Kensuke took the stand. His testimony dealt in detail with Hirota's term as prime minister and his following period as foreign minister, but Carr objected to it on the grounds that Hirota should give evidence himself, and considerable sections of the testimony were dismissed. Carr's objection, of course, was a typical move based on his awareness that Hirota had no intention of taking the stand.

The sections of Horinouchi's deposition which survived and were read to the court were devoted to showing the efforts Hirota had made for peace. They began by describing how Hirota's agreement to mobilization at the cabinet meeting held at the time of the outbreak of the China Incident had been given in response to an understanding from the war minister that this was a "preparing for preparation." They then gave accounts of Hirota's moves for a peaceful solution, the negotiations that were held on a number of occasions, and the declaration that Japan would "have no dealings with" the National Government, which was in fact aimed at leaving the door ajar, though closing it where Chiang was concerned.

There followed a fierce cross-examination by Carr. In setting out to attribute all responsibility to Hirota, he arbitrarily imposed on Japan the Western concept of civilian supremacy in government and ignored altogether the special circumstances involved in Sino-Japanese relations at the time. The man who headed the government at the time of the Incident—Konoe—had committed suicide, and so had his war minister, Sugiyama. Terauchi, war minister in the Hirota government, had since died. Hirota had been advised to let the dead take all responsibility and to concentrate his defense on that approach, but he rejected the idea. His mind was already prepared for the worst, and he had no desire to trample the dead in making his own escape to the world of the living; rather, he was filled with a quiet determination to shoulder responsibility for them. The one thing he regretted was that it was impossible to say such things when everyone else was struggling so frantically to escape death.

Horinouchi did his best to defend Hirota, fielding Carr's questions, occasionally arguing with him, explaining to him the precise powers wielded by a civilian minister under a system where the supreme command was a law unto itself, and the special relationship existing between Japan and China; but there were limits to what he could do, and it was perfectly apparent that Hirota's silence worked to his disadvantage.

When Horinouchi started to give evidence concerning the Hirota-Craigie talks, in which Hirota asked the British ambassador to act as intermediary in peace negotiations, Carr again raised an objection, claiming that such matters should be testified to by the defendant himself. His objection was admitted by President Webb. It was almost as though Hirota were being tried *in absentia*.

Another damaging question for Hirota's case was that of the "Bases of National Policy" approved at the time of the Hirota government. The prosecution treated this document as a comprehensive statement of national policy setting forth a program of totalitarian reform at home and expansionism abroad, and sought to install it in place of the Tanaka Memorial as prime evidence of a "conspiracy." Again, the only person who could really explain and defend the document and its aims was Hirota himself.

The man who as chief of a War Ministry policy-making team had drawn up the first draft of the document and presented it to Hirota was Lieutenant General Sato Kenryo, who was still barely in his fifties and the youngest of all the A-class war criminals. It was he who, in his days as a fiery major, had shouted "Shut up!" in the famous incident in the Diet, but since entering Sugamo prison he was among those who had been won over by Hirota's personality. He always tried to sit next to Hirota on the bus that took them to Ichigaya; merely to be next to him, he confessed later, seemed to give him an odd sense of inner peace.

Sato found it intolerable to watch Hirota walking unprotesting into the trap set for him by the prosecution, and urged him almost aggressively to take the stand. Hirota should make it clear, he said, that the "Bases of National Policy" was initiated by the army from fear of another attempted coup d'état. But Hirota shook his head. "No matter whether it was the army or anyone else," he said, "it was I as prime minister who gave it the OK. The whole responsibility is mine."

Sato also suggested that the "Bases of National Policy," in both the domestic and foreign fields, constituted a "gesture" designed to pacify revolutionary sentiment at home, and that for all the military's talk of "advancing to the south" or "advancing to the north," there was not the slightest intention in fact of resorting to war.

"The army intended a gesture in initiating it, and the general reaction was to see it as such," he insisted. "Surely the defendant himself ought to take the stand and point that out?" But Hirota looked displeased. "Do you mean that a prime minister should testify that his statement of national policy was no more than a gesture?" he demanded curtly. Even so, Sato continued to press his point. Agreed that there were some items in the document which they had intended to put into effect, he as its initiator still considered that, on the whole, it was only a "gesture." "I'm sure you felt the same way," he said. "I'm not asking you to take the stand and tell a lie; I'm asking you just to tell the truth about what you thought." But Hirota made no further answer.

On the seventh day of Hirota's individual defense, a former counselor at the embassy in China, Hidaka Shinrokuro, testified concerning the efforts made by the Foreign Ministry to get the Marco Polo Bridge incident in hand and prevent it from spreading to Shanghai. The consul general in Shanghai at the time, Okamoto Motomasa, supplemented this with evidence concerning the cease-fire talks and other related matters.

There was no cross-examination by the prosecution, and cables of instruction concerning these matters, together with excerpts from Grew's diary and a book by Craigie, were submitted as evidence and accepted.

Following this, Ishii Itaro, former chief of the East Asia Bureau at the Foreign Ministry, testified concerning the Nanking Massacre and warnings and representations made to the army at the time. He was cross-examined by Carr, who posed a series of questions concerning matters that had not been within the competence of the Japanese foreign minister at the time. "Did Hirota put it before the cabinet?" he asked. "Did Hirota take the necessary steps to have those responsible punished?" In most cases, Ishii answered with a very simple negative such as "I didn't hear anything," or "I don't know." The result was to give the court the impression that Hirota knew about the massacre but made no special effort to check it.

Ishii had been a protégé of Hirota's rival Saburi, and had clashed with Hirota while he was head of the East Asia Bureau. By nature he was frank and impulsive, but his evidence, undeniably, was different in its implications from that of others associated with the Foreign Ministry who had spoken up in Hirota's defense. The question involved, moreover, was such that the personal implications for Hirota were rather grave. Sato watched from the defendants' dock with a sense of acute frustration. On this matter too he had repeatedly urged Hirota to take the stand himself. "It's not just Carr alone—" he said, "the foreign judges, too, find it hard to understand that cabinet meetings were restricted to administrative business and had no jurisdiction over questions such as the Nanking incident, which involved military operations and the supreme command. Here at least you ought to testify in person and explain that the Japanese state as laid down by the Constitution clearly distinguished the fields of competence of the government and the supreme command—which meant that all the foreign minister could do in a case like the Nanking affair was to attempt to check things by issuing warnings to the war minister."

The last witness was former foreign minister Arita, but before he appeared in court there occurred another incident with unfortunate implications for Hirota. In his deposition, Arita described how, on the way to peace talks with China, he had met staff officer Itagaki of the Kwantung Army and been urged to take a tough stand. Hearing of this, Itagaki urged Hirota strongly to have this passage deleted, since it would be detrimental to his own—Itagaki's—case. Hirota agreed. He had no desire to submit evidence that contradicted or did harm to others.

His defense lawyers, however, were dissatisfied. Morishima in particular, who had served under Hirota at the Foreign Ministry, believed that the army's high-handed methods should be exposed, and had already gone to great trouble lining up evidence and witnesses to prove his point. Not surprisingly, therefore, he insisted that Hirota should not give in to Itagaki. Hirota, however, insisted that Itagaki should have his way. The outcome was that Morishima resigned as Hirota's counsel. To lose Morishima at this stage, when Smythe had already withdrawn, was a great blow. The other defendants sympathized with Hirota, but Hirota himself was unperturbed. "Morishima's the kind of man who always marches straight ahead," he said to Masao with a smile. "Even when he sees a wall in front of him he refuses to do the obvious and switch direction to left or right; but that's one of the interesting things about him." He observed the behavior of his counsel and former subordinate as though it were a matter of academic interest, rather than one of life and death.

There were some defendants who were ready to sling mud at anyone and everyone in the frantic attempt to save their skins. This was true of quite a few of the military defendants. On the other hand, there were civilians among the accused who asked their military counterparts to give false testimony. In such company, two men stood out for the way they attempted to take responsibility upon themselves: Tojo, whose death sentence was a foregone conclusion, and Hirota, who was completely unconcerned for himself.

After Hirota, counsel presented further individual defenses—Hoshino, Itagaki, Kaya, Kido, and so on, in alphabetical order. While Kido and Togo were giving their evidence, something akin to panic occurred among the military defendants who found them-

277

selves cast as the villains, and the two men were roundly cursed when the accused came together on the bus and elsewhere. There were exceptions: Itagaki, for one, seemed to have resigned himself to things, for he embarrassed Shigemitsu—who was then engaged in attacking the military—by calling out to him, "Have another good day today!" Far from being resentful about the withdrawal of evidence against Itagaki, Hirota actually praised him to family members who came visiting, telling them that Itagaki was a "straightforward fellow."

A marked change also occurred in Tojo, who had formerly looked glum most of the time, but was now sometimes seen smiling. "My future's decided, you see," he would joke.

The daily routine remained unchanged for the defendants in Sugamo. In the morning, voices were still to be heard reading the Kannon Sutra and the Lotus Sutra. By contrast, the voice of Oshima Hiroshi chanting Chinese-style poems sounded almost cheerful and lively. The prisoners were forbidden to have printed matter sent in, so books were brought on a trolley from the prison library and lent out to them. Many of them were in English, and they included a recent publication dealing with atomic energy. The prisoners were permitted to visit each other's cells, where they played cards, *go*, and *shogi* to while away the time. Hirota played patience in silence by himself; he would watch others playing *go*, and occasionally comment on the game, but could never be persuaded to join in himself. For this reason he was held by some to be very standoffish, but the fact was that this was nothing new for him, nor was he interested in explaining his reasons. He took everything as it came, without surprise or emotion.

American guards who were due to go back to the States would often go around collecting the defendants' signatures to take home as souvenirs. Their replacements included more very young men. They were noisy, talking and laughing in loud voices well into the night, sometimes even whistling or playing the harmonica. On the floor above, condemned war criminals were being brought in on their way to the gallows.

Surveillance of the A-class war criminals became even stricter.

When they took a bath, an officer and two or three men were always present. At night, their spectacles and even their pencils were taken away from them. A hundred-watt bulb burned all night in each cell, and guards paced the corridor unceasingly; one prisoner claimed to have counted up to ten thousand paces. For nights on end, it was impossible to do more than doze.

Hearing of the evidence ended on February 10, 1948, and the next day the prosecution's summation began. The individual summation against Hirota started on February 20. Symbolized by a sentence that occurred at the very outset—"His true purpose from beginning to end was to expand Japanese influence as far as possible through foreign policies backed up by military threats"—the argument was based entirely on the prosecution's one-sided interpretation of events. The process whereby Hirota's policy of conciliation was wrecked piecemeal by the army in China became, in the prosecution's version, a plot by the army of which Hirota had full cognizance and which he sought to cover up with policies of deception. Even so, comparatively few accusations of having positively planned or carried out a war of aggression were in practice leveled at Hirota; most of the accusations, rather, were of sins of omission: that he had "failed to take any action."

On March 2, the defense's closing argument began, and the summation of the individual defense for Hirota was carried out on the seventeenth and eighteenth by counsel Yamaoka. He began by remarking sarcastically that the prosecution's arguments were the product of "astonishing imagination and invention"; not a single event which the prosecution had dealt with had suggested the existence of a shared plan or conspiracy. Even supposing it had, there was not a shred of evidence to support the theory that Hirota as an individual had acted with the aims that the prosecution ascribed to him. The defense went on to deal with specific accusations, citing contrary evidence in each case.

Where relations with the Soviet Union were concerned, the Soviet side had been extremely satisfied with the part Hirota had played in arranging the sale of the Chinese Eastern Railway, and he had also worked with remarkable perseverance to solve other outstanding questions between the two countries. The conclusion of the anti-Comintern pact with Germany—which the prosecution had cited—had provided for exchanges of information concerning the activities of the Communist party, and had been motivated by fear of a possible threat from communism to Japan's ruling structure and by a desire to check the proliferation of its doctrines. Hirota had not foreseen that it would develop into a tripartite pact, and when the question of such a pact subsequently arose, he had expressed strong opposition to it.

Where the "Bases of National Policy" of his period as prime minister was concerned, it was not possible to prove, for example, that it had been enacted at the instigation of the army, since Hirota himself did not take the stand. However, in respect of prosecution evidence showing that he had advocated Japanese expansion in Manchuria and Inner Mongolia, and in Southeast Asia, defense produced counterevidence demonstrating that he had expressly stipulated that, in carrying out the "advance to the north," consideration should be given to relations with the great powers, and that in "advancing to the south" Japan should seek to extend her influence by "gradual, peaceful means, taking care not to offend other nations."

Around the same time, a document entitled "An Outline Policy for Dealing with North China" had been issued, but the original draft had been decided on at the War Ministry, and Hirota himself had tried to keep a curb on the army by adding the sentence, "Strict care must be taken to avoid any action that might be interpreted as showing that Japan's aim is to deny Chinese territorial rights in North China, or to encourage the birth of an independent nation detached from the Nanking government, or to bring about an extension of Manchukuo." Things such as these, the defense argued, bore witness to Hirota's strong initiative and efforts.

As regards relations with China, Hirota had struggled against the special position enjoyed by the supreme command, pursuing conciliatory policies throughout and making persistent efforts over a long period to adjust relations between the two countries.

Where the spread of the China Incident was concerned, the question, rather, lay in the negligence and procrastination shown by the Foreign Ministry of the Chinese National Government which, while maintaining an embassy in Tokyo for six months following the outbreak of the Incident, had not once put forward any proposal for a cease-fire or a normalization of relations.

Hirota had sought to check the hawks within the military, and had tried to get the situation in hand by means of cease-fire terms which showed an extraordinary willingness to consider the Chinese position. Just before the Incident had spread to Shanghai, he planned potentially effective means of achieving a settlement such as the dispatch of Funatsu and Arita. His moves to attain an agreement by relying on British mediation were frustrated by the army, and the attempt had been begun via Germany alone, but by then the National Government had already determined on an all-out battle of resistance, and no serious study was given to the Japanese terms.

Concerning the launching of the Pacific War, Hirota had expressed views warning against it at the conference of senior statesmen that preceded Pearl Harbor.

At the time when he received complaints concerning the Nanking Massacre, he was in no position to investigate the truth of the affair; even so, assuming that the complaints had considerable basis in fact, he had made prompt and repeated representations to the army, as a result of which the General Staff Office had sent Lieutenant General Honma to the spot. The suggestion that he should have put the matter before the cabinet missed the point; the cabinet could do no more than what Hirota had done. Neither it nor Hirota had any powers to issue orders to the army, or to punish those responsible.

Hearings were finally completed a little before 5:30 P.M. on April 16. The court was adjourned from the next day in order to give time for preparation of the verdicts.

The prisoners boarded their bus in the rain. When they got back to Sugamo, they found they had been driven to a different entrance from usual. They were stripped of all their clothing, submitted to X-rays, and even taken to the dental surgery for an oral inspection. The aim, of course, was to make sure they were not concealing poison or some other instrument of suicide on their persons. Their ordinary clothes were taken away on the grounds that they would not be appearing in court for some time, and they were issued with prisoners' uniforms marked with the letter "P."

Their quarters, also, were shifted to the second floor of Block 1. The first and third floors were both unoccupied. Each of the solitary cells, which were thick with dust, contained used army blankets and a mattress. The concrete building had been deserted for some while, and was cold through and through although spring was already well advanced.

The one improvement was that the evening meal, which arrived late that day, was a proper Western-style meal, and included both meat and fruit. It was personally served to them, moreover, by the American officer in charge of the kitchens. In the days that followed, their meals were to be the same as those eaten by the American forces. However, the reason for this lay not so much in any compassionate impulse on the part of the prison authorities as in cold calculation. If they continued to eat the kind of Japanese food they had had so far, there was a danger that the Japanese cook might contrive to bring poison or some other means of suicide concealed in the food.

It was the same with their exercise. If they walked on ordinary soil, there was a chance that they might pick up nails or pieces of glass, so one-third of one of the yards, containing several cryptomeria trees, was fenced off and boarded over. A number of benches were provided, but some of the prisoners chose to sprawl directly on the boards, so that the effect was rather like a cage at the zoo. All the while, they were under constant surveillance by guards stationed both inside and outside the enclosure, as well as at windows around the yard.

Inside the block, chairs were placed in the corridors for the guards, several of whom kept watch both day and night. They were as noisy as ever. Some of them practiced dance steps while others sang and clapped their hands.

The prisoners passed the time reading, or playing mah-jongg, *go*, *shogi*, chess, or cards.

The verdicts were delayed again and again. The word at first had been that they would be handed down in May; this was changed to the end of May, then to July, and then—this time with a more plausible air—to October 20. For the prisoners, these were days of cruel, wearisome leisure. Visits were restricted to twice a month, and almost the only pleasures left were taking baths and reading the newspapers. In his diary, Itagaki described those days when no newspapers came as "the most painful of all."

The thing that most interested them in the papers was the civil war in China. The Nationalist forces had suffered defeat after defeat at the hands of the Communist troops, and there was much discussion among the prisoners as to where Chiang Kai-shek would go. They also discussed the antagonism between the U.S. and the Soviet Union; many of the military prisoners— doubtless out of ill feeling toward their American captors—believed that future trends would favor the Soviet Union. In these discussions Hirota took almost no part at all.

At home, the appearance of a government headed by Katayama Tetsu—a Socialist—had caused surprise and, among some older men, disapproval at the elevation of such an "outsider." But the government, which had been drawn chiefly from the ranks of the Socialist party, resigned on the same day that hearing of the evidence at Ichigaya ended. Power was passed to the Democratic.party, which had provided some of the previous government's members, and a new cabinet was formed by Ashida Hitoshi, president of the party and former foreign minister in the Katayama government.

The postwar political world was marked by the emergence of former bureaucrats to replace the military men who had hitherto predominated. Ashida, for example, had been a contemporary of Shigemitsu's at the Foreign Ministry. Promotion had come slowly for him, however, and around the time of the Manchurian Incident, when he was ambassador in Belgium, he became a Diet member, taking over what had been his father's constituency. Following the war, he was a member of the Liberal party for a while, but switched to the Democratic party and became its secretary-general. Yoshida and Shidehara, with their ingrained bureaucratic outlook, were obstinate conservatives opposed to the Socialist party, but Ashida believed in cooperating with it if necessary in order to overcome the crisis. As a result, his star within the party rose as Shidehara's fell, and he found himself challenging the older man for the party presidency. In the end, he approached Shidehara personally and told him that since a majority of party members no longer looked to him for leadership, it would be better for Shidehara himself to take the opportunity to withdraw from the party. And he himself took the presidency.

Shidehara left to form his own body of supporters, which then amalgamated with the Liberal party in response to a call from Yoshida for conservatives to join forces. He was installed as the new Democratic-Liberal party's most respected adviser, and Yoshida himself became its president. Despite his seventy-six years, Shidehara remained active, setting off on a nationwide stumping tour on Yoshida's behalf to call for the overthrow of the Ashida government. Thus three of Hirota's fellow Foreign Ministry men—one his senior, one his contemporary, and one his junior, all of them prime ministers at some stage in their careers—found themselves doing battle at the same time.

Later that year, there occurred the "Showa Denko" bribery scandal, which finally drove the Ashida government to resign. The Democratic-Liberal party, which amalgamation had made the largest party of all, now took the reins of government, and its president, Yoshida, was about to become prime minister for a second time when word came from SCAP's Government Section that Yoshida, as an ultra-conservative, was not the right man; it would be better if Secretary-General Yamazaki were to head a national coalition government. Among the reasons for this move were Yoshida's contempt for the labor unions and his opposition to such democratization policies as the disbanding of the great financial combines and the dispersing of economic power. A less obvious reason was that Yoshida had constantly insisted on dealing directly with MacArthur, the highest source of authority, and made light of intermediate administrative agencies such as the Government Section and the Economic and Scientific Section. Even within his own party, there were growing moves to get rid of him, motivated by objection to his employment of bureaucrats and scholars in his previous cabinet, as well as to the pompous airs he affected.

Yoshida, who at this time was living in a house in suburban Tokyo that had once belonged to Prime Minister Konoe, was thrown into despair by this growing storm of opposition to him both inside and outside the party, but he hung on grimly nonetheless. By obtaining the backing of former bureaucrats and younger members in the party and insisting that the suggestion from SCAP's Government Section had been a piece of uncalled-for interference in domestic affairs rather than a formal directive, he managed to reverse the trend within the party. On October 15 he became prime minister designate once more, and formed a government. Even so, the Democratic-Liberals, though the largest party, did not have an absolute majority, and his cabinet was no more than a caretaker government designed to keep things going until the next elections.

Five days after the formation of the second Yoshida government, winter clothing was issued at Sugamo. The third winter since they had entered prison was already at hand. They had been waiting for the verdicts for half a year by now, and the rumored date of October 20 was looking more and more doubtful. Cold drafts whistled through the concrete building, and many prisoners went down with colds.

Thursday, November 4, dawned bright and clear. The prisoners, who were unusually spruce, having bathed and had their heads shaved the day before, had breakfast at an unaccustomedly early hour. Then, for the first time in many months, they boarded the army bus for the court at Ichigaya. The court opened at 9:30. The judges were all present, and the reading of their majority findings began at once. A defense request that the court should hear minority opinions also was dismissed with a promise that they would be made available in writing later.

After a recess on Saturday and Sunday, the reading was continued the following week. Hirota's name occurred frequently during the reading of the general findings, which closely approximated the arguments of the prosecution. The Japanese government, in short, had conspired with the military in their policies of aggression, and Hirota, as prime minister and foreign minister, had contributed to the conspiracy with his "Bases of National Policy" and other measures. Hirota's efforts in peace negotiations with China were dismissed as a mere cover, and his work to maintain friendly relations with the Western powers was similarly labeled as an expedient aimed at obtaining aid from the West. Where the Nanking Massacre was concerned, the judgment swallowed the prosecution's argument whole.

As the days went by, the unexpectedly severe tone plunged the defendants into increasing gloom. Even Shigemitsu who, it had been believed, would be the first to be pronounced innocent, began to face up to the possibility that all the defendants might be condemned to death in the end.

During the lunch hour on the eleventh, when the reading of the findings was approaching its climax, the defendants were allowed to meet their families, though separated from them by wire netting. Hirota's third son Masao, who came to see him that day, told his father that some of the spectators in the public gallery had been expressing concern for Shigemitsu because of the dejected way he sat, with his head in his hands, and suggested that Hirota say something to cheer him up. Hirota shook his head and replied, "There's nothing up with Shigemitsu; he's all right." Nevertheless, he remembered what Masao had told him, and the following day—the twelfth, the day the sentences were handed down—he came and sat down next to Shigemitsu in the court anteroom and made conversation about one thing or another. This was so unusual that Shigemitsu misinterpreted the gesture and thought to himself, "even Hirota must be feeling rather miserable." He had failed to appreciate just how imperturbable was Hirota's state of mind.

On the morning of the day on which sentence was passed, Masao came to see Hirota again. Though realizing that it was a subject one would not normally bring up, the sight of Hirota's composed countenance encouraged him to say,

"I imagine you're prepared for the worst, aren't you, Father? I mean, just supposing you should get the death penalty?"

"Of course I am." Hirota nodded and smiled.

"You wouldn't be lonely, after all. Grandfather and Grandmother, Mother and Tadao are all there waiting for you."

"That's right." He nodded vigorously, then peered into Masao's face. "Why, are you worried?"

". . . Just a little."

Hirota chuckled softly. "Don't be silly! Think of your grandmother in Fukuoka, now—she was a tough woman. You've heard about the way she died, haven't you? Well, I take after her."

Masao was silent, so Hirota smiled again and said, "And besides, I've been nearly throttled to death any number of times at judo. So I know that it's not at all an unpleasant way of dying."

Masao managed to nod agreement, though he could not help wondering what the average person would think of a father and son who could exchange such remarks at a time like this. But then he reflected that the very fact that they could talk quite calmly about such things, as though they were having a conversation over the dinner table, was what made their relationship what it was.

"They say you have to walk up thirteen steps," he said. "At the top a board gives way, and that's all."

"I know."

"Mind you don't slip on the steps."

"All right, all right." Hirota smiled gently, almost as though he were consoling a child.

The reading of the individual verdicts began at 1:30 that afternoon. Their indictment of Hirota, which traced his career back to the Genyosha—indirectly related to the Black Dragon Society—was severe in the extreme. He was found guilty on the first count (consistent conspiracy to gain control of East Asia, the Pacific, and the Indian Ocean), the twenty-seventh count (the waging of war against China), and the fifty-fifth count (negligence in the prevention of war crimes and crimes against humanity).

Reading of the text was completed at 3:30, and the court took a short recess, during which the defendants' benches were cleared away and armed MPs were stationed around the courtroom.

At 3:50, the judges took their seats, and the defendants were brought into court one by one, in the order in which they had been indicted, to hear sentence pronounced on them. The only other defendant within hearing was the next man, who stood waiting at the entrance to the corridor.

Araki: life imprisonment. Doihara: death by hanging. . . .

Hirota was the sixth to appear, and took the stand after hearing a sentence of life imprisonment pronounced on Hiranuma. He put on his earphones and, as always, listened with eyes half closed.

Death by hanging. He removed the earphones and, as had become his habit on leaving the courtroom, smiled at his two daughters, sitting in the section reserved for the press, as he went out.

A moment of tense silence fell upon the courtroom, then there was a sudden murmur of voices. Hoshino Naoki, who was waiting his turn at the end of the corridor, was shocked, unwilling to believe his ears.

Back in the anteroom, Hirota got his coat and was taken off to another room. Doihara had already taken his coat and disappeared from the anteroom. Around dusk, the seven men who had been condemned to death were taken back to Sugamo in a separate bus, somewhat before the rest.

That day Hirota's daughters Miyoko and Toyoko, though in a state of near collapse, waited outside the court and waved their handkerchiefs busily at the usual bus as it left. The previous day, Shigemitsu had noticed them waving through a crack in the paper covering the windows and had told Hirota, who stood up and waved his hat vigorously in the direction of the crack. It was something he had never done before.

But today he was not on the bus, which by now was reserved only for those who carried tickets to the world of the living.

Of the seven defendants who had received sentences of death, six were military men, and in each case the judges had voted 7–4 in favor of the death penalty. The exception was Hirota, the only civilian, whose sentence had been decided by a single vote, 6–5. The minority opinions published later revealed that the judge representing Holland had accepted the fact that civilian governments had been almost powerless in the face of the military, and that Hirota had done what he could within this narrow framework. Showing a remarkable understanding of Hirota's life, he found him not guilty on all counts. Thus the country where Hirota had once spent a cramped period as minister had, in the end, provided the most sympathetic verdict of all.

The judge representing France insisted that it was not fair to try these men who were, in the end, only accomplices of the figure who held ultimate responsibility and who was being allowed to go scot-free—the emperor.

Hirota's death sentence came as a surprise even to the prosecution. Chief Prosecutor Keenan declared emotionally that the verdict was stupid, and that at the very stiffest the sentence should have stopped at life imprisonment. Speculation was rife. Hirota's family heard, indirectly, that one prominent (civilian) figure among the war criminals who had escaped death remarked cryptically that "perhaps the medicine had worked too well." Presumably he meant that his own moves in court to save himself had worked for him but proved fatal to Hirota.

The Yoshida government expressed not a single opinion—much less criticism—of the verdicts, any more than it did of the main lines of SCAP policies. One might almost have thought, from its absolute silence, that the trials had taken place in a different country. It was the general public, rather, that expressed dissatisfaction with the verdict on Hirota and campaigned to have the sentence remitted. Hirota's two younger daughters both became ill following the sentencing, but friends and teachers took the lead on their behalf by going out on the streets of downtown Tokyo and appealing to passersby to sign an appeal for reduction of the sentence. Students resident at the Kokokyo and other students from Hirota's home prefecture joined them, taking their stand in front of the Marunouchi Building and on the Ginza, and in the end more than thirty thousand signatures were collected. Another seventy-two thousand signatures were collected in Fukuoka and submitted to MacArthur.

This awoke a response among those associated with the Foreign Ministry. Shidehara, as well as the speakers and deputy speakers of both houses of the Diet, lent their support to a movement to draw up a petition for clemency. This finally inspired Yoshida to act on behalf of his old acquaintance, and he set off for SCAP headquarters bearing the petition. MacArthur was not there, unfortunately, and General Whitney saw him instead. The result was that Yoshida was reproved for conduct unbecoming a prime minister, and left again taking the petition with him.

On November 19 the defense made a request to MacArthur for a retrial of all seven men who had been condemned to death, taking advantage of a provision that the tribunal's sentences were subject to reduction or alteration by the supreme commander. As a result, the representatives of the eleven-nation Far Eastern Commission in Japan held a meeting, ostensibly to make a recommendation on the matter to MacArthur. But its finding was a foregone conclusion, and the request for a retrial was dismissed. From this point on, the condemned men were not allowed any newspapers each day.

Alone in Block 1, the seven men awaited death. For Hirota, the other six were strange companions with whom to share the last journey. Former foes, they were all in the same boat now, but for Hirota it was as though, in one final piece of mischief, the men whose actions had plagued him for so long were carrying him with them into death. Generals Doihara and Itagaki were militarists whose intrigues in Manchuria, North China, and Inner Mongolia had frustrated Hirota's efforts, as foreign minister, to negotiate peace in China. Lieutenant General Muto was one of those who had brazenly interfered with Hirota's attempt to form a cabinet by demanding Yoshida's removal as candidate for the post of foreign minister. General Tojo had barred Hirota and other senior statesmen from access to the emperor, and ignored efforts to dissuade the government from commencing hostilities with America. General Kimura had assisted Tojo as undersecretary during Tojo's days as war minister, while General Matsui was the officer whose failure to control the troops under his command in Nanking had led eventually to Hirota's being accused of negligence in preventing the massacre. Hirota had been charged with the same crimes as these men—the notorious "military" personified—and now must wait under the same roof with them to suffer the same death penalty.

In one sense, of course, they were by now simply human beings and as such beyond hatred. Some of them proved to be unexpectedly gentle, others to have a boyish, almost innocent streak, so that it was difficult sometimes to imagine them as they had been in uniform and at the height of their power. Yet it was they, nevertheless, who with the help of a Constitution that gave independence to the supreme command had unleashed the savage forces that had now brought them to the threshold of death, dragging the "man in mufti" along with them. Fellow condemned though they were, there was little, basically, that Hirota could share with men such as these.

Around this time, the Buddhist scholar Hanayama Shinsho, who was acting as chaplain to the war criminals and to the condemned men in particular, had started a series of interviews with each of the seven men now under sentence of death, with the aim of preparing them for their end. His first meeting with Hirota, on November 17, lasted for an hour. Hanayama talked of the spiritual changes he had noticed in B- and C-class war criminals prior to their execution, but Hirota merely listened and said almost nothing himself. He had, in fact, been resigned to the worst long since, and there was little for which the chaplain could "prepare" him. If anything, he felt the interview as an intrusion. When all seven condemned men assembled in a room with a Buddhist altar and joined Hanayama in chanting the "Hail to the Buddha Amida," Hirota sat reading a sutra in silence.

The second interview took place a week later, on the twenty-fourth, and again lasted an hour. Hirota smiled occasionally as Hanayama gave him news of the signature campaign and of his family, but again had little to say for himself. He was a striking contrast to the other six, who showed great eagerness to hear about Buddhism, to talk of their own states of mind, and to hand over farewell poems for their families. The one thing that Hirota did was to give Hanayama some of his own hair and nail clippings, wrapped in toilet paper, and ask him to give them to his kin.

The third interview, which started at 3:00 P.M. on November 26, lasted twenty-five minutes. Hirota was as uncommunicative as ever, and Hanayama felt driven in the end to ask:

"Don't you have any parting poem, say, or any impressions you want to record?"

"The things I've done since I went into government service still stand; I don't think I want to add anything further."

Undeterred by this apparent indifference, Hanayama went on, "Not even any comments on. . . ?"

"Nothing. Just to die without fuss. . . ." He broke off.

"Nothing at all?" Hanayama pressed.

"I've always taken things simply, as they came," Hirota replied in a quiet voice as though talking to himself, "saying what I had to say and doing my job as well as I could, so in fact there's nothing for me to add now. Just to live naturally and die naturally."

Hanayama, who was a priest of the Shin sect of Buddhism, asked whether Hirota's state of mind derived from Zen, and Hirota replied that it was close to it. The only sign of emotion he showed was when Hanayama told him that five members of his family had come to see him the day before, but had been sent home because it was Thanksgiving Day. He immediately asked the American officer present, in English, when he would next have a chance to see them, and was told "Monday at nine o'clock."

That Monday, Hirota was able to see his children. Notice confirming the sentences had already been given to the prisoners, and SCAP's Public Information Section had announced that it would work around the clock beginning at 00:00 hours that day. The implication was that the sentences were to be carried out within twenty-four hours, and the prison had an air of unusual activity.

In his POW uniform, Hirota was as cheerful as ever. Although this was the last time, he talked of the same, everyday things as usual, in the same tone of voice, so that the children felt, almost, as though they were all chatting together at home.

"I was a brash kid in those days—" he said, recalling how he had taken a new name when he was a boy, "to change it after all the trouble they'd gone to finding a good one for me."

He also remarked that what pleased him most was that the children were in good health. The thought of Tadao, who had died while he was minister in Holland, must have crossed his mind as he said it. Tadao, Shizuko, his mother Take, and his father Tokuhei, who had died just before the end of the war—they had all preceded him to the other world. It was as though he were going to join them again, with a feeling as natural as the sun setting in the evening. He gave his children no last message, unless it was his remark, "As things will be from now on, it might be a good idea for you to learn some foreign language."

The next day, he sent a letter home. As usual, it was written in the simple *katakana* syllabary so that it could be easily translated and censored, and was addressed to Shizuko, as though she were still alive and he were talking directly to her:

> On Monday the weather was fine, and all five—Chiyoko [his eldest daughter], Hiroo, Masao, Miyoko, and Toyoko—came to see me. I was very very pleased. They talked a lot, and I talked, and it was thoroughly enjoyable.
>
> After I last wrote, Mr. Hanayama asked me about a post-humous name, but I told him that mine had already been decided on, so don't forget.
>
> I have signed a list of articles to be sent back home—apart from my clothes, just my spectacles and false teeth.
>
> That's all. Good-bye. My regards to everybody.
>
> Koki

In fact, this was not to be his last letter, since a postponement of execution was announced. Although counsel Smythe's sense of justice had brought him into conflict with Webb and eventually led to his return to America, he still concerned himself with Hirota's fate even after the end of the trials, and persuaded other defense lawyers to join him in appealing to the U.S. Supreme Court. The Far East Military Tribunal, they argued, was controlled by SCAP, who was in direct line of command from the U.S. Despite this, the supreme commander had not followed legislative and judicial procedures normal in the States, but had established rules for the court, created new crimes, and pronounced the sentences on his own responsibility. This was a violation of the American Constitution, and habeas corpus should be applied in order to rescue Hirota and the other defendants.

The Supreme Court accepted the appeal by a vote of 5–4 and began consideration of it. As a member of the U.S. forces, MacArthur was obliged to postpone the executions.

Thanks to this, Hirota was able to see his family once more in December. This time Masao and his wife (Izumi) were accompanied by Hirota's younger brother (Tokuemon), his eldest daughter's husband (Sugano), and his eldest son's wife (Haruko). The atmosphere of the meeting was the same as the previous time, and Hirota even said with a smile, "I couldn't see to the children's education as well as I would have wished." He was not the kind of man to say, "So please see to it for me." After that day's meeting, Hirota sent another letter to his home, again addressed to Shizuko:

> The other day, I had five visitors—Tokuemon, Sugano, Haruko, Masao, and Izumi. We talked of all kinds of things, and I very much enjoyed myself. I was happy too that Tokuemon was in time and I could see him.
>
> I've been spending my time since playing patience, but sometimes in the morning or the afternoon I go outside for about thirty minutes for a walk. My health is quite normal, so don't worry.
>
> I had a lot of postcards and letters around the time of the verdict. I enjoyed reading them. I feel better now that I know how people feel.
>
> The U.S. Supreme Court met on the sixth to consider the appeal, so presumably the execution will be postponed until the outcome is known.
>
> The weather is fine today, and the sun is shining. My cell is pleasantly warm.
>
> There's nothing more to write now. With prayers for Shizuko's soul,
>
> Koki
> December 7

Ever since he entered prison, Hirota's letters had been short, more like telegrams—an effect not solely due to their being written in *katakana*. They were full, moreover, of phrases such as "in good health" and "happy" with no sign of dissatisfaction or complaint. The "walk" mentioned in the letter just quoted is a good example: since receiving the death sentence, they had taken exercise hand-cuffed to a guard, who accompanied them round and round the boarded exercise yard. It was a disagreeable business, with none of the pleasure usually associated with the word "walk." One military prisoner became so irritated by the constant surveillance, extending even to their visits to the toilet, that he shouted at his guards, "I wish you'd execute us and get it over!"

The eighteen men including Shigemitsu who had escaped the death sentence were transferred to another block in the same jail formerly used for women prisoners. Here they started serving their sentences, which ranged from life to Shigemitsu's seven years. Not only were the facilities better than before, but supervision was less strict. During the day, the iron doors of their cells were left open so that they could come and go as they pleased, and meals were taken facing each other across tables in the corridor. They could bathe and take walks whenever they chose, a courtyard with a lawn being allotted for exercise. "It's like living in a residential hotel," said one of the inmates. "I wouldn't mind living here all my life." Even Shigemitsu would sometimes bolster his self-esteem with the remark that many of the outstanding figures of the beginning of Japan's modern era had had experience of life in jail.

Thus the A-class war criminals were divided clearly into two groups, one under the shadow of death, the other with the promise of life. Deep blue autumn skies stretched above the prison, the shrike cried outside, and at times they could hear the dying call of the last cicadas. Winter approached relentlessly.

The U.S. Supreme Court rejected the appeal made by Smythe and the other counsel. As expected, the reason given was that the Far East Military Tribunal was a trial conducted by the Allies, and that consequently the Supreme Court had no authority to question its findings. Justice Douglas concurred with the view that the Supreme

Court lacked jurisdiction, but later complained that the Far East Military Tribunal, as part of a chain of command stretching from the United States to SCAP, had been not a court of justice but a simple instrument of political power.

News of the denial of the defense motions reached SCAP on the morning of the twenty-first, and MacArthur immediately gave orders for the executions to be carried out at 00:01 A.M. on the twenty-third. That evening the prisoners, in handcuffs, were summoned and notified of the order.

Chaplain Hanayama went to the prison and on the morning of the twenty-second had an interview with Hirota. The previous day, when the prisoners were notified of the pending executions, he had been asked by several of them to take care of their wills, last letters, and so on, but Hirota, unlike the rest, had behaved almost as though the executions had no connection with himself. Today, therefore, Hanayama asked Hirota again whether he did not have some message for his family.

"As you can see," Hirota said simply, "I'm in good health. I have no message; just tell them, please, that I went to my death quietly and in good health."

"The others have given me farewell poems and so on," Hanayama said. "How about you—don't you have anything?"

"I gave up literary things when I was quite young," said Hirota. "Ever since, I've devoted myself to my career as a civil servant. I read what others have written, but I've given up composing anything myself."

"Don't you think your children would be glad to have something of the kind?" Hanayama pressed. But Hirota's reply was noncommittal:

"I gave up all cultural pursuits, you see. . . . The only thing I have to show for my life is the things I've done."

After this, Hirota continued to reply with polite sounds of interest or the occasional smile to whatever Hanayama said, but no more. Driven by a feeling that it was his duty to get what he could out of Hirota, Hanayama continued to ply him with questions. As a result, he elicited a few comments:

"There are major trends in our human world which one has to keep an eye on. If people had kept a watch on what was really happening in Russia, it might have been possible to avert a world war."

"America, you see, always follows the well-beaten track; Russia is a country that moves in accordance with great fluxes in society. I imagine the most important question of the future will be what changes occur in Russia."

His final remark before the interview ended was on a familiar theme:

"Somewhere in Japan, there should always be somebody who keeps a quiet eye on world trends. People are so busy nowadays that nobody has time to consider the larger pattern of world developments."

For their meal that evening they were served, at Tojo's request, broiled fish, rice, and bean-paste soup in addition to the usual U.S. army fare of meat, bread, and coffee. It was a lonely last supper for each of them, eaten facing the concrete wall of their solitary cells.

Afterward, they met chaplain Hanayama once more. Hirota's meeting lasted for twenty-five minutes. Nothing new was said, and the conversation ended with Hanayama's asking, to make quite sure, "Well then, you haven't written anything, have you? Not to your attorney, for example?" and Hirota's reply, "No. There didn't seem to be anything to write. Thank you for all you've done."

The first group to be executed consisted of Tojo, Matsui, Doihara, and Muto. The four men in their drab khaki clothing heard Hanayama read from the scriptures in the room with the Buddhist altar. When it was over, someone called for three cheers for the emperor and the Japanese Empire. Led by Matsui, the oldest among them, they twice raised three cries of "banzai," then entered the brightly lit execution chamber.

The second group—Hirota, Itagaki, and Kimura—were on their way to the chapel when they heard the cheers. "They were doing *manzai** just now, weren't they?" Hirota said to Hanayama.

*A frequently boisterous comic dialogue, closely resembling similar comedian-and-stooge turns in the West, which was popular in old-style Japanese variety halls and still features frequently in modern television programs.

"*Manzai*? No. . . . Perhaps you heard it from the next block?"

When they were in the chapel and had listened to the reading from the scriptures, Hirota said again, "They did *manzai* here, after the reading, didn't they?"

"Ah," Hanayama replied, realizing at last what he must mean. "You mean 'banzai.' Yes, they did. If you want to too, please go ahead."

But Hirota shook his head and turned to Itagaki: "You do it." Itagaki and Kimura gave three cheers, but Hirota did not join in. He had, of course, said "*manzai*" deliberately; it was his last wry little joke. Nothing, after all, could have been more comical than to shout "banzai" at such a time, especially if one considered where those earlier cries of victory beneath the onward-marching flag of the Rising Sun had finally led Japan. . . .

To Hirota, "banzai" was a chilling sound. It was the nightmare cry that time and again had shattered the dream of international accord cherished by "the man in an ordinary suit." Thanks to it he was now going to his death, the unwilling companion of the men who had plagued him throughout his life. A choice piece of comedy indeed. . . .

They entered the place of execution. The Allied representatives and officers who were to witness the carrying-out of the sentences stood there in a line. The other condemned men muttered to themselves, recited the scriptures, stumbled, but Hirota walked steadily, gazing calmly into each of the alien faces as he passed. He was like a judoist casting his eyes over the opposing team, or a diplomat sizing up a row of guests at a party.

He was executed at 00:20 A.M. on December 23.

The news that the sentences had been carried out was brought to the nation over the radio that morning.

Shigemitsu in his cell composed a haiku for his children:

> They went in silence
> To their deaths
> That frosty night

and followed it with another:

But your father
Is still alive—
A winter camellia.

On the same day, Hirota's contemporary Yoshida Shigeru dissolved the Diet. The opposition parties were still suffering the after-effects of the Showa Denko scandal, and Yoshida was assured of a great victory in the coming election.

The election was the first to be held since the promulgation of the new Constitution. It rang the death-knell of the old Meiji Constitution, the document that had laid the nation so low.

LIST OF SOURCES

The author wishes to express his gratitude to Aoki Hide, Owatari Junji, Kadowaki Yoshimitsu, Konoe Michitaka, Shindo Kazuma, Hagiwara Chuzo, Hidaka Shinrokuro, Hirota Hiroo, Hirota Masao, Hoshino Naoki, Horinouchi Kensuke, Yoshida Tan'ichiro, and the many others who gave him advice and assistance in the preparation of this book. The principal works on which he has drawn for his material are listed below.

Harada Kumao: *Saionji-ko to Seikyoku* Vols. I–VIII. Iwanami Shoten.

Kido Koichi Nikki Vols. I–II. University of Tokyo Press.

Shidehara Kijuro. Shidehara Heiwa Zaidan.

Hasegawa Shun: *Yamaza Koshi*. Ikuseisha.

Hirota Koki. Hirota Koki Den Kanko-kai.

Akojima Toshiharu: *Hirota Koki to Terauchi Taisho*. Homeido.

Shigemitsu Mamoru: *Showa no Doran* Vols. I–II. Chuo Koronsha.
   Gaiko Kaisoroku. Mainichi Shimbunsha.

Yoshida Shigeru: *Kaiso Junen* Vols. I–IV. Shinchosha.

Kosaka Masataka: *Saisho Yoshida Shigeru*. Chuo Koronsha.

Sato Naotake: *Kaiko Hachijunen*. Jiji Tsushinsha.

Ishii Itaro: *Gaikokan no Issho*. Taihei Shuppansha.

Miwa Kimitada: *Matsuoka Yosuke*. Chuo Koronsha.

Yabe Sadaharu: *Konoe Fumimaro* Vols. I–II. Kobundo.

Konoe Fumimaro: *Heiwa e no Doryoku*. Nihon Dempo Tsushinsha.
   Ushinawareshi Seiji. Asahi Shimbunsha.

Oka Yoshitake: *Konoe Fumimaro*. Iwanami Shoten.

Fujimoto Naonori: *Kyojin Toyama Mitsuru*. Sekkasha.

Nakano Yasuo: *Seijika Nakano Seigo* Vols. I–II. Shinkokaku Shoten.

Inomata Keitaro: *Nakano Seigo*. Yoshikawa Kobunkan.

Grew, Joseph: *Ten Years in Japan* (trans. by Ishikawa Kin'ichi). Mainichi Shimbunsha.

Itagaki Seishiro Kankokai: *Hiroku Itagaki Seishiro*. Fuyo Shobo.

General Staff Office (ed.): *Sugiyama Memo* Vol. I. Hara Shobo.

Aoki Hide (ed.): Shuyu Sammyaku. Nishi-Nihon Shimbunsha.

Nihon Seikei Hihankai: *Asu no Nihon wa Do Ugoku?* Kanda Shobo.

Araki Takeyuki: *Showa Gaiko Henrin-roku.* Shin-Shosetsusha.

Mitsuda Iwao: *Showa Fuun-roku.* Shin-Kigensha.

Takada Kazuo: *Seijika no Ketsudan.* Seiyusha.

Tatamiya Eitaro: *Showa Kenryokusha-ron.* Simul Shuppankai.

Suematsu Tahei: *Watakushi no Showa Shi.* Misuzu Shobo.

Abe Shinnosuke: *Gendai Seijika-ron.* Bungei Shunju.

Showa-shi no Tenno Parts 18, 20. Yomiuri Shimbunsha.

Matsumoto Seicho: *Showa-shi Hakkutsu* Part 3. Bungei Shunju.

Takahashi Kamekichi: *Taisho Showa Zaikai Hendo Shi* Vol. II. Toyo Keizai.

Otani Keijiro: *Tenno no Guntai.* Tosho Shuppansha.

Imai Takeo: *Shina Jihen no Kaiso.* Misuzu Shobo.

Takahashi Masae: *Ni-niroku Jiken.* Chuo Koronsha.

Kodama Yoshio: *Akusei, Jusei, Ransei.* Kobundo.

Hora Tomio: *Nankin Jiken.* Shin-Jimbutsu Oraisha.

Usui Katsumi: *Nitchu Senso.* Chuo Koronsha.

Hosokawa Morisada: *Joho Tenno ni Tassezu.* Isobe Shobo.

Tsurumi Shunsuke *et al.*: *Ajia Kaiho no Yume* (*Nihon no Hyakunen*, Part 4). Chikuma Shobo.

Shigemitsu Mamoru: *Sugamo Nikki*; *Zoku Sugamo Nikki.* Bungei Shunju.

Asahi Shimbun Hotei Kishadan: *Tokyo Saiban* Vols. I, II, III. Nyusu-sha.

Kojima Noboru: *Tokyo Saiban* Vols. I–II. Chuo Koronsha.

Eguchi Ko: "Tanaka Ryukichi to Kokusai Kenjidan" (Sept. and Oct. issues of *Nihon Oyobi Nihonjin*). Nihon Oyobi Nihonjin-sha.

Hanayama Shinsho: *Heiwa no Hakken.* Asahi Shimbunsha.

Sato Kenryo: *Ko Hirota Koki-dono o Shinobu* (personal memorandum).

Sasagawa Ryoichi: *Sugamo no Hyojo.* Bunkajin Shobo.

Shindo Kazuma: *Suishucho.* Shindo Kazuma Koenkai.

Takigawa Seijiro: *Tokyo Saiban o Sabaku* Vols. I–II. Towasha.